BOOTLEGGERS & BAPTISTS

HOW ECONOMIC
FORCES AND MORAL
PERSUASION INTERACT
TO SHAPE REGULATORY
POLITICS

BOOTLEGGERS
& BAPTISTS

ADAM SMITH
AND
BRUCE YANDLE

CATO
INSTITUTE
WASHINGTON, D.C.

Library of Congress Cataloging-in-Publication Data

Smith, Adam C., 1982-
    Bootleggers and Baptists : understanding America's regulatory journey /
Adam Smith and Bruce Yandle.
        pages cm
    Includes bibliographical references and index.
    ISBN 978-1-939709-36-3 (hardback : alk. paper)
        1. Trade regulation--Political aspects--United States. 2. Business and
politics--United States. 3. Pressure groups--United States. 4. United States--
Social policy. 5. United States--Economic policy. 6. United States--Politics and
government--Moral and ethical aspects. I. Yandle, Bruce. II. Title.

    HD3616.U47S546 2014
    320.60973--dc23

                                                                    2014017682

Cover design by Jon Meyers.

Printed in the United States of America.

                              CATO INSTITUTE
                    1000 Massachusetts Ave., N.W.
                         Washington, D.C. 20001
                               www.cato.org

Contents

Preface

Just over 30 years ago in the May/June 1983 issue of *Regulation* magazine, a short piece appeared in the publication's "Viewpoint" section. It was called "Bootleggers and Baptists: The Education of a Regulatory Economist" (Yandle 1983).[1] Only four pages long, the article set forth a new theory of regulation, one that seemed consistent with the facts surrounding a large number of regulatory experiences. Using the economist's standard concepts of supply, demand, and market forces, the theory was summarized as follows:

> Politicians need resources in order to get elected. Selected members of the public can gain resources through the political process, and highly organized groups can do that quite handily. The most successful ventures of this sort occur where there is an overarching public concern to be addressed (like the problem of alcohol) whose "solution" allows resources to be distributed from the public purse to particular groups or from one group to another (as from bartenders to bootleggers). (Yandle 1983, 14)

In 1999, after 16 years spent observing Bootlegger/Baptist dynamics, the theory was described again in *Regulation*, this time a bit more tightly:

> Here is the essence of the theory: durable social regulation evolves when it is demanded by both of two distinctly different groups. "Baptists" point to the moral high ground and give vital and vocal endorsement of laudable public benefits promised by a desired regulation. Baptists flourish when their moral message forms a visible foundation for political action. "Bootleggers" are much less visible but no less vital. Bootleggers, who expect to profit from the very regulatory restrictions desired by Baptists, grease the political machinery with some of their expected proceeds. They are simply in it for the money. (Yandle 1999b, 5)

The evolving theory filled a small niche in the growing field of public choice economics, a study area that represents a broad effort to apply economic principles to the area of politics pioneered by Nobel laureate James M. Buchanan and Gordon Tullock (1962).

The theory takes its name from the classic example of laws requiring liquor stores to close on Sundays, which were supported by both alcohol bootleggers and anti-alcohol Baptists—with both groups willing to spend valuable resources in pursuit of such laws. The happy bootleggers eliminated competition one day a week, and the devoted Baptists could feel better knowing that demon rum would not be sold openly on their Sabbath day. Of course, no one will ever see bootleggers carrying signs in front of a state house seeking political support when closing laws are up for reauthorization. The point of the theory is precisely that they don't have to: the Baptists lobby state house members for them. For success to occur, according to the theory, a respectable public-spirited group seeking the same result must wrap a self-interested lobbying effort in a cloak of respectability. Both members of the politicking coalition are necessary to win. The Baptists enable accommodating politicians to say the action is the "right" thing to do and have folks believe them. The bootleggers laugh all the way to the bank—and may occasionally share their gains with helpful politicians.

Since the publication of that original 1983 article, the theory has been applied to countless regulatory situations. Today, it seems just saying "Bootleggers and Baptists" in a conversation about a regulatory struggle is enough to trigger an explanation of an otherwise curious episode.

The *Regulation* article has become something of a classic in the small world of regulatory studies and has defined much of its author's career as a regulatory economist. As a rough measure of the theory's popularity, a June 2013 Google search for "Bootleggers and Baptists" yielded 51,700 hits. Obviously, not every one of these results is about regulation: some may actually be about bootleggers (with a lower-case *b*) and Baptists! To put this into perspective, a Google search for "Laffer curve" returned 269,000 hits, and a search for "Lady GaGa" yielded 507 million. We would be the first to admit that those who get their thrills from studying regulation constitute a small tribe.

Although the cumulative tally of Bootlegger-and-Baptist hits is interesting, we believe the phrase's profile over time is even more noteworthy. For the period January 2010 to June 2013, the count is 15,300. For the years 2007 to 2009, there were 1,920 hits. The three years 2004 through 2006 saw 329 hits, and 2001 through 2003, just 271. The theory is 30 years old, but the recent explosion in the number of hits generated suggests the word is just getting around. At least that is one explanation.

A more subtle explanation exists, however. First, regulatory activity is a growth industry. Growth in Bootlegger/Baptist media references is a product of that industry. Because of this growth, an extensive and dense lobbying network has been built that now encompasses every significant part of America's political economy. Instead of investing in new plants, private hospitals, and universities and taking their chances as capitalists in a relatively free market, Bootleggers and Baptists prefer regulations that wall out competition. They want subsidies that keep weak and obsolete enterprises afloat, and when things still don't work out well, bailouts paid with taxpayer dollars. Put another way, Bootleggers and Baptists, just like other normal people, respond to incentives. Lobbying for pork often pays a whole lot better than struggling to bring new and better goods to market—at least in the short term. Put another way, political incentives cause Bootleggers and Baptists to become anti-capitalists, participating in what former Office of Management and Budget (OMB) director David Stockman and others term "crony capitalism" (Moyers 2012). In that sense, the count of Google hits is a crude barometer of capitalism's health. More hits mean poorer health. We are pleased that the Bootlegger/Baptist theory is part of a growing conversation on regulation but alarmed that Bootlegger/Baptist interaction is occurring at such a high pace.

Other commentators are alarmed as well. Writing in *Newsweek* magazine, George Will (2009) called attention to the theory and applied it to health care legislation funded by an increase in the federal cigarette tax, implying that the government may need more tax-paying smokers. Making reference to our theory, Max Borders (2012) proposed the development of a crony capitalism mitigation index. Borders even devised components for the index that would include the dollars per employee firms receive from government grants and contracts along with the campaign donations, per employee, contributed to aspiring presidents. After commenting briefly on California's approval of funds for initiating a bullet train in the Central Valley with green jobs justification, Peter Gordon (2012) recommended that a Bootlegger/Baptist prize be awarded annually to recognize the most egregious examples of wasteful political action.

We aren't quite ready to manage an annual contest for the ugliest special interest engagements, but we are convinced that the rising tide of crony capitalism, or what we would call Bootlegger/Baptist capitalism, is drawing some seriously critical attention to capitalism itself. Capitalism has taken lots of hits recently. Everything from bailed-out banks and auto companies to subsidized solar product firms that fail spectacularly leaves the public with the feeling that the marketplace is seriously flawed. Anti-capitalist messages seem ubiquitous. Yet the proposed remedies for the system's failings all seem to involve more government regulation, which means more opportunities for Bootleggers and Baptists to line their purses with transferred rather than newly produced wealth.

How the Book Is Organized

With capitalism under misguided attack and with just over 30 years having passed since Bootlegger/Baptist theory first saw the light of day, we think it is time to update and add new muscle to the theory. This book seeks to do more than retell the Bootlegger/Baptist story. A lot has been learned about regulation over the last 30 years as a host of empirical studies and new economic theories have produced new insights. We seek to include the essence of this work in our book—but not just for the sake of padding our bibliography. Rather, weaving new knowledge into an old theory extends the theory and enables us to offer more carefully structured explanations of what is going on in our world—and why capitalism, the most productive way to organize wealth production that improves human well-being, is again threatened.

Our aims in this book are the following:

- To provide a richer, more detailed presentation of the theory and thereby situate it within a growing body of literature that seeks to explain government action in ways that yield richer forecasts of regulatory outcomes

- To present an illustrative collection of Bootlegger and Baptist episodes, organized in categories that can be linked to empirically observable economic effects

- To show that our account is not just a theory of political economy but rather a fundamental theory of human behavior that can be found beyond the halls of government because it emerges from basic and universal evolutionary forces

- To provide a series of in-depth applications that demonstrate the power of the theory in illuminating old and new regulatory episodes in a variety of governance situations

Our book has two parts. The first part focuses on theory while providing numerous applications. Chapter 1 describes federal regulation's explosive growth during the 1970s and 1980s, when the theory was germinating, and presents an array of Bootlegger and Baptist stories stretching from Magna Carta to President Barack Obama's 2012 efforts to coordinate U.S. energy producers. We organize these stories into four modes of Bootlegger/Baptist interaction, which we use throughout the book. The chapter also provides evidence of regulation's effects on U.S. gross domestic product (GDP) growth.

Chapter 2 connects the theory to the discipline of public choice economics with a focus on the Bootlegger side of the story. Here we examine a stream of economic thought that has emerged to explain regulatory activities. We build this account by reviewing discussions of regulation that have appeared in the *Economic Report of the President* over 45 years. Doing so enables us to illustrate how the ideas of academic scribblers shape the mental models of presidents and their senior staff as they attempt to explain and communicate their actions. Chapter 3 speaks to the question: Why Baptists? Why do politicians find offering moral justifications necessary for actions they seek to take when serving their constituents? Why not an economic or patriotic justification? This chapter reaches into philosophy, experimental economics, and evolutionary psychology to answer the question and concludes that politicians must always offer a "Baptist" justification for their actions if they hope to survive in the political realm.

The book's second part is a collection of specialized case studies, each illustrating an important facet of Bootlegger/Baptist theory. Chapter 4 begins, naturally enough, with the struggles over sinful substances that gave our theory its name. Here we describe regulatory episodes involving alcoholic beverages, tobacco products, and marijuana. In each case, Bootlegger/Baptist theory explains how certain rules arose in the first place and how they disappear when a Bootlegger/Baptist coalition breaks down. The alcohol regulation story is about the industry's successful cartelization by government, acting at the behest of moral lobbyists. Similarly, the tobacco story explains how anti-smoking crusaders successfully obtained regulation that actually strengthened the tobacco industry's profits. And as strange as it may seem, the marijuana story is about efforts to legalize pot openly opposed by the illegal growers themselves, with an unwitting assist from moralists committed to the view that everyone must not get stoned. This chapter exposes how Bootleggers undermine and manipulate even the most seemingly pure social causes, all while appearing to be at odds with the Baptists who—typically, though not always—are rallying against them.

Chapter 5 applies the theory to one of its most fertile fields—environmental regulation. We focus on the debate over global climate change, beginning with the 1997 Kyoto Protocol and then describing frustrated attempts by various interest groups to establish stricter U.S. regulation of greenhouse gas emissions. The story we tell is about Bootleggers who seize upon such regulations as a way to gain markets and grow profits, joined by environmental Baptists who lobby for emission reductions. Ours is a story of coalitions that form and split, of Bootleggers who openly join Baptist efforts, and ultimately of failed efforts to "do something" about carbon emissions. We show how the ultimate results of noble-minded efforts to effect change in the public interest prove to be neither noble nor in the public interest, but instead a product of Bootlegger manipulation.

The financial collapse of 2008 and the organization of the Troubled Asset Relief Program (TARP) are the subject of chapter 6. TARP's injection of federal funds into banking and other institutions was devised during some of the darkest days of the financial crisis, when White House officials were operating in uncharted territory. With all the constitutional barbed wire cut and pushed to the side, cabinet members acted to form cartels involving the nation's largest financial institutions. Our theory is used to explain the rise and fall of TARP support and to show how banks, initially eager to be on TARP's receiving end, became even more anxious to escape its clutches. This chapter in particular shows how Bootlegger activity without Baptist support is a dangerous business and detrimental to all parties involved.

Chapter 7 addresses the most significant Bootlegger/Baptist story of our time: the rise of Obamacare. The passage and implementation of health care reform simultaneously provided health care access to a larger share of the population, cartelized a major part of the U.S. economy, and guaranteed an expanded health care market for the insurance industry, all while disappointing many of the very parties involved with its construction. This chapter offers insights into how the interaction between the relevant Bootleggers and Baptists wound up producing a bill that many wanted but few are now willing to claim as their own, because of its failure to address health care costs.

Chapter 8 concludes the book by summarizing our key points and exploring a fundamental question: Is there a Bootlegger/Baptist endgame? We close with final thoughts on the theory and its ability to explain at least part of the political economy puzzle.

A Personal Note

We wish to offer deep appreciation to those who provided critical support to us in developing and expanding Bootlegger/Baptist theory and in producing and publishing the book. We acknowledge with deep appreciation the inspiration and guidance provided by regulatory scholar and former Federal Trade Commission chair and OMB director James C. Miller III. We hope that Miller's noted insistence on clear thinking, tough-minded analysis, and understandable prose are found throughout the book. We also thank Richard Wagner, whose inspiring, eclectic take on the relationship between market and political domains is both pathbreaking, and perhaps accordingly, underappreciated. For similar reasons, we thank Bart Wilson, who continues to push the boundaries, and thereby the veracity, of what experimental economics can teach us. Our universities, Clemson University, George Mason University, and Johnson and Wales University, provided invaluable support as well as inspiration for our scholarly activities.

Although the ideas and papers that have emerged from our academic work have been essential to the book's development, there would be no book if not for the support of the Searle Freedom Trust and Cato Institute, which respectively funded our enterprise and published the book. In addition to providing funds, Searle president Kim Dennis urged us to the task. Cato executive vice president David Boaz guided the publication process with the able assistance of Cato research fellow Julian Sanchez, who reviewed and commented on the entire manuscript. To Kim, Cato, David, and Julian, we extend our heartfelt appreciation. We are also deeply grateful to colleagues who read and commented on the manuscript. Chief among these is Roger Meiners, who worked through the complete manuscript offering many useful comments for revision along the way. We are indeed grateful to Roger and, as with other readers, we hold him blameless for our final product. Other readers include Dan Foster, David Rose, and Bart Wilson. Comments and criticisms received from these scholars made the book far better and much more readable. Of course, we note that the final product is ours. We alone are responsible for errors of fact or logic that remain in the pages to follow.

We close on a very personal note. The book is the product of a grandfather–grandson effort: Bruce Yandle, the grandfather; Adam Smith, the grandson. We are both economists and students of regulation, public choice, and the market process. Our collaboration has been ably assisted by a person especially important to us, Kathryn Yandle Smith, former newspaper editor and professional writer, who read and commented on the entire manuscript as it was being written, revised, and written again. We have already noted that errors that remain are ours; improved readability and logic of thought are due to Kathryn's generous effort. She did wonders while navigating the often turbulent waters occupied by her determined father and son.

1. Bootleggers and Baptists: A Winning Coalition

"Baptists question Amazon porn sales, oppose tax break."

That headline appeared in the Columbia, South Carolina, *State* newspaper (O'Connor 2011) in April 2011, above a story describing a controversy over an Amazon.com distribution center under construction in South Carolina. The facility would employ 1,200 people. Amid high unemployment, the state's previous governor attracted the company with the promise of a five-year exemption from sales tax on purchases by South Carolina residents. The exemption, which gave Amazon an advantage over conventional retailers, was seen as critical for bringing the center to South Carolina.

Construction of the Amazon fulfillment center was pretty far along when Baptist leaders rallied in opposition to the tax break—and to Amazon's presence—spurred by moral concerns about unrated videos sold by the website, which they considered to be pornographic. "We obviously have great concern about pornography, wherever it is sold in South Carolina," said Joe Mack, the director of public policy at the Christian Worldview Center at North Greenville University, a school affiliated with the South Carolina Baptist Convention. "We'd be opposed to anybody who is selling it" (O'Connor 2011). Of course, the location of the distribution center would have no effect on whether residents could buy videos from Amazon, but this fact appeared to make little difference.

While these Baptists bristled at the prospect of pornography consumption, an unlikely alliance had formed among competing big retailers—including Walmart, Best Buy, and Target—and small Main Street retailers. The common denominator linking these otherwise adversarial firms is a fixed brick-and-mortar storefront, which obligates them to pay sales tax on each purchase. Their common goal: to reduce loss of market share to Amazon, which they claimed was

1

subsidized by favorable tax policy. As William R. Harker, senior vice president at Sears Holdings, said of Amazon's sales tax edge: "I think it puts all retailers at a disadvantage. What we and other retailers are looking for is for the playing field to be level" (Kopytoff 2011).

These seemingly disparate forces—Baptist leaders; major retailers Walmart, Best Buy, and Target; and small Main Street retailers—worked in tandem to vehemently oppose the tax exemption. As far as we know, the Baptists never met with the retailers to strategize. Nevertheless, the retailers undoubtedly welcomed the implied support of South Carolina's largest religious denomination in the lobbying battle against Amazon's special tax treatment. After all, with support from religious authority figures, their battle against Amazon took on a meaning beyond a mere commercial dispute. Alongside arguments about fair competition, the retailers had been empowered to question the very morality of an otherwise routine, profit-motivated attempt to manipulate tax assessment.

The coalition of churchmen, major retailers, and Main Street merchants was initially successful. The South Carolina General Assembly reneged on the previous governor's promise and voted to deny the Amazon exemption (Adcox 2011). But the story did not end there. After all, the Amazon distribution center was already under construction. Shutdown costs would be sizable. Amazon responded to the makeshift coalition by promising to build a second South Carolina facility that would employ hundreds of additional workers. That offer proved enough to tilt the political scales, and a second Amazon vote was favorable to the online retailer.

We see the Amazon story as a perfect illustration of the Bootlegger/Baptist theory of regulation (Yandle 1983). As noted in the preface, the theory gets its name from two seemingly unrelated groups that both stand to gain from restrictions on the sale of alcoholic beverages. Baptist leaders lobby openly and enthusiastically for regulation of spirits; they prefer a world where less alcohol is consumed. Bootleggers, the illegal sellers of alcoholic beverages, happily support the laws as well; Sunday closings shut down legitimate sellers, thus expanding opportunities for bootleggers to sell their wares.

The resulting laws never restrict the Sunday consumption of alcoholic beverages—no bootlegger worth his salt would support that. Instead, the typical restrictions generate differential effects across sellers. The rules set an output restriction that is monitored by Baptists, enforced by government, and enjoyed by bootleggers.[1] Along the way, some of the resulting bootlegger profits are undoubtedly shared with cooperative politicians.

The Bootlegger/Baptist label is now applied to a wide variety of regulatory episodes where the term "Bootlegger" no longer implies illegal action but rather applies to political action in pursuit of narrow economic gains.[2] Moreover, the term "Baptist" does not necessarily indicate a religious motivation but rather group action driven by an avowed higher moral purpose or desire to serve the public interest. Since emerging in 1983, the theory has been used to illuminate countless examples of "strange bedfellows" who rally behind a shared political aim.

Bootlegger and Baptist interaction is as old as recorded history, but we limit ourselves to tales from the past few centuries in political contexts similar enough to our own that lengthy background exposition can be avoided. Every story we relate is told for a purpose, and each contains specialized content that contributes evidence to a richer theory of political action. Although historic legacy is interesting and may be instructive, it is the growing imprint of Bootlegger/Baptist–abetted regulation that we think deserves attention. Illuminating the dimensions of that imprint is the underlying purpose of this introductory chapter.

The chapter is organized into four parts. First, we introduce the Bootlegger/Baptist dynamic. In this part, we examine the growth of social regulation that has emerged because of Bootlegger/Baptist interaction and the impact of these relationships on economic performance. We explain how Bootlegger forces largely define how the regulation advocated by Baptist interest groups actually comes about in practice. The new set of opportunities afforded by social regulation biases the behavior of corporate leaders away from producing more and better goods and services in favor of regulation-seeking activities that reduce output. Then, we break down examples of social regulation into four modes of Bootlegger and Baptist interaction: (a) covert, (b) noncooperative, (c) cooperative, and (d) coordinated. We use these labels throughout the book to organize our various examples and episodes of Bootlegger/Baptist activity. Finally, we close out the chapter—as we do each chapter—with concluding thoughts.

The Bootlegger/Baptist Dynamic

The Bootlegger/Baptist theory provides a useful device for explaining crucial features of enduring social regulations that affect consumers and producers worldwide. The theory describes how special interest groups acquire gains through the political process, and why these two types of interest groups become more prevalent and vocal. Politicians are agents who serve the competing goals and objectives of special interest groups as well as the broader unorganized public. Bootlegger/Baptist theory tells a story of how public interest justification greases the rails for purely private pursuits.

Gifted politicians who seek to serve their constituencies can do more for economic interest groups if their actions can be clothed in public interest garb (Simmons, Yonk, and Thomas 2011). Politicians will rarely explain an effort to improve the profits of an economic interest group by saying, "I was just trying to help a good firm make more money." The Bootlegger/Baptist theory explains how the cost of organizing demand for political action can be reduced while at the same time easing the politician's burden when it comes time to justify those actions. When Bootleggers and Baptists unite, activity in the market for regulation flourishes.

We should hardly be surprised by private pursuit of regulatory benefits. None other than the patron saint of economics, Adam Smith, warned about efforts by early industrialists to seek political favors through laws and regulations. As Smith wrote in his magnum opus, *The Wealth of Nations* ([1776] 1827, 107):

> The proposal of any new law or regulation of commerce which comes from this order, ought always to be listened to with great precaution, and ought never to be adopted till after having been long and carefully examined, not only with the most scrupulous, but with the most suspicious attention. It comes from an order of men, whose interest is never exactly the same with that of the public, who have generally an interest to deceive and even to oppress the public, and who accordingly have, upon many occasions, both deceived and oppressed it.

Writing in 1776, Adam Smith had apparently not encountered situations where businesspersons were joined by clergy and others who wrapped the political enterprise in an attractive moral cloak, thereby improving the chances that politicians would respond favorably to their high-sounding petitions.

The government "pork" Bootleggers seek—with the witting or unwitting assistance of Baptists—can take myriad forms. The most straightforward example of Bootlegger/Baptist activity occurs when some private interest seeks a direct benefit from government—such as a subsidy, contract, or special tax break—on the premise that some higher moral aim or public interest will thereby be served. In these cases, nominal rivals within a sector of the economy may find themselves united in covert support of measures that benefit all, even if they subsequently find themselves at odds over the division of the loot.

Often, however, firms can profit as handsomely by hindering their market rivals as they could by seeking direct payouts from public coffers—and without the public scrutiny that typically attends such transfers. The simplest form of this situation is seen when regulatory measures are used to sock it to competitors (Salop and Sheffman 1983).

The noncooperative strategy of raising rivals' costs is hardly a novelty of the Internet era: a prime example appeared some eight centuries before the South Carolina Amazon episode, when London weavers exploited a stricture contained in the Magna Carta to gain an advantage over foreign competition (Yandle 1984). As the historian W. F. Swindler (1965, 311) explains, chapter 25 of the "Great Charter" established uniform measures of ale, grain, cloth, and other goods to facilitate trade—a classic case of consumer protection at a time when buyers, ill-equipped for comparative shopping, dealt with traveling merchants who moved from market to market, and "traders and merchants found it practically impossible to conform to the standards that were different in each locality."

Such imposed uniformity may have made sense on its own terms given the potential uncertainty of dealing with traveling peddlers, but enforcement of the standard was not uniform. As William McKechnie (1914) documents, the London weavers paid a bribe to local enforcement agents to avoid having the standard enforced on themselves but demanded that it be scrupulously applied to traveling merchants who came to London markets. Differential enforcement thus entered the picture, allowing the best organized merchants to raise rivals' costs, and— unsurprisingly given the state of communications at the time—traveling merchants from assorted far-flung locales had little chance of being as well organized as the London weavers (Thompson 1948, 100–121). In short, the "uniform" standard meant to protect consumers became a barrier to entry for disfavored sellers.

Such regulatory gamesmanship may also take subtler forms, as when looming government action prompts an industry to rally in support of stricter regulation—perhaps to avoid an even more costly outcome—ultimately forming a government-assisted regulatory cartel. Almost invariably, regulation generates differential effects across member firms in the cartel. In other words, when noncooperative strategies are at play, there are winners and losers.

The interaction between Bootleggers and Baptists in pursuit of these aims can itself take a variety of forms. Starting again with the simplest case, Bootlegger firms may covertly advance Baptist arguments, as when film studios advocate for more stringent copyright protection by invoking either the moral claims of artists to remuneration or the promise of increased creativity and innovation spurred by greater rewards to creators. Strictly speaking, these are not Bootlegger/Baptist scenarios at all, but rather cases of Bootleggers covertly posing as Baptists. Such cases, however, often signal the first phase of an evolving political process that yields more complex forms of cooperation. Moreover, considering some of the drawbacks of this one-man-band approach helps illuminate why we so often find a division of labor between Bootleggers and Baptists, with members of each group doing what they do best: the Baptists making the moral argument and the Bootleggers providing financial support for cooperating politicians.

When separate independent Baptist groups enter the picture, at least initially they may find themselves backing the same cause as Bootleggers through a happy confluence of interests, as in the early stages of the Amazon example. Each group, in effect, pursues its own noncooperative lobbying and advocacy strategy, happily reaping any spillover benefit from the other's efforts. Independence has its benefits—Baptist groups may seem more credible if they avoid any taint of association with self-seeking Bootleggers—but comes at the cost of whatever efficiencies might be achieved by pooling resources and acting under a unified strategy. In later examples, we will see how togetherness can work.

In other cases—whether by design from the outset or over time as sympathetic interests are recognized in the course of a protracted political struggle—cooperative partnerships emerge as Bootleggers fund Baptists to bolster support for the political outcome both desire. In economic terms, the Baptist groups have comparative advantage in providing public relations efforts supported by less attractive Bootleggers. An extreme form of this mode of interaction is the notorious practice of "astroturfing," in which corporate interests essentially create from whole cloth an advocacy group designed to seem like a grassroots effort by concerned citizens. Given the tendency of such charades to backfire when exposed, however, the savvy Bootlegger will typically prefer to bankroll an authentic, pre-existing Baptist group with a reservoir of public credibility to draw on, even when this strategy requires sacrificing some control.

Finally, as regulation expands and becomes all encompassing across national markets, a still more complex dynamic may emerge. In this fourth type of interaction, presidents or other political actors take the initiative to coordinate a desired mix of national interest groups and regulators to achieve their ultimate political goal by way of a grand regulatory cartel. One could refer to this as the "grand slam" of Bootlegger/Baptist initiatives. When this happens, high-level politicians and Bootleggers profit while Baptists achieve their goals and provide moral cover, making it easier for coordinating regulators to control the industry group. Taken together, these diverse modes of Bootlegger/Baptist interaction yield expanding regulatory activity and rising costs that constrain GDP growth.

The Rising Tide of Social Regulation

A veritable tidal wave of regulation has emerged in the last four decades from the confluence of Bootlegger and Baptist elements. Any investigation of U.S. regulation quickly reveals the explosive growth in federal regulatory activity that began in the early 1970s. An examination of the count of new pages in the *Federal Register* provides the most vivid indication of the rising tide of regulation, although some may argue that levels of regulation need to be considered in terms of the size of the economy being regulated. To account for this argument, we show the count of pages weighted by real GDP in Figure 1.1.

Figure 1.1
FEDERAL REGISTER PAGES PER REAL GDP DOLLAR
1940–2012

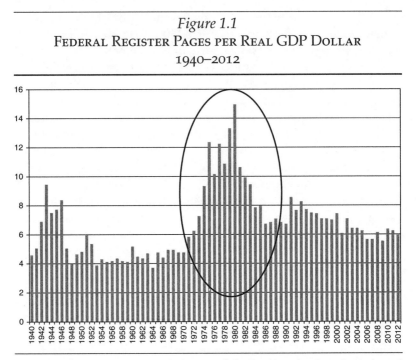

SOURCES: Crews 2012, *Economic Report of the President* (various issues), and authors' calculations.

The massive change in regulatory activity that occurred in the 1970s should prompt us to question whether an economy can absorb so much regulation in such a short time without significant production losses—and, indeed, whether that economy is still one driven primarily by private risk takers operating in a capitalist system.

When analyzing regulatory activity—like that reflected in the *Federal Register* pages—regulatory scholars divide regulation into two categories: economic and social. Economic regulation, the older of the two types, addresses such things as freight rates, permits to operate, interest rates, and geographic service areas. The economic regulatory agencies included the Interstate Commerce Commission, which regulated surface transportation; the Civil Aeronautics Board, which regulated air travel; the Federal Communications Commission, which regulates radio and television broadcast rights; and the Comptroller of Currency, the Federal Deposit Insurance Corporation, and the Federal Reserve Bank Board, which collectively regulated financial institutions. Joining these older economic agencies, the social regulators of the 1970s focused on safety, health, and the environment. These agencies included the U.S. Environmental Protection Agency, the Occupational Safety and Health Administration, the Consumer Product Safety Commission, and the National Highway Traffic Safety Administration.

The new wave of social regulation was fundamentally different from the older economic regulation for transportation, communications, and energy markets. Old-style regulation focused on single industries, yielding a natural constituency of regulated firms that sought to influence outcomes. Social regulation affected all industries. It created no natural constituency of targeted firms that might organize to influence outcomes—at least not easily.

Social regulation also brought something to the table that was lacking in economic regulation. Social regulation was about things that mattered deeply to ordinary people. Interest groups that formed to lobby for safer food, cleaner water, and more humane workplaces possessed a moral fervor that railway freight rules seldom inspire. Voters and interest groups alike became passionate about the new regulation that emerged full bore by the 1970s. New economic models and modes of thinking were needed to explain what was going on. Social regulation became a growth industry, partly because of accommodating Bootlegger/Baptist forces.

When the budgets (in constant dollars) of federal regulatory agencies are considered for the two categories—economic and social—the fast-paced growth of social regulation is astonishing (Dudley and Warren 2011, 5). Total spending on social regulation increased more than 19-fold from 1960 to 2010. By comparison, spending on economic regulation increased less than seven-fold, and total government spending for all federal activities increased just under four-fold across the same 50 years (OMB 2010, 26). Given that government revenues grew less than outlays for most of those years, we can say that regulatory growth was so important that it was funded with deficit dollars. With so much regulation occurring, what was the effect on economic performance?

Throttling GDP Growth

It is now more than 40 years (and 3.5 million *Federal Register* pages) since the surge of regulation that began in 1970. We believe the structure and performance of the U.S. economy has been significantly altered by the rise of what some call "regulatory capitalism," what others might call crony capitalism, or what we would term Bootlegger/Baptist capitalism. In Figure 1.2, we show the annualized rate of per capita real GDP growth over a series of decades, beginning with 1951 and ending with 2010.

Figure 1.2
GDP GROWTH ACROSS THE DECADES

Decade	Real GDP Growth, Annualized	Real Per Capita GDP Growth Annualized
1951–1960	3.05%	1.25%
1961–1970	4.40	3.14
1971–1980	3.16	2.11
1981–1990	3.32	2.36
1991–2000	3.81	2.58
2001–2010	1.60	0.66
2001–2007	2.56	1.59
Average, 1951–2010	3.10%	1.89%

SOURCE: Officer and Williamson 2011.

The data show the large reduction in growth that occurred from 1971 to 1980. Some recovery takes place in the 1990s, but severe deterioration in growth occurs in the most recent decade. Clearly, this is not merely a function of the recent recession: the growth rate for 2000 to 2007 is still anemic. Obviously, regulatory expansion is hardly the only factor that affects GDP growth, but the scholarship on the matter leaves no doubt that regulation has taken a toll on the economy.[3]

Regulating the Regulators

As the newly formed and expanded regulatory agencies followed their congressional mandates and started pumping out new rules, few observers of the political process could believe what they were seeing. According to Eads and Fix (1984, 46–47), President Richard Nixon became so concerned by the unexpected flow of rules from the EPA, an organization his administration had spawned, that he called on OMB director George Shultz to find a way to rein in the regulators. Shultz and the Nixon White House team responded with the Quality of Life Review, located in the OMB, which required agencies to subject regulations to benefit/ cost and economic impact analysis—and then to have the newly proposed rules reviewed by OMB officials.

The Quality of Life Review process was the first in a series of presidential initiatives developed to monitor and manage the growth of regulation. Following President Nixon's move, each subsequent president added new features to the review process that is today managed by the OMB Office of Information and Regulatory Affairs. A recent executive order issued by President Obama added a few important features to the review process, which we will touch on later. But in every case, presidents—who are in charge of all executive branch agencies and hire and fire their leaders—placed the review process within the White House.

Generally speaking, the regulatory review process has one official purpose: to reduce the cost of achieving stated regulatory goals. Put another way, the focus is on economic efficiency, reflecting a desire to serve the public interest. Very few scholars in the early 1970s and 1980s saw federal regulation as a way to serve private interests. Adam Smith's warning was not heeded. And there was little recognition that rules promulgated in the public interest might also win support by serving far narrower private ends. The theory of Bootleggers and Baptists had not yet seen the light of day.

Four Modes of Bootlegger/Baptist Interaction

Now that we have documented the rise of Bootlegger/Baptist activity in the form of social regulation, let's revisit the four modes of Bootlegger/Baptist interaction we introduced previously. These modes are listed here in order of complexity: covert, noncooperative, cooperative, and coordinated. We start with covert strategies, where Bootleggers have not quite found their Baptist and thus try to assume the role themselves, albeit "covertly."

Covert Strategy

Bootleggers aren't shy about advocating directly for their own interests, as the billions spent each year on professional lobbyists amply demonstrate. Even when Bootleggers push their interests without the help of a Baptist group, adopting Baptist rhetoric is often still to their advantage. Restrictions on trade, for instance, tend to protect domestic producers from foreign competition at the expense of consumers—but saying so overtly is a poor way to win political support for such measures. Unsurprisingly, domestic producers who lobby for higher trade barriers use a covert strategy by claiming to have just the opposite aim: protecting consumers from their foreign competitors!

Thus, we discover Francis Cabot Lowell, founder of the U.S. textile industry in Lowell, Massachusetts, successfully petitioning the U.S. Congress in 1816 to impose an 83.5 percent tariff on Indian cotton and English imports. The items, he said, "[were] made of very inferior materials and are manufactured in a manner calculated to deceive rather than serve the consumer" (Yafa 2005, 107). Again we find a public interest justification for constraining market supply. Lowell successfully agitated for legislation that raised his rivals' cost in the international market, and then he artfully obtained a tariff exemption for his own firm. This story's signal element is the two-fold process that raised rivals' costs: the U.S. industry gained a competitive advantage over India's producers, and Lowell gained a specialized payoff within the constrained market.

The limits of the covert strategy may be illustrated in a more recent case: the January 2012 debate over a controversial piece of legislation known as SOPA—the Stop Online Piracy Act—whose passage had been deemed a top priority by the music and movie industries, as represented by the Recording Industry Association of America and the Motion Picture Association of America (Schatz 2012). Among other things, the law would have created a streamlined process for designating foreign-based Internet sites as havens for copyright piracy, requiring Internet providers to block them and obligating search engines and certain other domestic websites to refrain from linking them. Eliminating piracy has a nice Baptist ring to it: at least that is what the Bootleggers thought when they built their argument.

Though it was not framed in this way, SOPA can be thought of as a concealed subsidy to copyright owners. Typically, copyright claims are enforced through civil litigation by the holder of the copyright at its own expense. Many online "file lockers" have indeed been sued by content companies; yet often it was the alleged "pirate sites" that proved victorious in court, because website operators are generally not liable for infringing files uploaded by their users unless the operators actively encourage illegal conduct. The blocking process that SOPA would have established was, in essence, a mechanism for offloading the costs of enforcing content-industry copyrights onto technology companies and taxpayers.

As might be expected, many major U.S. tech companies are not enthusiastic about being drafted into the role of copyright police, and given the government's spotty record of accurately identifying "pirate" sites, tech investors feared that startups enabling users to upload content could too easily be cut off from U.S. users—a potential death sentence for a fledgling firm (Morath and Fowler 2012). These groups lobbied against the proposed legislation as vigorously as the content industries had lobbied for it.

Baptist arguments were to be found on both sides. Supporters of the law condemned overseas file lockers for enriching themselves at the expense of American artists, and content-industry workers and warned that unchecked piracy would impoverish public culture by making the production of new creative works less economically viable. In addition to raising a variety of technical objections, opponents blasted the law's domain-blocking provisions as a form of censorship without due process and argued that it would symbolically undermine the global push for Internet freedom, emboldening repressive regimes to claim that even the liberty-loving United States did not adhere to its own rhetoric of openness.

While the pro-SOPA arguments were primarily advanced by the studios and labels themselves, covertly attempting to disguise their economic interests as a social benefit, opposition to the law was publicly spearheaded by an array of well-established civil liberties and human rights groups—real Baptists. These included the American Civil Liberties Union, the Electronic Frontier Foundation, Reporters without Borders, Human Rights Watch, the Center for Democracy and Technology, and the American Library Association (Kang 2011).

Internet users preferred the real Baptists to the fake ones. On January 18, 2012, constituents flooded congressional switchboards in such overwhelming numbers that by the end of the day, many of the law's own cosponsors declared they had seen the light and joined the ranks of the opposition (Kane 2012). Although many factors shaped the public's response—not least the objective merits of the arguments on each side—it seems plausible that many were predisposed to give greater credence to moral arguments delivered by Baptist groups whose perceived raison d'être was principle rather than profit.

Noncooperative Strategy

Moralized calls for political action may be initiated by Bootleggers deploying Baptist rhetoric, as seen in the case of SOPA and other proposals to crack down on copyright piracy. But often the shifting sands of economic interests bring Bootleggers in as latecomers to long-standing moral crusades, thereby providing Baptists with the decisive boost they need to achieve their aims. Economist Howard Marvel (1977) tells one such story in his account of the implementation of England's Factory Act of 1833, then known as Althorp's Factory Act. Marvel's analysis notes that the law was hailed as a humanitarian move that placed burgeoning textile mill operators under the authority of England's Home Office, banned the use of child workers under 9 years of age, and restricted hours and work conditions for those under 18.

Prominent members of England's landed aristocracy had long sought to bring cotton mills under the protective wing of government, without success. But the political balance was changing, along with the textile industry itself. Textile districts had gained seats in Parliament, and developments in cotton-processing technology—which dramatically altered production costs—were generating differential effects across the industry.

The effect of technology on Bootlegger/Baptist interaction is the unique feature of this story. A host of new manufacturing plants was being driven by steam engines rather than by water wheels. The newer steam-driven plants required less labor and were not affected by periods of low water flow, during which the older water-driven plants operated longer hours to catch up on production. The older plants were thus seen as abusive by some, because they employed more children to work the longer days.

Marvel's review tells us that the factory districts supported the new Factory Act, but the support was not monolithic. His study of the vote led him to conclude that:

> [The law] was, instead, drafted at the behest of the leading textile manufacturers who intended it to have a discernible impact on textile industry operations. Its purpose was to increase the cost of production of many of the smaller textile mills, thereby causing them to curtail their output. The legislation was designed to have differential impact on textile production, harming some manufacturers while benefiting others. The group standing to gain was the large urban manufacturers who relied on steam engines to drive their machinery. Such steam-powered mills not only employed relatively fewer very young children, but were less susceptible to production interruptions than were the water-powered mills. The latter were dependent on nature to keep their reservoirs full and often had to cut hours in dry spells while working extended hours when sufficient water was available. (Marvel 1977, 387–88)

Marvel found that industry output fell significantly more for water-driven mills than for steam-driven mills. Changing technology was thus the key to a story featuring Bootleggers (the operators of the steam-driven mills), Baptists (public interest groups that lobbied for improved working conditions), and a regulation that predictably imposed higher costs on a specific subgroup of manufacturers. As in the story of Francis Cabot Lowell, some of the law's supporters were covert Bootleggers in Baptist clothing—enlightened industrialists who, it would seem, found a profitable way to achieve improved working conditions in England's burgeoning cotton mill industry. Some might say they did well while doing good.

About 50 years after the passage of the Factory Acts, another Bootlegger/Baptist episode occurred in London, where William Booth's newly organized Salvation Army was working to improve the lives and save the souls of the city's downtrodden (Hattersley 1999). This time, instead of Bootleggers and Baptists, Methodists and brewers formed the coalition opposing Booth's efforts. But in this case, as we explain below, a critical element for success was missing—and the effect of the missing element is what makes this case interesting.

A visit to the Salvation Army website provides a brief history of this Protestant church, founded by Booth in 1852. A Methodist minister, he decided to take his ministry to the streets. According to the website: "Booth abandoned the conventional concept of the church and a pulpit, instead taking his message to the people. His fervor led to disagreement with church leaders in London, who preferred traditional methods" (Salvation Army 2013). The more traditional churches felt threatened by this new competition from Booth and his unconventional methods, whereas the minister's uncompromising attack on alcohol was too much for the brewers. Yet this seemingly potent coalition of brewers and Methodists ultimately failed.

Booth had been a minister in good standing with the Methodists before stepping out on his own to build his unconventional movement, dedicated to helping the urban poor wherever they might be found. Delivering the movement's message through uniformed marching bands and preaching in the streets, Booth and his noisy band of disciples began to attract huge followings wherever they traveled. Preaching against any consumption of alcoholic beverages, the Salvation Army called on sinners to repent and change their ways.

As Booth's effort gained momentum, the Methodists and brewers decided to take him on; yet they proved unable to gain meaningful political support for their efforts, largely by not cooperating in pursuing their common goals. Brewers in communities where the Salvation Army held services paid local beer lovers to disrupt the army's music and preaching. Meanwhile, Methodist bishops and other religious leaders struggled to shut down the army's successful efforts to attract members and funds for its growing enterprise. Instead of disrupting the preaching, playing, and singing in the streets, the bishops worked for the enforcement of city ordinances that would require permits for religious parades and noisy street gatherings. Though both groups were working toward the same end, they used distinct methods and strategies in doing so.

Roy Hattersley (1999, 253–54) describes the development this way:

> And it was in 1880 that there came into existence the strange alliance which menaced The Salvation Army for the rest of the century. "Professors of religion and haters of religion," Booth told his followers, "combined to drive you away." A collation of intellectually fastidious bishops and frightened brewers were coming together. The whole establishment, seeing the uniforms and the banners, feared that the church militant might take on a political or military form and that William Booth, having taught the working classes to pray, would encourage them to fight. They were joined in antagonism by the people who simply thought William Booth ridiculous. (pp. 253–54)

Opposition from brewers grew as the army experienced increasing success in converting London's street people. The Salvation Army (2011) explains how an opposing army rose against them:

> Despite its rapid increase in numbers and growing success, The Salvation Army provoked brutal and determined opposition, attracting many enemies. Pub and brothel owners were particularly angered when many of their former customers were converted in Booth's Army. Their profits fell rapidly and business suffered. Many persuaded their friends to join 'The Skeleton Army' whose main ambition was to get rid of The Salvation Army at any cost. (The Salvation Army 2011)

Disruptions of Salvation Army activities reached such a tempo that Booth appealed to Prime Minister William Gladstone for protection. Although Booth received no official government response, his appeal captured the attention of the *Times* of London, which did not endorse the army's activities but editorialized in favor of freedom of speech. Booth, prefiguring the more famous 20th-century campaigns of Gandhi and Martin Luther King Jr., instructed his people in the art of passive resistance. As a result, Booth and his Salvation Army gained national attention.

Salvation Army preachers were jailed for disturbing the peace with their sermons and music, and mayors, especially those who were also brewers, refused to offer police protection when the army came to town (Hattersley 1999, 239). As the disruptions continued, Booth described this situation this way:

> In nearly every town where there has been any opposition we have been able to trace it more or less to the direct instigation and often the open leadership of either Brewers or Publicans or their employees. The plan adopted is by treating or otherwise inciting gangs of roughs. (Hattersley 1999, 273)

In spite of the opposition, Booth's strategy gained momentum—and eventually the support of wealthy philanthropists. With its coffers and membership both swelling, the army captured the attention of the Church of England, which debated how it might affiliate with William Booth's successful program but made no official accommodation with the upstart group. The Salvation Army moved on to become a global ministry.

Efforts to regulate the Salvation Army, supported by brewers and Methodists, were unsuccessful. One factor in that failure may have been the lack of a political broker. Most Protestant denominations, including the Methodists, were fractured over doctrinal and other issues, and the Church of England no longer enjoyed its monopoly influence over Parliament. Put another way, no real cartel existed to oppose the Salvationists. Those opposed to the army were unable to gain parliamentary action that might have effectively blocked its efforts at the national level. Instead, the opposition had to rely on desultory efforts to step up enforcement of city ordinances. A successful Bootlegger/Baptist strategy must involve effective political brokers who can deliver effective restrictions across the relevant jurisdictions. Thus, the Salvation Army prevailed despite Bootlegger/Baptist opposition.

Cooperative Strategy

Our third type of Bootlegger/Baptist interaction—in which private firms fund public advocacy groups—is well illustrated by a recent regulatory episode involving Walmart's support for President Obama's 2009 Affordable Care Act. This case also provides a convenient demonstration of how politicians can spur firms to cartelize, either formally or informally, to gain political benefits (Adamy and Zimmerman 2009).

To understand this story, we must bear in mind that although the world's largest retailer is routinely attacked for not providing more generous insurance to all its workers, it has actually greatly expanded opportunities for its employees to obtain company-provided health care benefits, especially when compared with its smaller competitors. In 2009, some 52 percent of Walmart's 1.4 million U.S. employees were covered by company-provided insurance, up from 46.2 percent three years earlier (Adamy and Zimmerman 2009).

Walmart was a crucial supporter of President Obama's Affordable Care Act, which requires the mega-retailer's competitors to pony up health benefits as well. A story in the *Wall Street Journal* summarized the company's position with the telling headline "Wal-Mart Backs Drive to Make Companies Pay for Health Coverage" (Adamy and Zimmerman 2009). In this case, a host of groups supporting government-enforced expansion of health care played a highly visible Baptist role—and among the most prominent was the nicely named Center for American Progress (CAP), which received at least a half-million dollars in Walmart funding.

Also joining the fray on the Bootlegger side was the Service Employees International Union (SEIU), whose logo appeared alongside those of Walmart and CAP atop a letter announcing the retailer's support for the Affordable Care Act (Podesta, Stern, and Duke 2009). The union, too, backed its words with cash. Tax documents show that in 2010 alone, CAP's activist arm, the Center for American Progress Action Fund, received $625,345 from the SEIU.

Like Walmart, the union was interested in raising the costs of its competitor—nonunion labor. Although conventional wisdom often paints labor groups such as SEIU and capitalist employers such as Walmart as eternal and inherent antagonists, both had a shared interest in using government regulation to raise their rivals' costs. Yet the Bootleggers could have never done it without the Baptists leading the charge.

CAP is a genuine leftist advocacy group that promotes its values across a wide array of policy areas—and there's little doubt it would have backed the Affordable Care Act (though perhaps less effectively) even without corporate or union funding. Sometimes, however, Bootleggers find it more expeditious to organize and fund their own ad hoc Baptist associations—typically with high-sounding names designed to help them pass as public interest groups. For example, firms in the housing industry formed a group called the National Homeownership Strategy (NHS) that lobbied for more federal housing assistance for lower-income families.

Bootlegger-spawned Baptist groups may also serve a secondary function: when an industry's existing trade associations encompass members whose interests are normally aligned, but diverge on a particular issue, a subset of the industry may find it necessary to combine and focus its efforts through a new and separate entity that has more of a Baptist flavor. We find an example of this situation in a controversy that emerged in the trucking community. It exposed a division between larger commercial enterprises, such as Schneider National, and small driver-owned firms that compete for freight forwarding and delivery (Greenfieldboyce 2011).

The controversy started with a proposal from the U.S. Department of Transportation that mandated Global Positioning System (GPS) devices for all trucks. The devices cost roughly $2,000. They monitor and record a truck's location and activity, making possible more effective enforcement of adherence to Department of Transportation regulations limiting excessive driving time, which can lead to drowsy drivers and accidents. Most larger trucking companies already had their trucks equipped with the devices; they use them to encourage efficient hauling (Peter Klein 2011). Smaller operators keep written logbooks; these would be replaced by the more costly GPS monitors. Requiring small operators to go high tech would impose no cost on the already equipped larger firms.

The initial Baptist role in this story is played by Jackie Gillan, president of Advocates for Highway and Auto Safety, which is described on its website as "an alliance of consumer, health and safety groups and insurance companies and agents working together to make America's roads safer."[4] Tired truckers, Gillan argued, "are a major, major safety problem. Paper log books are easily manipulated. They are easily falsified" (Greenfieldboyce 2011).

Todd Spencer, executive vice president of the Owner-Operator Independent Drivers Association, an organization with about 150,000 members—many of whom own just one truck—thought otherwise. Spencer didn't buy the argument that GPS devices would detect tired drivers or catch cheaters: "The only thing that it will automatically record," he argued, "is when a truck is moving."

What about the Bootlegger element? The American Trucking Association, which represents thousands of trucking companies, supported the Department of Transportation proposal, but not all of the group's members were strongly committed to the effort. As usual, there were differential effects across industry members. Thus, five of the largest trucking companies formed a new lobbying group with a conspicuously Baptist name: the Alliance for Driver Safety and Security. The alliance supported the rule, perhaps expecting to raise rivals' costs.

An official with alliance member Schneider National praised the GPS plan as an effort to "elevate the expectations and the performance of all motor carriers" (Peter Klein 2011). The spokesperson for the independent owner-operator drivers' group took a more jaundiced view: "When they talk about leveling the playing field, what they are really saying is we need to get behind efforts that will increase costs of our competitors. We don't find that to be an especially noble effort."

One final intermediary type of scenario is worth considering. Instead of forming their own Baptist groups or merely funding Baptist efforts already under way, Bootleggers may seek to influence the positions or priorities of existing Baptist groups to ensure they align with the Bootleggers' interests. An example of this approach is seen in the debate over a controversial new technology called fracturing—more popularly known as "fracking"—that uses hydraulic pressure to access natural gas deeply embedded in shale. Old gas fields in Ohio, Pennsylvania, and elsewhere have become highly productive thanks to fracking. But the technique has also spurred environmentalist concerns about the potential for earthquakes, damage to water supplies, and harm from the disposal of chemicals used in the fracking process.

However, environmentalists also have reasons to welcome fracking: expanded natural gas production could help enable coal-fired electric utilities to switch to the cleaner fuel. The Sierra Club is the leading

21

environmental group dedicated to ridding the United States, if not the world, of high-carbon-emitting fuels—and coal, in its view, is the chief culprit. Natural gas producers are rather keen on this idea, because it favors their product over coal.

Now, enter the Bootlegger. Chesapeake Corporation is one of the nation's most innovative and successful natural gas producers. It, too, would like to see coal displaced by gas. Chesapeake made a $26 million donation to the Sierra Club to help fund an attack on coal directed to the EPA, with Sierra leading the charge (Martosko 2012). As it turned out, Sierra Club and other like-minded groups were successful. Citing the harmful effects of carbon emissions, the EPA issued final rules that, when implemented, will shut down or force fuel switching for 20 percent of America's coal-fired power generation. To the chagrin of environmentalists, President Obama postponed implementation of the rules.

But the story doesn't end there. Perhaps sensing growing concern among environmentalists about natural gas fracking, the Sierra Club shifted its stance—but only after receiving the Chesapeake payment. The organization disavowed support for natural gas but chose not to return the $26 million. One need not be an incorrigible cynic to wonder whether the group might have altered its view on the perils of fracking earlier had it not been for the promise of those Chesapeake funds.

Meanwhile, natural gas producers may have gotten what they wanted: a regulation that raises rivals' costs. Sierra Club got what it wanted as well: $26 million in funds. At first blush, the whole thing sounds like a case of gains from trade, but it is far from clear that society gains. Instead, vast resources have been devoted to restricting output and padding the pockets of a handful of businesses and advocacy groups.

Coordinated Strategy

The fourth and final category of Bootlegger/Baptist interactions involves political actors—often presidents—taking the initiative to yoke together interest groups and regulators in pursuit of national political goals. As a first example of this sort of activity, we turn to the recent financial crisis.

The 2008 credit-market meltdown brought with it the collapse and taxpayer bailout of Fannie Mae and Freddie Mac; the nation's gigantic quasi-public mortgage refinance units suddenly became fully owned by American taxpayers (Wallison 2008). For years, the two agencies formed a backstop for private mortgage lenders who made loans and sold them to the two agencies. The agencies in turn securitized the mortgages with their own bonds, which were sold in global credit markets.

In 1995, a new interest group emerged, dedicated to expanding government efforts to help Americans purchase homes: the NHS, which we mentioned in our last section as an example of a Baptist group created by Bootleggers. The 56 NHS members included the American Bankers Association, the Appraisal Institute, Fannie Mae, the Federal Home Loan Bank System, Freddie Mac, the Mortgage Bankers Association of America, the Mortgage Insurance Companies of America, the National Association of Home Builders, the National Association of Real Estate Brokers, the National Foundation of Consumer Credit, the National Urban League, and the U.S. Department of Housing and Urban Development (HUD) (Affordable Mortgage Depression 2010).

As should be evident, the alliance contained an impressive list of dominant private-sector and public-sector Bootleggers. The NHS coalition was not a winning one, however, because it had no true Baptists. But this oversight was addressed as quickly as one could say "homeownership." Led by sitting presidents, the housing coalition was soon supported by an array of public interest groups who followed a decades-old, if not centuries-old, tradition of promoting American homeownership.

With strong private-sector support, President William J. Clinton called on Freddie Mac and Fannie Mae to reduce their lending standards and greatly expand mortgage lending for families, even if the families lacked the funds for a down payment or the income to support homeownership on normal terms. In announcing the new strategy, President Clinton (1995) invoked a national commitment to the American Dream:

> One of the great successes of the United States in this century has been the partnership forged by the National Government and the private sector to steadily expand the dream of home ownership to all Americans. In 1934, President Roosevelt created the Federal Housing Administration and made home ownership available to millions of Americans who couldn't afford it before that.

Mr. Clinton then noted how prospects for achieving the dream had dimmed and pledged to brighten the light of government-assisted homeownership in America. The Baptist foundation for expanding home construction and ownership was easily laid and implemented.

After taking office in 2001, President George W. Bush blessed the idea that every American should have a home, whether or not the dream could be paid for, by signing the 2003 American Dream Downpayment Act. The new legislation provided up to $10,000 in direct government down-payment funding for low-income Americans (HUD 2003). Full of good cheer, the president, like his Democratic predecessor, offered a Baptist-flavored comment: "Today we are taking action to bring many thousands of Americans closer to the great goal of owning a home. . . . These funds will help American families achieve their goals, strengthen our communities, and our entire nation" (HUD 2003).

Alas, it was not to be. In 2008, as the subprime mortgage collapse loomed, CBS News reported:

> For decades, Fannie and Freddie fulfilled the American dream. . . . Consumers took out loans from banks, which in turn sell those loans to Fannie or Freddie. Then the mortgage giants repackaged those loans and sold them to investors, guaranteeing the mortgages would be repaid.
>
> As home ownership grew universal, Fannie and Freddie prospered. Their CEOs, Daniel Mudd and Roger Syron together earned around $30 million dollars in 2007. (CBS/ AP 2009)

A few months before the Fannie/Freddie takeover, a *Washington Post* story described the situation this way:

> Today, 3 million to 4 million families are expected to lose their homes to foreclosure because they cannot afford their high-interest subprime loans. Lower-income and minority home buyers—those who were supposed to benefit from HUD's actions—are falling into default at a rate at least three times that of other borrowers. (Leonnig 2008)

The picture was not pretty. The article explained that even as regulators warned that "subprime lenders were saddling borrowers with mortgages they could not afford, the U.S. Department of

Housing and Urban Development (HUD) helped fuel more of that risky lending" (Leonnig 2008).

HUD, Fannie, and Freddie were key players in the 56-member strong NHS group that included mortgage lenders, real estate developers and agents, bond-rating agencies, and the politicians who could speak glowingly about helping low-income people achieve the American dream (Yandle 2010a). By 2011, the bailout total for Fannie and Freddie was $259 billion (D. Wagner 2011). The presence of Fannie and Freddie, two government-sponsored enterprises, in a national-scale, presidentially coordinated Bootlegger/Baptist coalition is this story's distinguishing feature. The two housing finance agencies were the twin treads of a homeownership juggernaut driven by a supercharged engine. There was just no stopping the housing finance cartel from pumping out below-par debt until world markets finally said "enough."

Another example of government-coordinated coalition building occurred in 2009, when the Obama administration unveiled new fuel-economy and carbon emission standards for the U.S. auto fleet (Yandle 2009). The regulation made clear that the federal government, rather than the states, would set fuel-economy standards. State governments, which were actively pursuing tighter regulations at the time, were to be shoved to the side. Going further, the announcement said the new rules would be based on vehicle characteristics such as weight and size, rather than following a one-size-fits-all approach, as had been proposed previously. This more nuanced approach delivered a valuable differential effect: producers of larger cars were given a significant break relative to their South Korean and Japanese competitors that specialize in producing smaller, more fuel-efficient vehicles.

The group assembled in the White House Rose Garden for the fuel-economy regulation announcement comprised the largest visible collection of Bootleggers and Baptists in recent regulatory history, and this gathering is the distinguishing feature of the story. In a way, the episode marked the beginning of a new age of integrated Bootlegger/Baptist interaction, as the White House recognized explicitly.

As President Obama's press secretary put it in advance of the occasion, "You will see people that normally are at odds with each other in agreement with each other" (Yandle 2009, 6). In the garden that day were executives from Ford, General Motors, Chrysler, Toyota, BMW, Mercedes, Honda, Nissan, and Mazda. They were joined by United Auto Workers president Ron Gettelfinger and leaders of the League of Conservation Voters, the Natural Resources Defense Council, the Sierra Club, the Environmental Defense Fund, and the Union of Concerned Scientists (Hughes and Chipman 2009). As in other Bootlegger/Baptist episodes, the Baptist component sang the praises of Mr. Obama's environmental foresight.

The cheerful automakers saw the national rules as an honorable escape from more nettlesome state regulations brewing in California and elsewhere. The Bootleggers—even the Asian producers who were somewhat disadvantaged by the rule—wanted one national rule, not multiple state rules. As GM CEO Fritz Henderson put it, "GM is fully committed to this new approach. GM and the auto industry benefit by having more consistency and certainty to guide our product plans." Ann Mesnikoff, director of the Green Transportation Campaign at the Sierra Club, said, "The Obama administration is making automobiles go farther on a gallon of gas" (Hughes and Chipman 2010). In 2011, 13 major auto producers signed letters of commitment with the government to meet a fleet fuel-economy standard of 54.5 miles per gallon in 2025, up significantly from the 2012 standard of 24.1 miles per gallon (Zacks Equity Research 2012). The fuel-economy standards also embedded carbon emission limitations.

With the new federal rules in place, the auto industry had accomplished something it could not have achieved without the endorsement of environmentalists. The industry escaped a quiltlike pattern of state regulations, effectively pouring regulatory concrete around a long-term, foundational structure for future regulation. Because the rules set differential standards for cars vs. light trucks, dominant producers of light trucks—namely Chrysler, Ford, and GM—gained a potential advantage over Asian competitors. And domestic producers gained a slight fuel-economy edge over producers for the U.S. import market.

There were winners and losers, but on the whole, the Bootleggers did well. What about the Baptists? With significantly tighter fuel efficiency and carbon emission standards imposed on the entire industry, environmentalists accomplished more than they could have without the support of the auto industry. The new fuel-economy cartel is monitored and managed jointly by the EPA, the Department of Transportation, and the Department of Energy. With so many powerful agencies at the forefront of the process, it is little wonder that the auto industry saw the wisdom of joining the choir rather than trying to fight it.

Subsequent developments in energy markets paved the way for additional Bootlegger/Baptist activity. In 2012, natural gas (obtained in part through the new technologies described earlier) became so plentiful, and gas was flowing at such a pace, that storage locations were exhausted. Energy prices were falling. Electric utilities were switching from coal to gas, and major trucking companies were converting engines from diesel to natural gas. The rapid change in relative prices created disturbances across the oil and coal sectors, and the rapidly falling price of natural gas brought increased uncertainty to that industry's future prospects.

The situation was ripe for coordinated Bootlegger/Baptist interaction. On April 13, 2012, President Obama issued an executive order that demonstrated his expertise in extending an altar call to suffering industry leaders (White House 2012a). Following the blueprint for his highly visible fuel-economy cartel, the president appointed a multiagency task force that would coordinate clean production and distribution of natural gas.

Members of the task force included every federal agency that had anything to do with regulating, subsidizing, pricing, and planning energy production and use in the U.S. economy. Key trade associations were sent the draft executive order prior to its becoming final, along with a request for letters of endorsement. When industry groups responded to the invitation, offering glowing support for the president's foresight, their letters were publicized by the White House (White House 2012b). In effect, President Obama cartelized the government regulatory agencies by way of the task force, then he used this as leverage to cartelize the energy sector. The episode's truly interesting feature is the formation of a cartel within a cartel.

What does this have to do with Bootlegger/Baptist interaction? The environmental community forms the Baptist component. Highly critical of the new fracking technology that had dramatically increased natural gas production—and even more critical of coal—environmental organizations stood at the forefront of those supporting the president's effort. The American Petroleum Institute, the American Gas Association, the American Natural Gas Alliance, the American Chemistry Council, Dow Chemical Company, Marcellus Shale Association, and the National Association of Manufacturers each came forward with letters of support. And for understandable reasons. In a world full of federal regulation and price uncertainty, each organization had a lot at stake.

The president artfully circled the wagons. By bringing all the regulators to the table, he reduced infighting and the tendency of each agency to take its own bite from the apple. And by bringing all major energy producers to the table with supporting letters in hand, the president reduced the likelihood that the resulting regulatory cartel would fall apart. The results of this effort remain to be seen, but it seems a safe bet that pork will be divided up across sectors and interest groups, as the combined regulators create industry-wide rules that raise prices and reduce output.

Final Thoughts

This chapter laid out the basic theory of Bootleggers and Baptists, giving examples of four modes of interaction between them, and described the regulatory context from which our model emerged. Our examples have been drawn from as far back as the 13th century up to recent days. The operational content of the theory applies equally in the oldest and most recent episodes.

We have highlighted the extraordinary 1970–80 regulatory period, when the new social regulatory agencies were first emerging, along with thousands of new pages of rules focusing on the environment, safety, and health. The explosion of social regulations set the stage for Bootleggers and Baptists to converge in the regulatory process. The goals of social regulation were, more often than not, the goals of interest groups that included civic and religious organizations along with the newly emerging environmental and consumer groups. In many cases, the regulatory fine print sought by environmental and other public interest groups turned out to be precisely what major firms and industries wanted as well. The resulting rules often brought output restrictions, higher costs for smaller firms than for larger ones, and higher profits for firms well adapted to the new regulatory environment—even while often delivering the goods desired by the Baptists.

As we prepare to turn to the next chapter, which examines where Bootlegger/Baptist theory rests in the broader, evolving body of regulatory theory, we return to the previously mentioned executive order by the Obama administration, which we believe adds new vigor to Bootlegger/Baptist activity.

On January 18, 2011, President Obama issued an Executive Order for Improving Regulation and Regulatory Review, which affirmed the principles of the 1993 order specifying how executive branch agencies would manage development, review, and implementation of regulations (White House 2011). Broadly speaking, Mr. Obama's order represents the next stage in the evolution of White House regulatory review processes that date back to Richard Nixon.

Mr. Obama's order directed agencies to identify old regulations for retrospective review to ensure that they were still justifiable and called for more transparency in the regulatory process, so interested parties could more easily learn what is going on as regulations develop. But the order also, for the first time, allowed agencies doing the required benefit-cost analysis to consider effects far beyond the usual economic considerations.

The order states, "Where appropriate and permitted by law, each agency may consider (and discuss qualitatively) values that are difficult or impossible to quantify, including equity, human dignity, fairness, and distributive impacts" (White House 2011). With equity, dignity, fairness, and distributive impacts now part of the official regulatory lexicon, groups organized around a higher moral purpose should become even more valuable allies for Bootleggers who just want an easier ride to the bank. And with presidents showing new savvy in assembling interest groups for the purpose of forming regulatory cartels, we may expect still wider smiles and louder hallelujahs on the lips of Bootleggers and Baptists.

2. Bootleggers, Politicians, and Pork

Having introduced Bootlegger/Baptist theory and presented four modes of interaction, we need to take a step back and examine just who these Bootleggers and Baptists really are. As a simple definition, a "Bootlegger" is any individual, group, or organization that seeks political favors for financial gain. "Baptists" are individuals or groups that seek political favors for loftier reasons. The favors they seek might take the form of benefits to causes they favor or simply actions that magnify the importance of the values they embrace.

Most groups, of course, are not exemplars of either category: there's a bit of yin in every yang. Surely firms that pursue economic profit are not totally bereft of moral values (or at least, so they often assure us). Groups that pursue regulation for avowedly public-spirited reasons can't be wholly indifferent to whether a little cash falls into their coffers. Still, in most situations it is relatively easy to pick out those groups drawn to legislation more for economic gain and those with more of a moral interest in the outcome. It is easy because they identify themselves.

In this and the next chapter, we explore what motivates these Bootleggers and Baptists. We show how politicians find it in their interest to cater to each of these groups when crafting legislation or developing regulations. Our theory is largely a positive or descriptive one, in the scientific sense of aiming to understand and predict human behavior rather than to render value judgments. We want to know how the world works. Still, the theory has obvious policy implications, which we try to draw out. Let's put it this way. We also want to know if things work out well overall for a society that assigns high value to freedom and wealth-creating opportunities.

Bootlegger/Baptist theory also rests in a much larger body of work that applies economics to politics, which we navigate for the reader as well. The body of research called "public choice" was pioneered by Nobel laureate James M. Buchanan and Gordon Tullock (1962) in their seminal book, *The Calculus of Consent*. Public choice analysis uses standard economic logic to develop a model of how government works—as opposed to a model of how it should work—or what should be done by government regulators to alter human action. James Buchanan (2003, 16) calls it "politics without romance." Public choice exposes how incentives work in the realm of political theater, just as they do in markets. The differences arise from context, as political institutions create different incentives for people making decisions through politics rather than through economic markets.

We begin this chapter by giving a more complete discussion of public choice theory as it pertains to Bootlegger behavior. (Though we occasionally brush against Baptists as well, they get their turn in the next chapter.) As we look through the public choice lens, we describe four theories of regulation that have evolved in an effort to explain why so much regulation exists. We illustrate these evolving theories by drawing on comments from a series of the *Economic Report of the President*, starting in 1965 and moving forward to 2010.[1] By reviewing 45 years of focused commentary from the same source, we are able to describe in crude terms the linkage between theoretical work and recognition of the work by White House officials. In this way, we identify how and when academic theory came to influence political practice. We understand, of course, that White House recognition of anything will be politically biased—but knowing which biases prevail at different times may be illuminating. We close the chapter with some final thoughts about pork-loving Bootleggers.

Politicians, Incentives, and Pork

Let's start with a simple notion: politicians are people just like the rest of us. They weigh costs and benefits when taking actions. Like most of us, they attach substantial weight to career concerns: which is to say, they want to keep their jobs or advance to better ones. Even the most idealistic politicians, after all, have little opportunity to implement their ideals unless they first get elected and then manage to hold on to their offices. For politicians, employment requires votes. Securing votes requires running costly campaigns that run costly ads. Politicians need revenue. And revenue can come from happy Bootleggers. Like the rest of us, politicians are smart about some things and naive about others. They cannot know everything, so they logically choose to become best informed about things that matter most to their day-to-day pursuits. They, too, are rationally ignorant about many things except those things that keep their enterprise afloat.

Starting from these premises, we infer that what will matter most to politicians, in practice, is whatever matters most to the special interest groups who support their reelection prospects. For example, if an auto assembly plant, diesel engine manufacturer, or major bank headquarters is located in the politician's state or district, we can bet safely that he will know a great deal about proposed regulations that affect the fortunes of these particular enterprises. If instead the politician hails from a soybean-producing region without a manufacturing plant or bank headquarters within 500 miles, we can just as safely bet that he will know little about regulations affecting manufacturing and banking but an awful lot about agriculture policies related to soybeans.

Politicians, then, predictably engage in activities that provide concentrated benefits to well-identified special interest groups located in their states or districts. But not just any old benefit will do. Improvements in Yellowstone Park or cleaner rivers in faraway regions may be sentimental goals for Bootleggers and their friends, but none of these political outcomes puts money in Bootlegger bank accounts. Businesses, we assume, can most easily justify spending money—whether on capital goods or campaign donations—when they expect to make a return on investment as a result. If they hope to induce Bootleggers to open their pocketbooks, politicians need to provide the sort of benefit that the recipient can take to the bank. Such benefits may come directly, in the form of cash or a government check, or more indirectly, through a restriction on competition in a Bootlegger's business or industry that increases the Bootlegger's revenue—as long as the Bootleggers know whom they ultimately have to thank for their fattened wallets.

Effective politicians want to find low-cost ways to reward Bootleggers who favor them. Doing so is easier when the cost of those rewards is spread across so many naive taxpayers that no one really notices what's happening. We know a lot about our homes, our families, and the ins and outs of earning a living. Only a few people know a lot about the finer details of 2014 EPA fuel-economy standards for motorcycles, diesel engine emission protocols, the Food and Drug Administration's proposals for regulating the sale of mentholated cigarettes, and proposals to limit the charges retailers incur when debit cards are used. Even when a particular ill-conceived policy imposes costs on the ordinary taxpayer, it seldom makes sense for any given individual to spend hours researching the issues—let alone mobilize resources to seek policy changes.

The ideal scenario, from a politician's perspective, occurs when he can provide valuable benefits to a few firms or organizations in his district or state and spread the costs across the entire nation. The smaller the number of Bootleggers pursuing a fixed benefit package, the better. This not only lowers the cost of organizing and agreeing on desired outcomes but also enlarges the benefit each Bootlegger receives. Small is beautiful as far as pork-hungry Bootleggers are concerned. Therefore, concentrated benefits and diffused costs are the stock in trade of the successful politician. And this is just when the Bootlegger side of the matter is considered. Things get more interesting when the Baptist side of the story enters the picture—but we'll get to that later.

The political distribution of benefits to specific local interests often goes by the name of "pork barrel politics," and Bootleggers love pork. Perhaps the best-known pork delivery system is the much-maligned "earmark," where a legislator writes into the government's budget expenditures that benefit specific parties or groups in his district alone while sticking the larger population with the bill. In recent years, the U.S. congressional practice of making such targeted distributions of government largess to home states and districts through earmarking has received enormous attention. The practice is condemned as though it was a chief cause of the yawning federal deficit or as if earmarking is somehow anti-American.

The fact is, however, that most government-provided goods and services are not really "public" at all. They are bundles of private goods that redound to the benefit of specific individuals, communities, and organizations rather than society as a whole (Aranson and Ordeshook 1981). These benefits do not spring randomly from public wells but are generated by the behavior of particular special interests—Bootleggers—working with particular political entrepreneurs (R. Wagner 2007, chaps. 4–5). Earmarking is clear evidence of Bootlegger success in bringing home more pork. But the competition for pork is tough. And pork does not fall from the sky; flying pigs are rare! Bringing home the bacon requires work—and that work takes time, money, and resources.

Tullock's Foundation for Thinking about Bootleggers and Baptists

This brings us to a key public choice insight developed by Gordon Tullock (1967). Tullock's seminal idea relates to just how much Bootleggers spend when they lobby politicians for more pork. Are there limits? What determines them? Tullock looked at the standard model of monopoly found in any introductory economics textbook and asked a simple question: How much would a budding monopolist be willing to spend for a government license that delivered full monopoly power with all the associated profits? Put more concretely: How much would you be willing to pay for the exclusive right to serve all cell phone users in the state of Illinois?

Tullock argued that in a chase with other firms in pursuit of the same goal, the budding monopolist would logically be prepared to spend up to the expected value of what might be gained from the resulting monopoly power. In a political economy where special interests struggle to obtain political benefits, firms eager for government protection may exhaust their hoped-for gains in a vain pursuit of the political prize. Of course, not every bridesmaid becomes a bride, and not every aspiring monopolist wins the permit. But everyone who tries will spend valuable resources doing so.

Monopolies generate an obvious loss to consumers when they produce below competitive levels, but Tullock identifies another loss or waste of resources that occurs in the course of pursuing the monopoly. All those visits to politicians and contributions to campaigns take time, money, and other resources—resources that could otherwise have been devoted to producing goods and services. Sadly, especially from the perspective of the Bootleggers, the amount spent on wasteful lobbying efforts can be as large as the expected profits sought.

Now, just for the moment, let's get some Bootlegger and Baptist interaction in the story. When considered in the context of the Tullock model, a winning Bootlegger/Baptist coalition lowers the cost of organizing demand for political favors. Because passing legislation with some plausible public interest justification is itself an electoral benefit to politicians, Baptist support may reduce the other forms of inducement—such as campaign contributions—needed to motivate legislators to act in particular instances. As those costs go down, regulatory activities increase, and with that increase come more lobbying expenditures from more Bootleggers and larger corresponding losses that spring from the resulting output restrictions.[2]

Declining lobbying costs on the demand side reinforce falling costs on the politician-supply side because enormous fixed costs are associated with forming trade associations, opening Washington offices, and keeping lobbyists on retainer. Once the office doors are open, the average cost of chasing bundles of pork gets smaller and smaller (Murphy, Schleifer, and Vichny 2003). In contrast, running a business or operating a factory tends to be an increasing or constant cost endeavor.

Business firms then have a choice. Will they seek gains at the margin through lobbying or by putting more scarce capital into producing products and services? Once the lobbying machinery is built, the calculus will be biased in favor of the former. Indeed, fledgling Bootleggers may even be spared the trouble of building their own machinery by channeling resources through Baptist groups that have already built the necessary infrastructure. We thus get fewer bread factories but more lobbying lawyers and economists doing benefit-cost analysis. Bootlegger/Baptist interaction helps grease the rails that lead to increased regulation and an expanded public sector.

But All That Glitters Isn't Gold

As we saw in chapter 1, regulation takes the edge off GDP growth. Fortunately, the Bootlegger's search for pork has limits. We must remember that the political process is competitive. Lots of Bootleggers would love to bend the politician's ear, but only a few can be successful. Chasing politicians and sharing views with them—lobbying—is costly business. As Tullock teaches us, even the most successful Bootleggers may end up with little in the way of additional net cash flow once the costs of currying favor are tallied. Even the winners of the pork race may discover that their barbecue cookout on the National Mall doesn't serve up the prime cuts they'd hoped for.

It may seem counterintuitive, or at least ironic, that those who pursue government favors can find themselves suffering from a kind of buyer's remorse, but this phenomenon has long been recognized in public choice scholarship. In another insightful article, Gordon Tullock dubbed this apparent paradox the "transitional gains trap" (Tullock 1975). His story describes a multistage process in which special interest groups first gain a profitable advantage but then must keep spending to hold their favored position. With profits seemingly assured, owners and managers of politically favored enterprises tend to spend more on fancier digs for themselves and share some of the wealth with their employees. As operating costs head skyward, producers of substitute goods—including novel types of goods that may fall outside the bounds of the monopolizing regulation—cheerfully expand to serve price-sensitive consumers. The market enjoyed temporarily by the favored interest groups contracts, profits fall, and the federal rules that protected the interest group—now with higher built-in costs—become handcuffs that won't let go.

Tullock uses the example of the U.S. Postal Service to illustrate the point. By maintaining its status as a monopolist in the delivery of first-class mail, the Postal Service garnered plush revenues for decades. With this income came generous pay and fringe benefits for postal workers. Prospective employees flocked to obtain the cushy positions on offer, and with more bright people looking to sign on, hiring standards rose—as did wages, benefits, and of course, postal rates. Costs then were locked in at a permanently higher level. The attendant higher prices attracted more-efficient competitors who took advantage of technological change and new forms of communication. With the advent of e-mail and online billing services, the Postal Service discovered that its legal monopoly no longer guaranteed it a captive audience. Captured by an old technology and a labor force spawned by it, the Postal Service held on to its disappearing first-class mail delivery system while caught in a transitional trap.

The essence of Tullock's lesson is that a regulatory advantage is not necessarily a goose that perpetually lays golden eggs or, indeed, any eggs at all. Successful government favor seekers enjoy only temporary gains that are soon eaten away as windfall profits translate into locked-in costs. If earnings should then be driven to competitive levels—whether by technological innovation, changing consumer preferences, or a shift in the political winds—the organization will find itself desperate to meet its inflated costs, as we've seen in the case of the Postal Service. Having been reared in a regulatory hot house, the "lucky" Bootlegger discovers it cannot sustain itself with mere competitive returns.

We find a similar dynamic at work in the surface and air transportation sectors. In both cases, regulation purposefully set up monopoly arrangements, to the benefit of owners and workers. As the regulated industries prospered, their competitiveness languished. Substitute services emerged, often based on new technologies. Some who had favored more regulation called for reform, until eventually, the regulatory structures came crashing down. The ICC, which had regulated trucking and rail transportation for decades, was eliminated in 1995. Trucking was deregulated; rail passenger transportation was nationalized. The Civil Aeronautics Board, which regulated airline pricing and service, was dissolved in 1984. Even the U.S. Postal Commission loosened its grip on the sale of stamps beyond the confines of post offices, cut hours of service, and allowed competitors such as FedEx to place receiving boxes on Post Office property. Deregulation is not complete, but the days of golden eggs for these industries are over.

To sum up, Bootlegger/Baptist theory rests on several key public choice insights. First, each of us tends to be naive about a vast number of subjects but intensely informed about matters that have an immediate and direct bearing on our own well-being. As a result, large benefits can be provided to well-informed special interest groups (Bootleggers) through government transfers without the majority of the population being aware that anything is going on— or having much incentive to find out.

Second, smaller Bootlegger groups have lower organizing costs than larger groups, and average gains per member are higher for smaller coalitions, given a fixed payoff. Startup costs are associated with organizing a lobbying effort. Once that initial investment is made, however, a lobbying group will be ready to go for the pork when another political opportunity surfaces.

As politicians redistribute pork to Bootleggers, the number of organized groups expands. At the upper limit, a rational Bootlegger will be prepared to spend the expected value of a political prize in pursuit of that prize. Once obtained, political restraints on competition or other benefits can improve profits for a time. But higher profits tend to feed higher costs in Bootlegger organizations.

The costly political machinery that provides all this must be maintained. Meanwhile producers of substitute goods and services are attracted by Bootlegger profits. With costs rising and profits falling, Bootleggers find themselves caught in a regulatory trap. The process has limits. Redistribution cannot continue indefinitely without killing the goose that laid the golden eggs or chasing off the pigs that provide the pork.

Four Explanations for "Why So Much Regulation?"

Having laid a public choice foundation, we now consider several accounts of why regulation flourishes and how the Bootlegger/ Baptist theory explains the workings of the regulatory world. We review four theories of regulation and trace their appearance in successive editions of the *Economic Report of the President* spanning 1965 through 2010. We examine which theories White House officials used to explain their regulatory policies and when the various theories seemed to be important. Though the goal of theory is to describe political action, how politicians and the public understand regulation can also have an enormous impact on how political outcomes unfold. That underlies our interest in discovering when the essence of Bootlegger/Baptist theory shows up in the reports.

Serving Everyman (and Everywoman)

The first and oldest theory of regulation—so old it has no clear inventor—is the public interest theory. This theory holds that when they take office, politicians and their appointees also take on a new life, putting aside their personal interests to serve the common good. Once ensconced in Washington, representatives lie awake at night trying to find better ways to provide broadly appreciated public benefits, their thoughts unsullied by any narrower interests.

Whether the problem to be addressed is pollution, unhealthy working conditions, or teenage smoking, a public interest legislator seeks to achieve as much improvement as possible given realistic budget constraints. He is constantly searching for lower-cost ways of achieving public interest goals. The legislator works to build institutions that strengthen (and in some cases repair) beneficial market forces so that markets will be robust. The public interest theory recognizes that politicians are, alas, human—meaning errors and even deliberate acts of chicanery will occur. But these failings are the exception, not the rule.

English economist Arthur Cecil Pigou (1920) is often (mistakenly) seen as the godfather of the public interest theory. Pigou famously argued that governments could take steps to correct all kinds of problems that plague unregulated private markets. Leaders could address the uncompensated harm done when sparks from railway engines set woods aflame, when land management practices caused rabbits to invade neighboring property, or even when construction practices tended "to spoil the lighting of the houses opposite."[3] Pigou worried about automobiles that wore out the surfaces of roads, the sale of intoxicants that then required additional expenditures on law enforcement and prisons, and in his own words "[p]erhaps the crowning illustration of . . . the work done by women in factories . . . for it carries with it, besides the earnings of women themselves, grave injury to the health of their children" (Pigou [1932] 2009, 134, 186–87, 196–203).

The remedy? Pigou called on enlightened leaders to address these problems by taxing unwanted activity, subsidizing desirable activities that tended to be underproduced, and imposing regulations on producers who disregard the social costs of their behavior.[4]

Now, let's take a peek at President Lyndon Johnson's *Economic Report of the President* (1965, 135–36), in which we get more than a hint of Pigou and the public interest theory:

> In the vast majority of industries, competition is the most effective means of regulation. But in a few industries, technological and economic factors preclude the presence of more than one or a few firms in each market. When these industries provide an important service to the public, direct control is substituted for competition. The independent federal regulatory commissions were established in the transportation, power, and communications industries because competition could not be expected to protect the public interest. In other areas, regulation is aimed at

> providing the public with reasonably full knowledge of
> the market. In particular, securities and certain commodity
> markets become so complex and technical that regulation
> is necessary to insure that buyers and sellers have access to
> accurate and reasonably comprehensive information.

The statement, prefiguring much of the recent rhetoric aimed at banks by the Consumer Financial Protection Bureau, makes a case for antitrust enforcement as well as regulation of certain consumer markets. Government, in President Johnson's view, was there to protect and further public interests that would be jeopardized by unchecked private action.

We see a more detailed expression of market failure and public interest theory in President Johnson's *Economic Report of the President* (1966). After describing the emerging problems of air and water pollution, the report claims that "in the case of pollution, however, those who contaminate the environment are not charged in accordance with the damage they do. . . . Public policies must be designed to reduce the discharge of wastes in ways and amounts that more nearly reflect the full cost of environmental contamination" (*Economic Report of the President* 1966, 119–20). Without acknowledging the possibilities for enhancing common law and other private action-based remedies, Mr. Johnson's economists took a cue from Professor Pigou. Their rhetoric expands the domain of public interest from antitrust regulation and consumer protection to dealing with external costs imposed by firms on their neighbors.

By 1978, the ever-ballooning domain of public interest had led to such extensive regulation that President Jimmy Carter's *Economic Report of the President* (1978) began to address regulatory reform. Still, the report indicates the need for government intervention as a means of limiting the unfettered private pursuit of profit: "In a mixed market economy like that of the United States, government regulations of the marketplace sometimes play a vital role in meeting social goals, curbing abuses, or mitigating the hardships that would flow from the unconstrained play of economic forces" (*Economic Report of the President* 1978, 206). Even as late as 1978, the *Economic Report of the President* did not recognize what historians and political scientists had known for decades: that the regulatory process can be captured by the regulated.

Capturing the Regulator

The second theory of regulation, called capture theory, builds on the public interest theory but recognizes that even politicians and regulators dedicated to serving the broad public interest face a fundamental information problem: they have no handbook that defines "the public interest." What the dedicated legislator and regulator do have is an ample supply of private- and public-sector advisers eager to offer their own ideas—not to mention the lobbyists.

It is important to recognize that lobbyists do more than curry favor and plead for pork: they also often provide a high level of valuable technical expertise. That can make them important adjuncts to the politician's office given the breadth and complexity of the myriad issues a modern government is expected to address. If fact, some lobbyists are so helpful that they get called on to assist in defining the public interest! Thus a thorny problem for elected officials becomes a golden opportunity for the lobbyist, a nascent Bootlegger. Increasingly dependent on the representatives of the very firms they are expected to regulate, politicians are effectively captured.

It is perfectly logical that a president's report would not discuss this element of political action. Admitting that politicians can be captured would seem to suggest that public servants are not up to doing their jobs. But in the real world, even the most dedicated public servant must obtain detailed information about prospective law and regulations somewhere. Generally speaking, those with the most information are the parties who will be directly affected by regulatory action—and they are typically only too happy to share it, along with their recommendations on the best course of action.

The reason is simple: with the stroke of a pen, a politician can cause vast wealth to be transferred from taxpayers to the providers of all this valuable information. Capture theory helps explain how eastern high-sulfur coal interests influenced key members of Congress when the 1977 Clean Air Act Amendments were being developed. These amendments required the use of "scrubbers" to remove sulfur oxides from smokestacks. Massive machines that used as much as 10 percent of the power generated to operate, scrubbers were mandated even though cleaner low-sulfur western coal could have accomplished the same thing without scrubbers.

The cost of the rule was spread over an enormous number of electricity users; most consumers never knew that their power bills were slightly larger because of the rule. Meanwhile, the benefits were concentrated among a relatively small group of coal mine owners and operators, and coal workers. Additionally, eastern coal was produced by organized labor spread over several states, whereas cleaner western coal was produced by nonunion workers concentrated in lonely Wyoming. Because unionized labor is well organized, unions can far more easily speak with one voice to help influence the debate.

Capture theory also explains how the railroads won the day when Congress empowered the ICC to regulate motor carriers in 1935 (Felton and Anderson 1989). This occurred after carriers began cutting prices for carrying freight, in spite of organized opposition from agricultural and other shipper interests. The rail interests were successful in forcing ICC controls on truckers.

If all this sounds a little too simple, that's because it is. After all, regulatory tradeoffs are made: political decisions create winners and losers. Thus, the question is not just whether a politician will be captured but which particular Bootlegger will do the capturing. Suppose a legislator is considering an array of proposals to set tighter limits on the nitrogen oxide emissions from diesel engines. Which of the several standards being considered serves the public interest? Is the burden of achieving cleaner emissions best placed on the producers of diesel fuel, on engine manufacturers, or on some combination of the two? Is a simple, uniform rule preferable to a more nuanced one that is sensitive to human exposure and differences between urban and rural operations?

Agents of Bootlegger engine and fuel manufacturers are only too glad to join the discussion—indeed, they better be at the table. Baptists from environmental groups, organized religion, and regulatory agencies are on hand to assist the legislator's search for a public interest solution as well. Some will even arrive with draft legislation already prepared to guide the politician.

The politician's search for the public interest is confused by the fact that many lobbyists will claim to be serving the public interest, even though disagreement exists as to which nitrogen oxide standard is most desirable and how best to achieve it. But time is precious, and the politician has to make a decision. Persuaded by some of the lobbyists' arguments, the legislator takes a position that turns out to be advantageous to certain Bootleggers.

Suppose the politician opts to place the burden of reducing emissions on fuel manufacturers. Perhaps without realizing it, the politician has been captured by the engine manufacturers, one of several competing Bootleggers, while still believing that he or she is serving the public interest. In specific instances, the belief may even be accurate! The point is that whichever choice the politician makes, he or she will necessarily rely on information and analysis provided by parties with powerful vested interests in the outcome.

Stigler's Special Interest Groups

So how does one predict which Bootlegger group will prevail in regulatory struggles? Our third theory was developed by Nobel laureate George Stigler and is called the special interest theory of regulation. Stigler suggests that if we wish to predict which of several parties will prevail in a valuable political struggle, we should imagine that the specific content of proposed legislation is simply auctioned off to the highest bidder.

By focusing on which parties have the most to lose (or gain) in the struggle, we can begin to understand outcomes. Of course, this is just a first step in the process. To participate in the auction, the agents doing the bidding must know the consensus position of the group they represent. Organizing an interest group is costly, and the more numerous and diverse the players, the greater the cost. Once organized, the group must reach consensus on a preferred policy outcome, which may itself be costly, requiring research, analysis, and internal deliberation.

With Stigler in mind, let's reexamine the Clean Air Act scrubber case. Suppose the case had simply involved pitting western against eastern coal producers. The eastern producers were located in relatively populous states, had been organized and working the halls of Congress for decades, and had more members of Congress to confront and more support from other interest groups who wanted to keep local economies humming. The producers were not strictly homogeneous. Some produced metallurgical-grade coal, and some were diversified across industries, but a small number of large producers dominated the industry. When speaking to politicians, the voice of the United Mine Workers came through loud and clear.

Now consider the western producers. They were comparatively younger firms with nonunionized workers and were located in remote corners of less populous states. They operated in towns that had yet to flourish, so these towns had not yet given rise to the school districts, Main Street merchants, and others who might later have lobbied for western coal. Although the bulk of the market for western coal was in the east, most consumers and voters were rationally ignorant about where their coal came from. Pushed to pick which region mattered most, concentrated eastern interests with a lot to lose outweighed scattered western interests that had yet to enjoy the fruits of an expanded market for their coal. Using this scorecard, a prediction that eastern interests would carry the day should have been easy to make.

What about the conflict between truckers and rail interests, which led to the truckers being brought into the regulatory web? First, far fewer railroad companies existed than trucking firms at the time. The large rail companies had been organized and politically active for decades. Furthermore, railroad companies owned vast amounts of land in many states. These fixed assets meant railroad companies were all but certain to be around a long time, were in a position to extend significant favors, and had a long-term interest in political decisions affecting the value of their land spread over many states. By contrast, thousands of small, local trucking firms had few employees in the average firm. The truckers, being new to the game, faced high upfront organizing costs. They lacked both deep roots in important political territories and experience in working Washington. The transaction costs of organizing and securing beneficial regulation were lower for railroads than for trucking interests. Unsurprisingly, the railroads won the day.

Now, let's return to our survey of the president's annual economic reports. By 1981, President Jimmy Carter's *Economic Report of the President* finally recognized the importance of special interest groups. So much new regulation had been placed on the books that steps were being taken to systematically review and control the flow of new rules. Although the report understandably makes no mention of regulatory theories, ample evidence indicates that the capture and interest group models were understood. Consider the following:

As government involvement in the economy has grown, so have the overtly political aspects of economic decisions. Representative government is quite responsive to claims from individuals, groups, or regions that proposed policies will benefit them or do them harm. Since all interventions, no matter how small, have the effect of harming some and benefiting others, there has been growing pressure to "manage" these gains and losses to produce "fairness" rather than economic efficiency. Many of the recent arguments over deregulation, for example, have tended to focus less on the benefits of deregulated markets than on the economic losses of the persons or industries that have been protected in the past by Federal economic regulation. (*Economic Report of the President* 1981, 89)

Eight years later, and following a change in the party in power, we find recognition of special interest demand for regulation—and even the possibilities of Bootlegger/Baptist alliances—in President Ronald Reagan's *Economic Report of the President* (1989). Along with this came discussion of government failure. Ideas developed by economists in the 1960s, 1970s, and early 1980s had made their way into mainstream discussion of regulation. In a discussion of rationales and motivations for regulation, the report indicates the following:

Until recently many economists viewed market failure as a sufficient rationale for government intervention. Because it is now widely recognized that government intervention is not without its pitfalls, however, market failure is seen as a necessary, but not sufficient, condition of government intervention.

Economists sometimes refer to situations where government intervention results in a less efficient policy as "government failure." (*Economic Report of the President* 1989, 191)

The discussion continues with direct references to special interest demand and the possibilities of Bootlegger/Baptist explanations for regulation:

Many firms attempt to use the regulatory process to enhance their competitive position. Barriers to entering an industry may increase with the introduction of new regulations, not

46

only increasing profits for regulated firms, but also yielding a less efficient industry structure. The existence of incentives for firms and individuals to manipulate the political process means that regulatory programs may not be implemented so as to promote economic efficiency; nor is such efficiency necessarily an important criterion for politicians designing such programs.

Over the past 20 years some economists and political scientists (especially those of the "public choice" school) have attempted to understand what motivates different approaches to regulation. A key insight from this research is that much regulation can be explained by an interest in redistributing wealth from the general public or taxpayers to special interest groups. . . . For example, the legislation requiring scrubbers on power plants appears to have been motivated as much by the self-interests of environmentalists and high-sulfur coal miners as by a desire to promote cleaner air. (*Economic Report of the President* 1989, 191–92)

There we have it. Environmentalists and coal miners, two very dissimilar interest groups that share one common interest: a requirement for technology-based standards in pursuit of cleaner air, even though clean coal could accomplish the environmental goal.

The very next year's economic report for President George H.W. Bush acknowledges the influence of successful lobbying efforts on the regulatory fine print (*Economic Report of the President* 1990). After all, it is not environmental protection per se that brings Bootleggers and Baptists to the table, but rather specific kinds of environmental regulation. The report tells us that "firms routinely seek to keep their existing products and facilities under the current regulatory regime when more stringent regulations are implemented for new products and facilities" (*Economic Report of the President* 1990, 188). Emission reductions can be obtained by setting clear performance standards—backed by high penalties—without specifying how air quality improvements are to be achieved. Alternatively, emission fees or taxes can be imposed; these can be raised or lowered to obtain the desired reductions. Finally, tradable permits can be put into play, with the total number of permits establishing a maximum emission level.

The Bootlegger/Baptist theory predicts that legislators will steer away from these three alternatives in favor of technology-based standards that set stricter rules for new sources of pollution than for existing sources. Environmentalists often seem to put more trust in technology than in economic incentives, and polluters prefer "polluter profits" that can accrue when output is restricted across an industry by technology-based barriers to entry (Buchanan and Tullock 1975).

Mr. Bush's 1992 economic report discussed the scrubbers required for electric power plants and then explained why they were required:

> One reason that command-and-control regulations remain in place is that the decision to introduce regulatory reform or to deregulate an industry affects the distribution of wealth among consumers and regulated companies. *The outcome of the regulatory process may be determined by the strength of interest groups rather than by an assessment of whether a proposed regulatory action maximizes net benefits to society.* A regulated company that produces inefficiently, for example, knows that competition will force the company either to go out of business or to invest in a more efficient production process. Such a company is highly likely to resist regulatory reform. (*Economic Report of the President* 1992, 163 [emphasis in original])

In 1993, President Bush's report echoed the notion, familiar from previous reports, that markets can fail to account fully for the costs of pollution or to adequately inform consumers of risks associated with products they may buy. Having acknowledged market failure, the report continued:

> *There are costs associated with regulation, however. Attempts at regulation must be tempered by the understanding that the rules may be as imperfect as the market they are trying to improve; that is, governments as well as markets may fail.* (*Economic Report of the President* 1993, 170 [emphasis in original])

From 1993 to 2010, discussion of regulation in the *Economic Report of the President* emphasized efficiency concerns and focused primarily on finding ways to improve the regulatory process.

In a sense, all the reports carry an implicit assumption that government is ultimately capable of getting it right—but increasingly tempered by an awareness of how easy it is to go wrong. For example, President George W. Bush's 2002 discussion is dedicated almost totally to institutional design, which is to say, making regulations inherently more efficient and marketlike. In addressing the need for regulatory reform, Mr. Bush's 2003 report indicates that "although some demands for regulation reflect a desire to improve the efficiency of intrinsically imperfect markets, other demands for regulation seek to change market outcomes, for reasons that range from the compassionate to the opportunistic" (*Economic Report of the President* 2003, 135).

In our earlier discussion, we mentioned the fleeting nature of advantages gained by the lucky and hard-working Bootleggers. In some cases, recall, this is a function of changing technology, but in others, it is the result of policy changes that strip away legal protections that firms had come to rely on—leaving them ill adapted to a more competitive market. Can these sheep somehow escape being sheared just when their wool is beginning to flourish?

Generally speaking, avoiding such haircuts requires legislation and regulation with a long half-life. When Congress passes major statutes that require regulatory action, there are typically preset dates when those actions must be taken and when the legislation must be reauthorized. These dates set predictable limits to the political gains from a successful lobbying effort. They also allow canny members of Congress to get entrepreneurial when seeking campaign contributions—which brings us to our fourth theory.

Money for Nothing

University of Miami Law School professor Fred S. McChesney (1987) developed the fourth theory of regulation. But unlike the others, this one will never be featured in an *Economic Report of the President*. Instead of focusing on political favors that politicians may provide in exchange for reelection support, McChesney developed a theory of political wealth extraction. Crudely put, politicians run a kind of legislative protection racket in which they are rewarded for doing nothing. As McChesney explains, the legislative vehicles for this kind of wealth extraction are sometimes called "Milker Bills," proposed statutes the politicians then offer to defeat for the right price (McChesney 1987, 107). Those who get "milked" may simply view the process as political extortion.

Here's one version of the story. Suppose a group of independent businesses has not yet been subject to regulation. The businesses are not organized politically and provide little in the way of campaign contributions to politicians. In a sense, a politician can do little to benefit or harm an unregulated industry. And that is the point.

To get the industry's attention, a politician announces that hearings will be held on the possibility of "consumer protection" regulation targeting the industry's main product or services. Assorted bills are drafted. Some include rather draconian rules. Hoping to escape these burdens, the industry organizes, hires lobbyists, and makes prudent campaign contributions to strategically important politicians. The politicians relax the threat somewhat but make certain to leave a few clouds in the sky. The newly formed Bootlegger organization, however, is unlikely to fade away: having paid the fixed costs of starting a trade association and hiring lobbyists, the businesses are primed to search for fresh opportunities to seek political favors.

This is the theory; McChesney (1987) relates a real-life example. The year was 1975, and Congress had ordered the Federal Trade Commission (FTC) to develop a rule regulating the warranties offered by used car dealers. The FTC delivered a rule tougher than any dealer wanted—one that required costly warranties and defect disclosures, which put small operators without mechanics at a distinct disadvantage.

The draconian FTC proposal brought Congress to the rescue, as solicitous legislators pledged to "save" the industry from the merciless clutches of the FTC. In fact, Congress had conveniently given itself authority to veto the FTC rule. Members of the industry responded on cue; descended on Congress, promising support to those who would help them; and successfully beat back the harsh rule. McChesney reports that of the 251 legislators who supported the regulatory rollback and ran again, 89 percent received contributions from the National Automobile Dealers Association.

Of course, even in Washington, undisguised extortion is unseemly. The FTC Used Car Rule in its original form posed a credible threat because it enjoyed the support of an array of Baptist groups, including national consumer organizations and state attorneys general. But who were the Bootleggers? It seems likely, of course, that new car dealers were interested in raising rivals' cost. But in this case, perhaps the real Bootleggers were the politicians who, abetted by good Baptists, seized the opportunity to feather their reelection nests just by preserving the status quo.[5]

Final Thoughts

The public choice perspectives we've explored shed considerable light on the Bootlegger side of our story. Our theories view politicians as highly specialized brokers who seek to balance competing demands for valuable political favors. If the brokers are to survive, the balance they strike must yield benefits to appropriately located special interest groups while at the same time providing citizen services to the folks back home. These theories remind us that all special interest groups are not created equal. Larger is not necessarily better. Those who have the most to gain or lose will persist longer and pay more in pursuit of political favors, and groups that are smaller and more homogeneous will be better equipped to play politics than larger, more diverse groups.

The Baptist element has not been the focus of this chapter but still plays a critical role in the story. Votes for a policy that transfers wealth from the broader electorate to a small interest group can be obtained far more cheaply if the supporting rhetoric includes a Baptist appeal—transforming a potentially embarrassing political liability into fodder for a politician's press releases. Even when politicians themselves play the Bootlegger role, as in our tale of wealth extraction, Baptist support is critical.

The survey of White House economic reports gave us the opportunity to show how regulatory reasoning made its way into official political dialogue. As regulation became a larger force in the life of the nation, presidents learned there was more to the story than straightforward efforts to serve the public interest. Implicit references were made to capture theory, to special interest theory, and finally to Bootlegger/Baptist explanations.

So what can we say about the Bootlegger's story? First, it is a story we can tell on its own: even when Bootleggers lack Baptist allies, they will always seek political favors, sometimes successfully. But far better days arrive when Baptists join the Bootlegger cause—and the time has come to put the spotlight on the Baptists' side of the stage. We begin the next chapter with a simple question: Why Baptists?

3. Why Baptists?

In the last chapter, we examined how Bootleggers influence political action. Baptists entered the story along the way to show how the political costs facing Bootleggers could fall when Baptists joined their cause. In a sense, though, this is question begging. Indeed, we are so used to the sentiment that American politicians need to offer a moral explanation for their actions that we seldom ask the question that motivates this chapter: Why Baptists?

The question may seem trivial, given that we all seem to know instinctively that making naked deals with big business is bad politics. But why? Why is it that the typical person seems to have a hard-wired understanding that moral justification is required for successful politicking? Shouldn't a political party's justification be enough? Or just an appeal to economic necessity? After all, big business does mean big jobs, higher incomes, extended life expectancies, better health care, and lots of other things people love. Charlie Wilson, a former auto executive who served as secretary of defense under Eisenhower, famously claimed, "What's good for General Motors is good for the country—and vice versa." So why can't politicians get away with saying that the Bootlegger groups represent vital economic interests that must be served? Why not straight talk?

Economist Paul Rubin, who has worked at both the Consumer Product Safety Commission and the Federal Trade Commission, notes that special interest groups routinely claim to deserve politically provided benefits for specific public interest reasons. Rubin offers a sample of public interest rhetoric: "Farmers are the backbone of America; steel producers are suffering from 'foreign excess steel capacity and market-distorting practices'" (Rubin 2002, 166). So why is interest group advocacy not enough? Why do groups, Bootlegger or Baptist, invariably describe their efforts in terms of fairness and serving a broad public interest? Is something deeply ingrained in the electorate that demands a moral justification for political action? And if so, why do some groups manage to satisfy that demand while others fail?

We address these questions, not just because doing so serves our theory but because the questions, often assumed away as obvious or trivial, are relevant to anyone interested in understanding American political behavior. Accordingly, this chapter focuses on the Baptist element in the Bootlegger/Baptist theory. Standard economics assumes that politicians will respond to those who contribute to their campaigns, employ their constituents, and invest in the communities, districts, and states they represent. Quid pro quo is explanation enough for these actions. But as James M. Buchanan (1994, 73) indicates, there is no obviously comparable quid pro quo with the moral community. Instead, there are evolved habits of the heart that, in every functioning society, operate as low-cost order-generating bonds. Seeking to serve private interests alone is not enough: successful politicians must clothe their actions in a public interest cloak woven from the familiar moral fiber that binds together the community they serve.

We begin our analysis by drawing on the moral philosophy of Adam Smith and David Hume. We then relate their notions of other-regarding or unselfish behavior to research in experimental economics, which directly tests the hypothesis that an other-regarding element is indeed at play when ordinary people engage in trade or other economic transactions. The literature we survey suggests that unselfish human behavior is every bit as fundamental as the self-interested striving of "homo economicus"—a fact that can and will be accounted for by successful political agents. Our discussion at this point lays the foundations of our answer to "Why Baptists?"

Evidence of other-regarding behavior observed in experimental economics can be seen as grounds for a genetic tendency to cooperate and thus survive in groups. We pursue this line of reasoning by delving into an evolutionary explanation of what may be going on in the experimental economics studies we survey. Here we describe the role and rise of religion, first as a survival mechanism in human communities and later as a governing mechanism. Communities with a high degree of cooperation and other-regarding behavior—a prerequisite for successful defense against raiders from other bands—were better adapted for survival. Groups that cooperated best in battle lived to see another day. Groups whose members fought isolated struggles, refusing to risk their individual safety for the benefit of their fellows, never left the field of battle. Evolutionary psychologists, zoologists, and religion scholars tell us that over the millennia, human communities characterized by a high degree of cooperative behavior survived (Ridley 1996; Wade 2009; Wright 1994). Those characterized by defection did not (Nowak 2011). Group survival in a Hobbesian jungle required altruistic behavior that religion can promote (Rubin 2002, 59–63; Wade 2009, 72). Religion and religious practices evolved as apparently low-cost mechanisms for inducing cooperation and perpetuating community social norms and moral values (Wade 2009, 48–51). Populations in surviving cooperative communities passed on cooperative genes. Those in defecting communities did not. Having laid another round of stones in the Baptist foundation based on evolutionary forces, we then show how moral appeals by politicians can be seen as necessary and desirable. Bootleggers and Baptists then emerge as a winning coalition.

In the chapter's final section, we turn to both recent and historical American protest movements to show how rational ignorance inflamed protesters' passions—and how politicians seized the opportunity to pass pork to favored Bootleggers. This gets to the heart of our theory: the good intentions of the many often unexpectedly pave the way for the private interests of the few. Our final message is a cautionary one: when unconstrained favor-seeking behavior becomes endemic, bets on Bootlegger/Baptist coalitions yielding efficiency gains will tend to be losing wagers. Instead, as Tullock (1975) argued, the pursuit of government favors ends up consuming resources while producing little or no wealth.

A note to our readers before proceeding. We get a bit technical in some of the discussion that follows, which may turn off some readers. Others may simply find the answer to the motivating question "Why Baptists?" to be self-evident. Nevertheless, we believe those who are interested in more than just an unpacking of the old familiar story of private interests swindling the public will find something new here. Indeed, the Bootlegger/Baptist theory is far deeper than most realize. It is not only about pork and politics but also about what ultimately binds us together as a society—and accordingly, about how politicians must appeal to that underlying fabric.

Morality, Trust, and Swapping Favors

All special interest groups are mutual admiration societies. They are formed by self-selection. Those who join agree with the group's purpose, and members tend to like each other. More to the point, special interest groups believe so strongly in their cause that they find it odd that further justification may be needed for the political support they seek. Downtown merchants associations see themselves as forming the economic backbone of downtown, something every citizen should welcome. Isn't that enough to justify a tax break when big-box retailers threaten? Engineering societies believe their members are making the world a safer and more humane place. Petroleum trade associations express deep belief in the broader purpose they serve: providing safe, low-cost energy to light the nation's homes and power the factories. Labor unions see themselves as serving the interests of hard-working people who may not always get a fair deal from their employers. The difficulty comes in getting the outside world, the political world, to agree that these justifications are sufficient grounds to deliver pork. To get their way in the political arena, the Bootleggers must move beyond claims that their group is especially deserving and make an appeal to commonly held norms of what is right.

Organization leaders can't simply walk into a senator's office, unarmed with broad public interest justification for their particular pursuit, and expect a positive response. Bootleggers must appeal to a common value to which the public will respond. Put another way, the Bootleggers have to help the politician prepare a good explanation for assisting them. When pursuing ethanol subsidies, for instance, the Bootlegger corn producers made an environmental appeal. When opposing free-trade agreements that would allow more low-cost Asian goods to enter U.S. commerce, U.S. producers and labor unions may invoke the immoral foreign use of child labor.

As the philosopher David Hume (2000, 266) said most famously in his magnum opus, *A Treatise of Human Nature*, "Reason is, and ought only to be the slave of the passions." Translated into our narrative (and southern vernacular), he might well have said, "Any Bootlegger worth his salt better make a Baptist appeal if he hopes to bring home the bacon." We all fancy ourselves sterling examples of reason and common sense. Yet more is going on in our heads than what our conscious minds report. Lurking behind the rational mind is an unconscious mind laden with emotional beliefs that shape our actions. If Bootlegger organizations want to win the day on Capitol Hill, they must send the appropriate signals to the treacherous domain of the passions.

All this may sound a bit deep and curious, but if we stay with it, we face another question: How exactly do special interest groups know what passions to appeal to? Why not patriotism? Buy American? Why not saving downtown from price-cutting big-box stores? What about keeping the wheels of American industry turning? After all, lots of gods, idols, and demigods might do the job. The answer to these questions is important in guiding our narrative of what constitutes the winning Bootlegger/Baptist coalition. We ask the reader to indulge us as we digress into an exploration of several areas of the academic literature, starting with a look at Adam Smith and experimental economics. When we reach the destination, the patient reader will understand why we took the trip.

Adam Smith and the "Impartial Spectator"

The great Scottish philosopher Adam Smith ([1759] 1982) offered in his "other" great book, *The Theory of Moral Sentiments,* a compelling thought experiment to illustrate how humans interact with one another in a community setting. Smith claimed that we all have an "impartial spectator" embedded in our genetic makeup that can be called on to help us understand how our actions will be viewed by others. The impartial spectator is impartial in that no person's preferences or interests are considered more important than any other's and is a spectator in that this "man within the breast," as Smith described it, focuses on the larger community and helps the searching individual figure out what is morally right and wrong.

By appealing to this impartial spectator, we are able to figure out where the sympathies of others truly lie (Adam Smith [1759] 1982, 132). According to Smith, the spectator helps us constrain our actions and offers guidance in what will be met with approval and what with disapproval. This is not to say that the impartial spectator is always accurate, as of course each person has his own underlying bias, or that people always follow what their impartial spectator dictates; we are free to ignore our consciences. But the idea is still a powerful one: the impartial spectator in general exists to ward off disagreeable behavior that could lead us into trouble with others. Think of it as a mental referee, helping people play the game of life.

In evolutionary terms, the impartial spectator can be seen as an emerging means of cooperating with others, allowing us to avoid constant conflict that would reduce our chances of survival. Those who find themselves in conflict with others are not long for this world, because their DNA risks being unceremoniously dumped from the gene pool. Those who survive are likely to have some innate sense of what will be met with approval from society and what will provoke ostracism or punishment.

Of course, the impartial spectator is no fool. Just as it can seek approval and facilitate social cooperation, it can also condemn inappropriate behavior by others. When the actions of others cause the impartial spectator to recoil in disgust, we react with an appropriate response. This mix of cooperation and censure is beneficial, because it ensures that those who do not deserve trust will more often be left out in the cold. As the saying goes, "Fool me once, shame on you. Fool me twice, shame on me."[1]

Our interactions with others thus involve a peculiar form of cooperation, one marked by not only sympathy but also potential hostility. Put another way, this form of other-regarding behavior is intricately related to the notion of reciprocity. How we act toward another person is informed by the other person's behavior as much as by our own. Please be patient, dear reader. We are on our way to discovering the answer to "Why Baptists?"

Reciprocity Observed in the Laboratory

Adam Smith's notion of the impartial spectator suggests that we trust others but only so much as this is validated by subsequent actions. That is, trust is guided by reciprocity. Because trust in others is fragile, wealth-accumulating communities must find ways to strengthen the tendency to cooperate. Social norms that embody moral standards such as religious teachings, for example, form an impartial spectator that must be nurtured to sustain cooperation.

A large body of laboratory evidence from experimental economics illustrates the extent to which these norms of cooperation prevail. Vernon Smith (1998), winner of the 2002 Nobel Prize for his seminal work in experimental economics, wrote specifically on the link between Adam Smith's impartial spectator and the lessons of the laboratory. According to Vernon Smith, our ability to reason what others are thinking is responsible for the community of personal relationships that ultimately facilitate economic growth. By relying on an inherent sense of trust, validated by subsequent reciprocal interaction, people may overcome short-run, selfish tendencies and instead engage in trade.

A set of economic experiments, known as the "trust game," illustrates this lesson. In the trust game, each person is given a certain amount of money and paired with another person for a series of interactions. The first person, a "trustor," decides whether to send the second person, a "trustee," any of his cash. If he does, this money is automatically tripled upon receipt by the trustee. Once the transfer occurs, the trustee then decides how much of this tripled amount to send back to the trustor.

Simple self-interest would predict that the trustor would never send money to the trustee, since the trustee loses nothing in keeping it all. But the results show that actual human beings behave quite differently. In the original experimental sessions documented in Berg, Dickhaut, and McCabe (1995), more than 90 percent of the subjects decided to trust their counterpart by transferring at least some of their money. Of these trusting subjects, half were met with reciprocity that resulted in positive returns: their partners returned earnings greater than the original amount sent. Furthermore, the returned earnings were higher when trustors sent a greater portion of their original endowment. In other words, not only were most of the subjects more trusting than strict self-interest would predict, but at least half the trustees given the opportunity to "take the money and run" failed to do so. Though limited, trust clearly emerged in a manner unanticipated by strict self-interest in this experimental environment.

Although this evidence is not universally in favor of our implicit sense of trust with one another, it does provide support for the larger theory of reciprocity. Most of the trustors initiated trust with their counterpart, and of those who did, half were met with reciprocated trust. This result is remarkable given that these trustees were essentially giving up free money. From a narrowly self-interested perspective, the trustee could gain more by exploiting his partner's trust than from cooperation. Nevertheless, trust emerged.

Remember, though, that if trust is violated, the impartial spectator beckons us to respond in kind. Another series of experiments, known as the "ultimatum" and "dictator" games, illustrates just how precarious trust can be once violated. These experiments pair persons up to determine how a certain amount of money will be split. In the ultimatum game, the first person decides how much money to offer the second person. The second person then decides whether to accept or reject the offered amount. If rejected, neither subject gains anything. The money is simply returned to the experiment. In the dictator game, the same rules apply except now the second person has no decision to make. Whatever the first person decides is final.

In the ultimatum game, strict self-interest would predict that the first person would send a trivial amount (that is, the minimum transfer, usually one dollar), and the second person would accept any distribution that resulted in his receiving anything more than zero dollars. In the dictator game, in contrast, strict self-interest predicts that the first person sends nothing, because the second person cannot reject the distribution.

Again, experimental results challenge this strict self-interest prediction. In the vast majority of reported experimental results, the first player in the ultimatum game chooses a percentage distribution between 70:30 and 50:50 (with the first player's percentage shown first in the ratio). If the first player calls for a larger payoff than 70 percent for himself, the second player will tend to reject the deal. In the dictator game, the first player still tends to send a positive amount to the second person, though less than the typical amount offered in the ultimatum game, despite the second person's inability to punish the first player.

Laboratory evidence shows just how hard it is to switch off our innate sense of trust and reciprocity. Take the ultimatum game. Not only does the second person tend to reject low distributions, at his own cost, but the first person already anticipates this, because very few grossly unequal distributions are even offered. In other words, both subjects are able to appeal to their respective impartial spectator in determining how to navigate the exchange in a way that helps both parties (or as Vernon Smith [1998, 7] calls it, "mindreading"). In the dictator game, the first person still recognizes the social context of the interaction. By offering a positive amount, he exposes a trustworthy nature.

This body of research supports the notion that human experience dating back several millennia generated genetic material that predisposed us to the cooperative behavior necessary for collective survival. For cooperation and cooperating communities to flourish, widely known and embraced social norms must embody wisdom of the ages. Again, the impartial spectator must be nourished. As we show in the next section, the lesson in all this is that successful Bootleggers and all other political agents must make a Baptist appeal.

Cooperation, Religion, Politics, and Wealth

The experiments we have described suggest that trust and reciprocity play an enormous role in human decisionmaking. In a sense, high degrees of trust and reciprocity provide low-cost mechanisms for inducing cooperation and perpetuating community social norms and moral values. From an evolutionary perspective, populations in which communities passed on cooperative genes and social customs thrived. Those in acrimonious communities did not. Making this point in his discussion of group survival, Matt Ridley (1997) builds on the work of zoologist Richard Dawkins (1976) and argues that human beings are genetically predisposed to cooperate.

But what about religion and political rhetoric? Again, why Baptists? Richard Dawkins (1976) argues that "actions" taken by the selfish gene "cause" human beings purposefully to seek genetic survival, which includes engaging in cooperative behavior. These efforts are fortified by cultural "memes," such as those found in religious rituals, songs, poems, slogans, and political speech that replicate survival knowledge. Political memes—words, phrases, flags, and drumbeats—that systematically appeal to and reinforce religious, moral, and civic values replicate survival wisdom and strengthen the genetic predisposition to cooperate in surviving groups (Dawkins 1976, 192–94). Nelson and Greene (2003, 4) put forward another explanation that relates to meme replication by way of signaling theory. They "maintain that a person signals that he is trustworthy to some group by imitating its members' behavior. In particular, he imitates their political behavior. This imitation is why ethnic groups and religious groups play such an important role in political behavior and civil strife."

With meme replication and trust signaling, cooperation can yield far more than survival. As Robert Axelrod (1984) points out, mutual cooperation, or what he calls mutual altruism, contains the seeds of community-derived economies of scale for producing life-enhancing resources. Division of labor and specialization follow cooperation. Survival costs fall and cooperative communities flourish where less cooperative ones languish.

But there is still more. Institutions that promote cooperation may also promote trust, truth telling, and promise keeping. The cost of maintaining order falls as these habits of the heart become a community's dominant moral values, which in turn form a basis for principle-based and duty-based moral advocacy (Buchanan 1994; Rose 2011). Political leaders who promote these high moral values may indeed promote a more efficient wealth-producing community, or at least so it would seem at this point in our story.

Separating the Politician from the Preacher

To bring us back to the original question: What about moral values and political rhetoric? Again, why Baptists? Religions that promote cooperation, conservation, and truth telling can be survival mechanisms. Priests and religious leaders, because of the critical role they play as interpreters of otherwise inexplicable events, often emerged to play the dual role of spiritual authority and tribal or community strongman. In this way, the religious or moral logic behind collective action merges with political mobilization of the group. Edicts that in another world might be viewed as strictly political, or as a strongman's ranting, could be seen as interpretations of God's will—providing a stronger motive for compliance than the displeasure of even the toughest tribal chief. Thus, in earlier periods—and even today—religious and political leaders could be the same people. Theocracies have been commonplace across time and space. If there were Bootleggers and Baptists, they were the same individual or entity.

Along these lines, James Montanye (2011, 40) notes that in "religiously homogeneous societies, such as ancient Rome, public provisions of religious ceremonies and rituals also might be warranted on public goods grounds," which is to say homogeneous beliefs helped maintain order. The Roman model for maintaining order by way of the gods and deified emperors was adapted elsewhere by people who believed in just one God. Montanye (2011, 40) notes that the Massachusetts 1780–1833 constitution gave the people of the commonwealth the right to invest the legislature with authority to require mandatory church attendance and support of churches with public funds. The almost iron-clad Puritan link between religion and politics that emerged in America's early history made it only natural that in his inaugural address, John Adams would thank an "overruling Providence for so signally" protecting the country from the outset (Micklethwait and Wooldridge 2009, 75). Seemingly, in this state of affairs, Bootlegger/Baptist coalitions with separable components would seldom arise. The Bootleggers were the Baptists, or vice versa. We find the early Massachusetts model applies across numerous countries today that have official state religions often subsidized by the public purse.

Separation of church and state and the rise of heterogeneous religious preferences— including no religion at all—changed all this, especially in the American experience. Fascinated by America and its promise, Alexis de Tocqueville ([1848] 1990) wrote extensively in the 1840s about the importance of religion in America as well as on the relationship between religion and politics. As he saw the situation, high participation in religious life was crucial to the success of American democracy. Indeed, he claimed that freedom of choice in an appropriate institutional setting would lead the human mind to "regulate the temporal and spiritual institutions in a uniform manner, and man will endeavor . . . , to harmonize earth and heaven" (Tocqueville [1848] 1990, 300). He described the form of Christianity brought to the New World as a "democratic and republican religion."

At the time he was writing, Tocqueville ([1848] 1990, 304) noted that "in the United States, religion exercises but little influence on the laws and on the details of public opinion; but it directs the customs of the community, and, by regulating domestic life, it regulates the states." If religion regulates the state, albeit only partially, then politicians must show respect for the regulatory mechanism and signal their understanding of its power when molding laws and regulation. Within the American landscape, successful politicians must bridge the religious/political/market divide when explaining their actions and in doing so acknowledge, if only by the content of their rhetoric, the critical importance of ethical norms in preserving order.

Ethical behavior can lower the costs of transaction in an ever-evolving political and economic order. This gives rise to the possibility of increased cooperation and economic growth by way of uncoordinated but vigorous support of ethical behavior, rather than constant monitoring to punish shirkers and cheaters. Of course, it must be the right kind of ethical behavior, which includes truth telling, promise keeping, hard work, and thrift. These habits of the heart can be encouraged by political rhetoric that extols the beneficial moral behavior. But there is another darker possibility.

What Happens If the Bootleggers Start Leading the Baptists?

This carefully constructed order can be perverted when the wrong kind of ethics enters the picture. If the state itself is viewed as the proper source of education, housing finance, risk mitigation, consumer protection, environmental protection, care and sustenance for the helpless, and even recreational activities for inner-city young people, then religious and civic groups will focus their energies on influencing the body politic to expand its redistributive activities. We have increasingly seen this result over the 20th century.

This was most evident in the early 1970s when the United States experienced a kind of civic religious awakening. Environmentalism emerged as a powerful social force that reflected characteristics common to conventional religions. Environmental leaders and politicians harmonized and called for a new ethic, a new morality that accorded almost divine status to the natural environment. Similar appeals were raised for federal regulation of food and auto safety, workplaces, and consumer products. As the machinery of government accelerated, a host of new rules and regulations emerged in an effort to change human behavior for the better, at least as seen through the eyes of the environmental leaders. But real-world policies don't spring fully formed from moral intentions or even from the will of the voters—neither of which can be counted on to derail the lobbying locomotive.

How Polling May Mislead and Voting Can Make Things Worse

Recall that voters are rationally ignorant. They may not know much about the inner workings of policy, but they're not suckers either. Telling voters that a special interest group just wants its share of government largess simply won't do. Representatives have to appeal to our other-regarding sympathies. So to gain voter trust, special interest groups have to apply sympathetic cover. Otherwise, the public's other-regarding tendencies will fail to emerge and may even spur voters to oppose the efforts of the organization. The problem, however, is that the sympathies engendered by this Baptist cover do not provide a reliable constraint against Bootlegger gaming of the policy process. In fact, they usually encourage it.

Let's suppose that voters will reward what they perceive as other-regarding behavior and punish pure self-interest. The question then becomes what political activity is truly other regarding and what is motivated more by special interests. It is not enough, after all, that people act in a public-spirited manner: their well-intentioned decisions must also be well informed if political outcomes are to be beneficial. But polling data overwhelmingly show that the public is largely ignorant of political outcomes—and as a result often inadvertently facilitate the seemingly "irrational" behavior so often found in politics (Caplan 2001, 2008).

Economist Bryan Caplan's theory of "rational irrationality" encapsulates this result and operates as follows. The first law of demand states that when the price of a good falls, the quantity demanded increases. Caplan simply applies this basic principle to the "good" of political decisionmaking. As the price of making irrational decisions decreases—meaning the cost of making a dumb but symbolically satisfying decision plummets—the quantity demanded of irrationality increases. The lower the cost of making irrational decisions in a particular domain, the more such decisions we should expect to see.

Bootleggers, of course, understand this and react accordingly. Although it is necessary to provide Baptist cover, this cover need not be especially coherent in terms of standing up to intellectual scrutiny. Detailed scrutiny is usually the last thing on the public's mind. Instead, all that is needed is a credible appeal to sympathy that the public can recognize as being trustworthy.

As we argued previously, human beings do not always behave as simple economic models predict: they will often accept substantial costs to behave morally, and in principle that might include the information costs of learning about the complex effects of legislative proposals. It may also mean that voters are willing to forgo losses on certain public projects simply because "it is the right thing to do." As we detail further below, massive expenditures are put toward environmental causes every year with little in the way of public complaint. Indeed, voters cheer these efforts for their tough stance on pollution. In a way, voters relish the opportunity to have their "impartial spectator" nourished with no real effort on their part. Nevertheless, the result of these outcomes is to privately reward Bootleggers, who bask in the glow of all this moral sympathy.[2]

Recall that these moral impulses evolved in small communities to govern individual conduct whose relationship to social outcomes was relatively straightforward. A voter's "impartial spectator" would surely condemn the choice to remain "rationally ignorant" about the bad social consequences of a policy, but only if the spectator already understands what those consequences really are. Morality cannot help us escape the problem of rational irrationality if the impartial spectator is never awakened. Put another way, voters do not know what they do not know. This can yield disastrous outcomes when our sympathies are engaged on behalf of policies whose consequences are not obvious—especially once the Bootleggers have exerted their influence on the details of implementation.

Thus, the presence of the Bootlegger changes the dynamic. Instead of ethical behavior leading to a superior expansion path that generates higher income and improved human well-being, Bootleggers routinely generate an inferior expansion path with lower income and diminished human well-being. In a world of naive voters, strategic political appeals based on a higher morality may lead to hoodwinking of the worst kind. When Bootlegger/Baptist coalitions form, resources that otherwise might be used for enhanced production and consumption will be dissipated in political struggles that consume more wealth than they produce.

Writing in 1810, American politician and political theorist John C. Calhoun ([1810] 1992) addressed this dynamic as it applied to taxing and spending, but the larger issue he spoke of was political redistribution. He put the problem this way:

> It must necessarily follow, that some one portion of the community must pay in taxes more than it receives back in disbursements; while another receives in disbursements more than it pays in taxes. . . . The necessary result, then, of the unequal fiscal action of the government is, to divide the community into two great classes; one consisting of those who, in reality, pay the taxes, and, of course, bear exclusively the burthen of supporting the government; and the other, of those who are the recipients of their proceeds, through disbursements, and who are, in fact, supported by the government; or, in fewer words, to divide it into tax-payers and tax-consumers. (Calhoun, [1810] 1992, np)

Unaware of what today we call public choice theory, Calhoun's concerns embodied much of what we have discussed. By providing moral sympathy—on the cheap no less—to voters, special interest groups become armed by others wearing breastplates of righteousness; then even larger transfers can be made from the uninformed body politic to the lurking special interest groups.

The theory of Bootleggers and Baptists thus puts a new spin on an old tune, that of who really benefits from public largess and at whose expense. Although the narratives on this point differ depending on political alliances, Bootlegger/Baptist arrangements clearly point to a common answer; that is, the primary beneficiaries of public choice are economic interests using moral suasion to dilute public coffers. The providers of such a delightful service are essentially everyone else. The Bootlegger/Baptist dynamic accordingly gives new clarity to the recent outrage in 2011–12, which entailed the "99 percent" protesting against the powers that be for supporting the remaining "1 percent" at the expense of everyone else. We turn to this example along with its historical counterparts.

Protesters and the Rationally Ignorant 99 Percent

Numerous movements have sought to "change the world" yet ended up greasing the rails for Bootleggers waiting in the wings. We trace several historical protests and social change movements, all the way up to the recent 2011–12 Occupy Wall Street movement, which emerged in the wake of the 2007–09 credit market collapse and became famous for slogans naming the disgruntled occupiers, the 99 percent, who were fleeced by the wealthy 1 percenters occupying Wall Street skyscrapers. As is typical of the movements we explore, theirs was an anti-capitalist protest, but it could have been more focused. It could have been an anti-Bootlegger/Baptist protest, an opportunity so often missed by those who misidentify the culprit behind "bad" capitalism outcomes.

In *Grand Pursuit*, Sylvia Nasar's 2011 book on economic thought, the author describes similar turmoil that arose in the aftermath of the panic of 1893 (Nasar 2011, 153–63). By 1895, some 500 banks had failed, 15,000 firms had given up the ghost, major railroads had gone bankrupt, and unemployment gripped one of every seven workers. There was famine in the land, and popular anger was directed toward familiar targets: bankers, moneymen, and the wealthy owners of the great enterprises of the time. Whereas most of today's Wall Street protesters are unemployed young people, farmers stood front and center then. The farmers were facing bankruptcy while Wall Street seemed to be rolling in money. Then, as now, the protesters zeroed in on the most immediate target they could find: the banks, rich people, and fat cat corporations. But then, as now, the deeper cause of the problem was far more complex.

These 19th-century protesters were angry and frustrated and somehow felt that Wall Street bankers were the source of the problem. The 99 percent of that day, for the most part, were rationally ignorant about how the international gold standard operated at the time. They did not understand how deflationary swings could force down agricultural commodity and other prices and bankrupt farmers, Main Street merchants, and manufacturers, leading to massive layoffs. All that was clear to them was that somehow, through all this, the Wall Street bankers survived or even flourished.

At the time of the 1893 panic, America was just becoming a regulated national economy. The Act to Regulate Commerce, which formed the Interstate Commerce Commission (ICC), had been passed in 1887, mainly at the urging of a farmers' movement calling for fair railroad rates. The farmers, who saw higher freight rates when they shipped their goods to larger cities, had wanted short-haul and long-haul freight rates to be equal. But instead of bringing lower rates, the

ICC became dominated by former railroad executives and lawyers. The ICC went for equal rates all right: the commission raised rates for everyone. The ICC functioned as a cartel manager that favored railroad survival, not farmer prosperity.

Along another dimension of the economy, the Sherman Antitrust Act had been passed in 1890. The stated purpose of the law was to rein in the power of the trusts and large enterprises that seemed to be controlling major markets nationwide. This satisfied the populists who supported it, but the statute's first application was against organized labor, not industrial firms.

A partial response to the 19th-century outcry came later when major banking legislation was passed in December 1913, forming the Federal Reserve banking system, a cartelization of national banks that fundamentally changed how U.S. financial institutions would operate, how they would avoid bankruptcy, and how the older risk of deflation would be converted to a new inflationary reality. In short, the 19th-century protest can be seen as a Baptist element in a Bootlegger/Baptist story where leading national bank operators played the Bootlegger role. The protest, far from ending special interest regulation, served to stimulate it.

There is another well-known, highly focused Washington protest: the Bonus Army's march to Washington in the late spring of 1932 (Shlaes 2007, 127–28). The marchers, some 20,000 strong, were World War I veterans who had been promised a bonus for their service, to be awarded in 1945. As the economy tanked, a movement arose to give the veterans an early payment. With sympathetic support among some members of Congress but staunch opposition from the White House and Treasury Department, these middle-aged and older men, caught in the difficult backwaters of the Great Depression, occupied abandoned government buildings, pitched tents in Washington's Anacostia Flats, and settled in for the duration. Their leader, an unemployed veteran named Walter Waters, "decided that if bankers could lobby, so could hungry veterans" (Alter 2006, 121).

President Herbert Hoover, concerned that the veterans represented a threat to the government, chose not to meet with them. On July 28, 1932, two veterans were killed when police attempted to empty a building they had occupied (Alter 2006, 122). That in itself was bad enough, but that afternoon, the U.S. Army was ordered to clear out the rest of the Bonus Army. A young General Douglas MacArthur aided by two deputies, Dwight D. Eisenhower and George S. Patton, led a contingent of troops supported by tanks and forced the veterans to abandon their camp. The tragic event occurred in the midst of a presidential campaign that would bring Franklin Roosevelt's New Deal to office. On hearing about the army's attack, Roosevelt is said to have turned to his aide Felix Frankfurter and remarked, "This elects me" (Hiltzik 2011). Mr. Roosevelt was swept into office in 1932 and installed New Deal programs that established the largest Bootlegger/Baptist playground yet to exist. The veterans received their bonus payments in 1936 (Nasar 2011, 330).

We now move forward to that grand epoch of social regulation that started in the 1970s with Earth Day. The event, organized by Wisconsin senator Gaylord Nelson with a lot of help from others nationwide, generated a 20 million-person turnout and ushered in the heyday of federal environmental regulation. Earth Day activities included marches in cities, programs in grammar schools, speakers at universities, and a surprised recognition by politicians that environmental protection was a hot-button topic that must be considered in an election bid. The Earth Day activists had one message: the Earth has been abused, and we environmental sinners must change our ways. Much like the Wall Street protesters, the anger of the Earth Day protesters was focused on corporate America. There was a clarion call for the federal government to get tough on corporate polluters. Unfettered greed was the problem, as the protesters saw it.

Interestingly, the federal government was just on the verge of taking action in 1970, but most politicians had no way of knowing that 20 million people cared enough about the environment to march in the streets. The first Clean Air Act was being formulated in Sen. Edmund Muskie's Senate Public Works Committee, and another statute creating the EPA was winding its way through Congress. Meanwhile, what would become the Federal Water Pollution Control Act of 1972 was just getting organized.

The 20 million Earth Day protesters had an effect, perhaps more than they could realize. They became Baptists for early emerging environmental Bootleggers. At stake at the time was the presidency. Sitting president Richard Nixon had sponsored the formation of the EPA; he wanted to be known as the environmental president, especially after learning that 20 million Americans were turning green. Senator Muskie also wanted to be president. The two competed in an effort to be tough on polluters while singing the praises of the Earth Day movement (Yandle 2013).

Senator Muskie's draft Clean Air Act had called for the creation of incremental performance standards that would be imposed on all major sources of air pollution across the land (Manheim 2009, 41). These standards would set the precise pollution reduction goals to be accomplished in a stated time. Polluters could accomplish the goals any way they wished; what mattered was cleaner air. The use of performance standards would encourage competition and creativity in finding new, lower-cost ways to clean up. But just what specific technologies would emerge—and whom they would benefit—was surely less clear than the effect of a mandate laying out concrete engineering standards. Unlike other regulatory approaches, performance standards offered few opportunities for corporate Bootleggers seeking pork. Mr. Muskie's performance standards were soon to be scratched. Ralph Nader, a leading public interest voice at the time who was inspired by the Earth Day crowds, accused Muskie of being soft on polluters (Manheim 2009, 41). In response, the good senator lowered the boom on corporate America: his committee revised the draft Clean Air Act to require costly technology.

Now enter the Bootleggers. The revised Clean Air Act not only required a one-size-fits-all technology-based solution, it imposed stricter standards for new sources than for old sources. The act thus created barriers to entry for new competitors. Existing manufacturing plants had to adopt specified machinery to clean up, but new competitors had to spend even more money. In this case, the protesters were successful. They got what they wanted, and some Bootleggers made the most of it. Bootleggers and Baptists both wanted a one-size-fits-all approach, and established manufacturers must have liked the fact that the new laws would raise competitor costs.

Now fast-forward one last time to the fall of 2011, when hundreds and then thousands of protesters took to parks and streets, first in America, and then across the globe, as part of a movement called Occupy Wall Street. On September 17, 2011, Occupy Wall Street began with a few hundred disgruntled citizens camped out in Zuccotti Park in the heart of New York's financial district (Pepitone

2011; Walters 2011). They were young, for the most part, with a heavy contingent of unemployed recent college graduates. One of the protesters dubbed their camping area Solyndra Park, named for the solar energy firm that had recently received a half-billion dollars in taxpayer loan guarantees, only to go bankrupt and default on the loans (Graham 2011). Solyndra's baptism with taxpayer money had been a much-celebrated event in the Obama administration's effort to stimulate green energy production while stimulating the economy. In a way, even Solyndra had some Bootlegger/Baptist flavor. Clean energy, which is moral high ground for environmentalists, was the political rationale offered for corralling and distributing taxpayer money. Bootleggers like Solyndra, General Electric, and others were simply looking for lower-cost funds. Unfortunately, however, neither Solyndra nor the economy responded favorably to the money shower.

Though perhaps inspired by the 2011 Arab Spring, which saw young people in another world taking to the streets to protest and foment revolutions, these American autumn protesters were not interested in toppling the government. They were angry about the U.S. political economy. Over time, every gripe possible was aired: bailed-out banks, corporate greed, bankrupt homeowners, the vanishing middle class, growing income inequality, war, and even natural gas extraction by way of hydrofracking (Lallanilla 2011). By one observer's count, the two dominant signs held high in the protester parades were "The banks got bailed out. We got sold out." and "We are the 99 percent" (Hedler 2011).

As the protest moved across major American cities to smaller towns and then to Europe, there was a recurring theme of dissatisfaction with special interest influence in politics and a burgeoning sense that American democracy just doesn't seem capable of righting itself. Indeed, some of the 99 percent held signs quoting the Declaration of Independence about the right of the people to reform government. As one protester put it: "It doesn't matter what you protest. Just protest" (Driscoll 2011). The number of locations and people involved eventually rose to the point that media commentators, politicians, and others tried to determine just what they were saying. What was the protest about? And, if and when that was understood, how could their concerns be addressed?

The 99 percent were clearly onto something in recognizing the massive Bootlegger/Baptist economy that has emerged in the United States since 1970. Occupy Wall Street was a sign that the 99 percent were finally recognizing the vast plunder of public coffers by well-organized Bootleggers—even if they routinely misdiagnosed it as a symptom of "free-market" policies run amok. This is understandable because the 99 percent are rationally ignorant about most political activity; they are busy earning a living, looking for jobs, and trying to figure how to make ends meet. They generally have no time to read daily issues of the *Federal Register* and track special interest lobbying in Washington. Indeed, many have probably never heard of the *Federal Register*, but they know something is wrong.

This episode also demonstrates just how Bootlegger/Baptist coalitions constantly evolve to provide benefits across this moral divide. For example, Mary Kay Henry, president of the SEIU, endorsed the Occupy movement and added a pure Baptist signal urging support of President Obama's American Jobs Act. That statute, coincidentally, calls for funds to expand the ranks of public service employees (Henry 2011). Perhaps Ms. Henry hoped that she had joined the moral high ground. When asked about the burgeoning movement, President Obama said this about Occupy Wall Street, "I think people are frustrated, and the protesters are giving voice to a more broad-based frustration about how our financial system works" (Isidore 2011).

The Zuccotti Park occupants called capitalism the problem, but the culprit needs to be a bit better identified. The problem is regulatory capitalism and what some call crony capitalism. We understand how easy misidentification is in the opaque world of special interest legislation. After all, what could be more noble than enabling people everywhere to experience the American homeownership dream, even if they lack the income to qualify for regular loans? Yet perhaps it is not so noble when families by the thousands are bounced from their homes when they cannot pay their monthly mortgage. Very few of the protesters had reason to know that the great housing bubble and its collapse were rooted in a complex witch's brew of special interest legislation and that Bootlegger/Baptist–driven legislation had spurred the expansion of such risky loans.

Most of the Occupy group were aware that huge financial firms were indeed bailed out with taxpayer money, but they may not have realized that this happened after the Federal Reserve changed policy, tightened credit, and in doing so, pricked the housing bubble. By then, it was too late to do much more than bail out the banks so that our monetary system would continue to operate. Yet in all this, the black hats were placed on the heads of bankers who earned lots of money moving the money. And the white hats? They generally went on the heads of the good public servants who, while earning millions, ran the federal housing finance organizations, the very organizations that went belly-up because of poor management and were nationalized, bailed out by the 99 percent.

We can only speculate about where Occupy Wall Street may take us. But we can be more certain regarding what happened in the aftermath of the 1893 panic, the Bonus March on Washington, and Earth Day. In those cases, the protesters satisfied a necessary Baptist requirement for later legislation that would feather the nests of some important Bootleggers. We hasten to say that this does not mean that real problems were not resolved, or that the world, on balance, was necessarily made worse off. What we do claim is that the early protest movements did not bring an end to Bootlegger and Baptist lobbying. We also note that the 1893 protesters, Bonus March veterans, and Earth Day protesters were not tightly focused on precisely how our political economy had gone awry. They had specific, self-interested outcomes in mind. Thus, the more focused the message, the more helpful the cover for the eager Bootlegger.

Final Thoughts

We began this chapter with a series of questions about political rhetoric and why politicians and special interest group leaders systematically speak in moral if not religious terms. The questions were a predicate for the larger question: Why Baptists? The question we have addressed goes far beyond the theory of regulation that motivates this book. The question is fundamentally about human nature, social order, and the interaction of politics and religion. The wisdom of Adam Smith and David Hume provided a foundation for examining what experimental economics tells us about human behavior in simulated exchange-and-bargaining situations. Human subjects in experimental interaction are systematically other regarding in their behavior. Put another way, the experiments tell us we are dealing with a moral animal. This discovery sheds important light on our question: Why Baptists?

Having observed what appears to be a preference for moral behavior, the literature from evolutionary psychology and the biological sciences helps explain why moral behavior tends to dominate some categories of human action. Humans survived in groups, and group survival requires cooperation. The genes of cooperators were passed on. Those of defectors were not. Modern man is predisposed to cooperate, to be other regarding in his behavior. Being predisposed, we hasten to add, does not mean that all humans will be altruistic. There is more to human behavior than genetic predisposition. In addition to nature, nurture and incentives affect outcomes. But the moral predisposition shows that the cost of long-run survival can be reduced when people cooperate, as when they engage in mutually beneficial exchange.

Another finding in our search for an explanation of political rhetoric relates to how knowledge of cooperation's critical value is passed from one group to another and from one generation to another. The story we constructed emphasizes the economic importance of ethical behavior and illuminates why economically successful communities maintain a moral or religious sector. If truth telling and promise keeping can be made a common part of community culture, then transaction costs will fall, and markets will flourish. With this in mind, politicians have even more reasons to use ethical, moral, and religious terms when communicating with the public, as do interest groups. But this is not the end of the story.

When the state is seen as the provider of basic human needs and the protector of the weak and downtrodden, and when regulation and fiscal policy activities expand to address these basic human demands almost without limit, then Bootlegger activity expands and politicians become even more engaged in brokering politically determined benefits across competing groups. Instead of putting a society on a superior growth path to higher wealth and well-being, moral rhetoric becomes associated with a state that is engaged in almost perpetual political resource churning that in the end reduces human well-being.

Why Baptists, then? The Baptist component of the Bootlegger/ Baptist theory is present because of deeply embedded genetic and cultural habits of the heart. Politicians and others who wish to gain the support and patronage of the larger community must earn the public's trust by speaking in symbolic terms that signal membership in the ethical community. Interest groups that seek political support must do the same. When constitutional constraints limit the domain of political action, ethical engagement can lead to a stronger, more efficient economic outcome. When those constraints are lacking, the same behavior writ large can lead to a weakened, high-transaction-cost regulatory state where Bootlegger/Baptist and other anti-capitalism coalitions flourish. As we show in the next four chapters, these appeals to our moral sympathy have the unfortunate effect of lighting the fires that fuel the barbecue feast for Bootleggers in line for pork.

4. Sin and Substance: Who Are the Real Bootleggers and Baptists?

We now explore the most obvious candidate for applied Bootlegger/Baptist analysis: illicit substances and their regulation by government. Readers familiar with the American television series *The Untouchables*, *The Wire*, or *Boardwalk Empire* are armed and ready to hear about the dubious dealings of politicians who declare "war" on drugs and alcohol, at least in the world of fiction. But friends, we are not weaving prime-time drama: the stories to follow are real.

Life is often stranger than fiction. In the televised world, it may be hard to tell the difference between the drug lord and the precinct boss as they go about organizing a cop-protected market for crack cocaine. But in the real world of booze, cigarettes, and weed, which we explore, things are a bit more complex. Helped along by good Baptists, Bootleggers can obtain legal protection for their enterprises by way of federal or state regulation. Everything is seemingly above board. But when we look beneath the boards, there are surprises galore.

As we explained in the preface, the "Bootlegger" and "Baptist" labels were chosen in homage to the original coalition of unlikely interests that was so successful in championing Sunday closing laws, which shuttered liquor stores one day a week. At the height of its success, this coalition entirely shut down the legal sale of alcoholic beverages in counties, states, and— ultimately, during Prohibition (1920–33)—the nation as a whole.

What was the moral motivating force for the closings? Sin. The behavior engendered by alcohol created an obvious target for moral crusaders but an equally meaningful, if less obvious, opportunity for Bootlegger interests. Alcohol markets have been deeply regulated for decades if not centuries. The Bootleggers and Baptists did their work years ago. As we show, alcohol distribution takes place within a well-protected cartel arrangement, which has been tested in the courts many times. When threats arise that might disturb the cartel, as they have recently with the sale of retail wine, Bootleggers and Baptists rise to the challenge.

In contrast, the regulation of tobacco marketing practices, while well established in important ways, is still evolving. This means that Bootlegger/Baptist interaction is more frequent—and more valuable to interest groups such as tobacco companies seeking to lock in their profits. The result has been a string of important, though transient, cases of Baptists winning small victories while Bootleggers win the larger war. Tobacco interests have effectively achieved a government-enforced cartel that succeeds in limiting output, while seemingly placating the interests of concerned Baptists.

Finally, marijuana is an illegal substance at the federal level but tolerated to varying degrees in some states—particularly for medicinal purposes. Because of these exceptions, some regulatory walls are beginning to crack, with specialized markets emerging and increasing calls for legalization. In 2012, voters in Colorado and Washington approved ballot initiatives to add those states to the ones that legalized the recreational use of cannabis. As a result, Bootleggers that operate in the illegal market are threatened, and Baptists are somewhat uncertain how to position themselves. Alcoholic beverages and tobacco products are examples of Bootlegger/Baptist–assisted cartelization of markets for legal products. In sharp contrast, marijuana is largely an illegal product that is only now approaching the point where a government-managed cartel is possible.

In each of these cases, Bootlegger/Baptist interaction is highlighted in the evolving political market where regulatory institutions are devised. This chapter makes the point that even with substances that society generally discourages, actual efforts to constrain their use are often guided as much by self-interested Bootleggers as they are by public-spirited Baptists.

Alcohol, Retail Wine, and the War between the States

The state of Georgia, until quite recently, required that each alcohol supplier designate just one wholesaler as the sole product distributor for an entire region of the state. Bootlegger motivation enters the picture immediately. Wholesalers, endowed with a distribution monopoly in a particular region, sold their wares to retail outlets at prices well above the competitive market rate. In other words, "the state not only permits but in fact *requires* that each wholesaler hold a monopoly on the brands he carries for his particular territory" (M. Smith 2002, emphasis in original). The arrangement can be viewed as a long-standing, profit-sharing, government-protected cartel that is light years away from free-market capitalism.

In return for this generous market position, wholesalers provide certain services to the state. Most important, wholesalers are responsible for collecting excise taxes for Georgia's Department of Revenue. In fourth quarter 2012, these amounted to $46.0 million of $4.4 billion in total revenues (U.S. Census Bureau 2013). In addition, wholesalers coordinate with retailers to restrict price-cutting, keeping the resulting regulatory cartel profitable. Wholesalers must post prices with the Department of Revenue and maintain them for a set amount of time (M. Smith 2002).

Such arrangements prove supremely beneficial to wholesalers but limit retailer price flexibility and restrict supplier choices in brands carried. The controls also cause consumer prices to be higher. One would expect such an arrangement to be politically unpopular. Nevertheless, as we show, the structure of this industry survives through cooperative efforts by highly motivated Bootlegger and Baptist interests.

Prohibition and the Onset of the Three-Tier System

Prohibition (1919–33) was the ultimate Bootlegger/Baptist arrangement and a watershed event in the history of alcohol distribution in the United States. The national shutdown of legal producers and sellers had a lasting impact not only on how alcohol is consumed—for example, through various blue laws—but also on how alcoholic beverages navigate through various channels of distribution. Although the Twenty-First Amendment, which ended Prohibition in 1933, may have again legalized the consumption of alcohol, it also endowed states with an unprecedented discretion to intervene in alcohol markets, an outcome that resonates today.

Prior to Prohibition, various temperance groups—such as the Prohibition Party, the Women's Christian Temperance Union, and the Anti-Saloon League—lobbied state-by-state to curtail the consumption of alcohol. In a series of Supreme Court cases, the temperance movement gained momentum one decision at a time. In *Mugler v. Kansas*, 23 U.S. 623 (1887), the Supreme Court decided that states could ban alcohol production within their borders, not only for commercial distribution, but for private consumption as well. In other words, people could be prohibited from making booze for personal consumption because those actions "would tend to cripple, if it did not defeat, the effort to guard the community against the evils attending the excessive use of such liquors" (quoted in Anderson 2004, 5–6). The decision set the stage for an expansion of illegal—genuine bootlegging—activity.

The bootlegger heydays were short lived. The anti-saloon movement was stymied in its effort to control interstate shipments. In *Bowman v. Chicago & N.W. Railway Co.*, 125 U.S. 465 (1888), the Supreme Court held that the Commerce Clause barred interstate prohibition through state enforcement, because Congress had made no exception for alcohol distribution in the original language of the Commerce Clause (Anderson 2004, 6–7). Invoking a doctrine often dubbed the "dormant" Commerce Clause, this decision appeals to the principle that states cannot bar interstate commerce, even when state practices do not explicitly violate an existing federal statute, because to do so would intrude upon the exclusive purview of Congress.

This setback for the temperance movement and bootlegger profits was buttressed by the Court's holding in *Leisy v. Hardin*, 135 U.S. 100 (1890). States could not bar sales of imported alcohol even if a statewide prohibition law was in effect (Anderson 2004, 7–8). This effectively gutted the ability of states to control alcohol consumption, because consumers could simply have alcohol imported from states that had not banned production. As explained below, the issue with interstate distribution of alcohol and its tension with the Commerce Clause became a focus of contention not only for early legislation but also in debates that continue to the present day.

Clearly, following these decisions, legislation at the national level was required to cartelize the production and sale of alcohol. The first such legislation was put into effect in 1910 with the Wilson Act, which stipulated that alcohol imported into a state was subject to the same laws as alcohol produced within the state (Anderson 2004, 8–9). With alcohol distribution now regulated at the federal level, states no longer faced the obstacle presented by the Commerce

Clause in regulating consumption. Later court decisions limited the constraint to regulation of direct sales, as opposed to imports in general—a bootlegger's dream come true! Now, a state could limit the internal legal market by way of state regulation, but illegal sellers remained free to bring in the booze.

Not until the enactment of Prohibition with the Eighteenth Amendment, ratified in 1919, was alcohol distribution effectively regulated nationwide. By barring production altogether, states now had the power to control alcohol distribution—at least in theory. We will not go into the details of the epic disaster that was Prohibition, beyond noting that it was a national nightmare for all but the illegal sellers (Meier 1994; Okrent 2011; Thornton 2007). Cooperation between state and federal authorities was largely absent, with rampant corruption undermining any possibility of credible enforcement. Violent organized crime networks, meanwhile, came to control the entire alcohol distribution supply chain.

Prohibition ended with the enactment of the Twenty-First Amendment, ratified in 1933. Alcohol production was again legal but with the substantial caveat that states could control how it was distributed within their borders. In particular, section 2 of the Twenty-First Amendment states, "The transportation or importation into any State, Territory, or possession of the United States for delivery or use therein of intoxicating liquors, in violation of laws thereof, is hereby prohibited."

Now, states could decide for themselves how alcohol would be distributed—not only when it was produced internally but also when imported. When it came to alcohol, the Twenty-First Amendment superseded the Commerce Clause. Alcohol, unlike any other product or industry, received special treatment. No other constitutional amendment has been aimed at one class of products (Melzer 2004, 282).

Three Tiers for Wholesalers

Exercising their newly endowed powers, most states adopted what is known as the "three-tier" system of suppliers, wholesalers, and retailers. Ostensibly, the three-tier system was created to avoid the rampant corruption and mob-engendered control of liquor rackets so prevalent during Prohibition (Freedman and Emshwiller 1999). By breaking the alcohol industry into three separate, independently operated—or in some cases state-operated—distribution components, state governments could use the tiered system to reduce the proliferation of alcohol. This consigned so-called alcohol empires to the dustbin of history. Of course, there is far more acceptance of alcoholic beverage consumption today than in the heyday of the anti-saloon league. States persist with the three-tier system largely for its considerable value in raising tax revenues and, most relevant to our theory, because of the deep Bootlegger/Baptist coalitions it inspires.

Coalitions form in response to a particular aspect of the three-tier system. As described previously, wholesalers are given an extraordinary amount of protection within their market domain, allowing them to collect higher profits than would be possible in a competitive market. Instead of mob monopolies, the system created legal wholesaler monopolies. In general, the profit-maximizing strategy for wholesaler organizations is not the same as for suppliers (B. Klein 1995). Wholesalers are eager to keep the market to themselves. Suppliers, in contrast, have an economic incentive to increase the number of wholesalers, which ensures greater exposure for their product—thanks to increased marketing effort by wholesalers competing with one another—and competitive pricing for wholesaler services.

This privileged position led to a wholesaling industry boom. By the mid-1960s, more than 10,000 wholesalers were in operation, mostly dealing with liquor. At present, the nation's two largest wholesalers, Southern Wine & Spirits and Republic National Distributing Company, generate roughly $13 billion in annual revenues.

Eventually, this dynamic shifted, at least in terms of the number of firms, as more and more wholesalers consolidated because of economies of scale and certain wholesalers being more politically savvy than others in dealing with their political supporters. The National Beer Wholesalers Association maintains the third-largest political action committee in the country, donating $15.4 million from 2000 to 2010 to candidates seeking federal office (White 2011). Good politics has become as important as good business to wholesalers as the political cover generated by sympathetic representatives maintains the lucrative status quo for their operations.

While Bootlegger activity is rampant because of the generous subsidies provided through protection from market competition, Baptists are no less prevalent in this arrangement. Going back to

Prohibition, the religious right made an indelible impact on the restriction of alcohol consumption. Britton, Ford, and Gay (2001) document the effect on alcohol regulation associated with high concentrations of Protestant conservatives in the regulated community. Greater restrictions on alcohol importation are significantly associated with a high concentration of Protestant conservatives. We return to shed further light on genuine Baptist activity shortly.

Direct Shipping As a Threat to the Three-Tier System

Perhaps the greatest challenge to the three-tier system has come from the expansion of interstate alcohol sales. Recall that restricting importation of alcohol is the cornerstone of effective state regulation. The three-tier system requires that all alcohol go through wholesalers before ultimately reaching consumers. But what if alcohol is purchased directly from outside retailers and then shipped directly to these ultimate consumers? Left to their own devices, outside suppliers would charge competitive market prices, which—even when accounting for shipping charges—undercut in-state establishments, thus eroding the previously well-entrenched market structure.

Historically, states have been largely successful in curtailing interstate shipping. As noted previously, interstate shipping was one of the crucial concerns of the temperance movement, because without the power to enforce restrictions on cross-border shipping, any attempt at control within states was bound to fail. This is why the suspension of the Commerce Clause contained in section 2 of the Twenty-First Amendment was critical to the control of alcohol distribution. The Commerce Clause has long been interpreted to forbid states from banning interstate trade, including trade in alcohol.

In several important early cases, the Supreme Court upheld this suspension. For example, in *State Board of Equalization v. Young's Market Co.*, 299 U.S. 59 (1936), the plaintiffs sued to prevent the state of California from assessing a $500 importer's license fee on all companies wishing to import alcohol into the state. The Court's opinion, as expressed by Justice Louis Brandeis, held that it is perfectly legal for the state to determine how alcohol may enter its border. The fee remained. Furthermore, discriminating between in-state and out-of-state vendors lies within the scope of discretion conferred by the

Twenty-First Amendment. These powers of the state were further reinforced in *Mahoney v. Joseph Triner Corp.* 304 U.S. 401 (1938) and *Indianapolis Brewing Co. v. Liquor Control Commission* 305 U.S. 391 (1939) (Melzer 2004, 287–88).

Exceptions were made limiting state authority over alcohol distribution in national parks (*Collins v. Yosemite Park & Curry Co.*, 304 U.S. 518 [1938]) and in international airports (*Hostetter v. Idlewild Bon Voyage Liquor Corp.*, 327 U.S. 324 [1964]). These marginal market cases were followed by a more substantive decision in *Bacchus Imports, Ltd. v. Dias*, 468 U.S. 263 (1984).

In that case, a high liquor tax (20 percent) instituted in Hawaii had clear benefits to local distillers who were exempted. Noting this unfair advantage, the Court overturned parts of *Young's Market* and *Joseph Triner*, clarifying that the Twenty-First Amendment does not wholly supersede the Commerce Clause, because this would mean the federal government has no control over how alcohol is distributed. Rather, the Court determined that the amendment allows for restrictions on imports only when these restrictions are applied to domestic distributors as well. Accordingly, the Court found that price restrictions imposed against out-of-state distributors exceeded the mandate set by section 2. States were no longer allowed to price discriminate but could still maintain barriers to importation, as long as the barriers were uniformly applied to in-state and out-of-state distributors. Future cases would need to weigh the benefits of the amendment against the economic costs of constraining commerce (Melzer 2004, 293).

These exceptions to the power of state control over alcohol distribution have coincided with changes in the underlying market structure. As noted, wholesalers have consolidated into a few large organizations, thus narrowing access to lucrative profits. In addition, the rise of the Internet—and the online retail industry that emerged from it—has caused conflict between consumers and wholesalers. The greatest source of tension has come from wine connoisseurs, fed up with the obstacles created by state-maintained monopolies. Using online retailers, these individuals found new opportunities to purchase expensive, rare wines but have come up against import restrictions enforced by wholesaler monopolies (Freedman and Emshwiller 1999).

"Won't Somebody *Please Think* of the *Children?*"

Wine connoisseurs apparently have enough political panache to challenge the status quo. Some states have passed laws in the past decade to eliminate the requirement that outside suppliers must contract with state-supported (or state-run) wholesalers. This development has not gone unnoticed by wholesalers. Wiseman and Ellig (2007) show that legalization of direct shipment to consumers in McLean County, Virginia, reduced the spread between interstate and in-state prices by nearly 40 percent in the sample of wines they survey. By circumventing this apparatus, interstate competition succeeded in decreasing retail prices, cutting into the profits received by Virginia wholesalers.

Bootleggers have continued to fight aggressively against measures that would disrupt the status quo. Part of this effort has involved calling upon their ever-willing allies, the Baptists. But there is more, as cooperative interactions evolve to coordinated ones. Wiseman and Ellig (2007) describe the formation of a grand Bootlegger/Baptist coalition, coordinated by state-government regulators and 31 state attorneys general. These coordinating efforts allowed wholesaler trade associations (both state and national organizations) to pair with a dream team of Baptist interests including the National Association of Evangelicals, Phyllis Schlafly's Eagle Forum, Gary Bauer's American Values, and Concerned Women for America.

It may at first seem surprising that religious organizations would cooperate in opposing such an innocuous market practice as interstate shipping. As one incredulous headline put it, "Bizarre Coalition Opposes Direct Shipment of Wine: Big Money and the Religious Right Join Forces against Wine Lovers" (Marcus 2005). Nevertheless, wholesalers convinced religious organizations that such interstate competition would cause an increase in underage alcohol consumption. Their argument is that direct shipping lacks the sort of enforcement found at "bricks and mortar" retail outlets. Despite a variety of safeguards designed precisely to prevent this outcome—such as age verification both by online vendors and by shipping agents and strict penalties for suppliers found shipping to minors—the notion that direct shipping causes spikes in underage drinking has proven successful in motivating the religious right.

Marcus (2005) reports how a certain Rev. Mark Creech, echoing arguments made by Juanita Duggan, CEO of the Wine and Spirits Wholesalers of America, proclaimed that direct shipment would lead to a "shadow alcohol trade that is unchecked and unaccountable" and further that "Jesus would have never approved the actions of a bunch of greedy Internet wine retailers who were determined to distribute 'strong drink' at the expense of the nation's children." It appears that wholesalers have relied on an age-old sentiment in mobilizing their moral cover: by invoking a danger to the plight of the nation's children, no matter how unfounded, these Bootleggers have succeeded in bringing Baptists on board.

Granholm v. Heald and the Potential End of the Three-Tier System

Still, the onset of online shipping created ongoing headaches for the three-tier system, as evidenced by testimony delivered before Congress by Todd Zywicki, director of the Federal Trade Commission's (FTC) Office of Planning and Policy, in 2003. Among other things, Zywicki reiterated that the three-tier system both reduced access to certain wines and increased prices for consumers. Furthermore, he noted the results of an FTC staff report, which had found that "on-line wine sales do not add to the problem of underage drinking" (Zywicki 2003).

Yet at the same hearing, Juanita Duggan, CEO of the Wine and Spirits Wholesalers of America, testified that direct sales create a slippery slope toward greater underage consumption that will eventually involve beer and liquor as well. Although her emphasis was mostly on the greater opportunities for underage drinking, she also alleged that the FTC had exaggerated the price discrepancies between online and brick-and-mortar retailers and claimed the agency had not properly accounted for true shipping charges. She even took a swipe at wine connoisseurs, reminding her audience that they represent an elite fringe of consumers— the broader majority of whom, she argued, favor current policy (Duggan 2003).

This acrimony among wholesalers, the religious right, and wine connoisseurs reached a peak with the landmark Supreme Court case *Granholm v. Heald*, 544 U.S. 460 (2005), which consolidated two separate disputes from New York and Michigan. Both dealt with bans on direct shipping from out-of-state wine vendors.

In a 5-4 decision, the Supreme Court ruled in favor of consumers against wholesalers, finding that bans on direct shipping were unconstitutional. The Court reasoned that section 2 of the Twenty-First Amendment, which states have repeatedly invoked to justify the bans on direct sales, does not supersede the dormant Commerce Clause, which bars states from discriminating against out-of-state vendors.

Aftermath: Don't Count a Good Bootlegger Out

The *Granholm v. Heald* decision struck a significant blow to wholesalers. Since the decision, many states have moved to repeal bans on direct sales. According to the Wine Institute, 39 states currently allow at least some limited form of direct shipping to consumers (Wine Institute 2012). Although the tide may be turning against this particular Bootlegger/Baptist coalition, it would be premature to forecast its demise. A recent House resolution calls for a strengthening of state-based alcohol regulation that would remand to the states their authority over alcohol distribution in their borders (H.R. 1161, 2011). It is too early to tell how successful such legislation will be in turning back the tide of market competition. Regardless, its mere appearance shows that this coalition may be made of sterner stuff than its antagonists had hoped.

Thank You for Smoking! (No Advertising Necessary)

We now move to our second sinful substance, tobacco. On June 22, 2011, the U.S. Food and Drug Administration (FDA) issued an order requiring cigarette companies to have graphic labels on cigarette packages that warn of the harmful effects of smoking (FDA 2011; McKay and Kesmodel 2011). The action resulted from the 2009 Family Smoking Prevention and Tobacco Control Act,[1] which mandated labels that cover the top 50 percent of cigarette packages (front and back), nine specific rotating warning messages, and a requirement for graphic presentation of harms caused by smoking.

Aware that the label warnings were in the works—because the FDA rule emerged from earlier negotiations with Congress—members of the tobacco industry challenged the regulations in court. They argued that strict FDA regulation would keep the industry on the straight and narrow but also claimed violation of their First Amendment rights (Strauss 2011).

One example of the imagery then mandated by the FDA, but now moot, shows a picture of a dead man in a casket with a label reading, "Warning: Smoking Can Kill You." In July 2012, the U.S. Court of Appeals for the District of Columbia Circuit left the broad regulations standing (Yost 2012), but another industry suit focused exclusively on the advertising mandate. In August 2012, the U.S. Court of Appeals for the District of Columbia Circuit ruled in favor of the industry, arguing that the FDA had provided no evidence linking the mandated ads to a reduction in smoking (Dooren 2012). For now, the Supreme Court has declined to rehear the case. The government is not seeking further review, leaving the industry with a highly profitable cartel formed by decades of regulation and now managed by the FDA.

The FDA's dramatic intervention in the marketplace generated extraordinary benefits for some members of the industry. Legislation that placed the tobacco industry under FDA control was just what some Bootleggers wanted. Members of the industry, rather counterintuitively, supported the 2009 legislation that mandated the gruesome messages, as did anti-smoking groups that fought long and hard for FDA control of the industry. Once again, Bootleggers and Baptists formed a winning coalition—at least for the Bootleggers.

In more ways than one, the stories we tell here can be linked to the polluters' profit theory. Over decades, each major federal regulation has established restrictions on competition or costly activities that combined with a price-insensitive product to generate "polluter profits." And, of course, each restriction seemed to offer the prospect, but not the substance, of tough government regulation, thereby inspiring anti-smoking interest groups to stay the course. Just as Br'er Rabbit feigned dismay at being thrown into his briar patch home, so did these Bootleggers appear subdued while secretly rejoicing at their good fortune.

We next discuss four episodes involving federal regulation of tobacco marketing practices and explain how the actions fit the model of Br'er Rabbit's briar patch. Two of the episodes involve warning labels. Another concerns television advertising, and the final episode involves extreme cartelization of the industry by way of the 1996 Master Settlement Agreement (MSA) that was negotiated in a coordinated effort by state attorneys general. The MSA allowed the industry to raise prices to fund a transfer of some $200 billion to the 50 states.

Each episode displays a noncooperative Bootlegger/Baptist inter-action that nonetheless saw tobacco come out on top, even when the Baptists thought they were winning.

Early History of Tobacco Product Regulation

Regulation of marketing practices is nothing new to the tobacco industry. In what is now U.S. territory, government control dates at least to 1629, when colonial authorities in Massachusetts Bay pro-hibited settlers from planting tobacco except in small quantities used for medicinal purposes (McGrew 1972), much as medicinal marijuana is tolerated today in some states. Tobacco bans reach even further back than colonial times. In 1604, King James I of England wrote *A Counterblast to Tobacco*. He described smoking as "a custome loathsome to the eye, hateful to the nose, harmeful to the brain, dan-gerous to the lungs, and in the black stinking fume thereof, nearest resembling the horrible Stigian smoke of the pit that is bottomeless" (Gascoigne 2001). Modern anti-smoking groups would suggest King James got it right.

As might be expected, anti-smoking and other health interest groups—one of several categories of Baptists in this story—have a long history of activism; there were several hundred anti-cigarette leagues in the United States with more than 300,000 total members by the turn of the 19th century (Thornton 1997). Partly owing to their efforts, 26 states banned the sale of cigarettes to minors by 1890, and 16 states totally prohibited cigarette sales by the end of 1909 (Troyer and Markle 1983, 33–34).

The health interest groups were numerous and apparently effec-tive at the state level, at least initially, but unable to mount a focused national movement when smoking first became a federal issue. The tobacco interests, in contrast, were consolidated early on by James Duke, who in 1890 formed and led a tobacco trust that accounted for 90 percent of the industry output. Keep in mind, however, that the principal product was plug tobacco meant for chewing.

Cigarettes rose in popularity during World War I. By 1927, all state bans on sales to minors had been repealed, with an important quid pro quo. As bans declined, state tobacco taxes were imposed, begin-ning in 1921 in Iowa and spreading to "nearly all" states by 1960 (Chaloupka, Wakefield, and Czart 2001, 42; Robert 1967, 256, 276).

After an antitrust breakup of the tobacco trust in 1911, six firms dominated the U.S. market. By 2004, there were seven tobacco firms, but just two, Philip Morris and R.J. Reynolds, had a combined market share of over 80 percent. With just two to tango, tobacco industry political action was not very hard to coordinate.

In this early period of tobacco dominance, state legislatures joined hands with the tobacco producers and overwhelmed the fractured anti-smoking leagues. The anti-smoking groups relied primarily on impassioned moral appeals. Scientific discoveries linking smoking to a variety of health problems, which would later galvanize public interest in tobacco regulation, had yet to arrive. This early history shows how tobacco's fortunes have long been intertwined with government, with the state acting as a sort of cartel manager for the industry.

In the struggles that ensued, both tobacco interests and their opponents engaged in a continuing political battle over market practices and the appropriateness of individual tobacco use. The government-protected tobacco cartel won repeatedly. Winning, after all, meant higher profits for the industry, larger campaign contributions to accommodating politicians, and a reliable source of tax revenues to state governments.

Eventually, health interest groups grew more influential as they became national in scope, smaller in number, and ultimately armed with scientific evidence that linked smoking to adverse health effects. Still, direct regulation of tobacco did not immediately follow. Consider the FDA, which would seem to be the most logical place to find federal regulation of tobacco. Until 2009, Congress consistently denied the FDA explicit authority over tobacco. The statute creating the FDA, the Pure Food and Drug Act of 1906, granted the agency jurisdiction over drugs but defined them as only: "(1) medicines and preparations recognized in the United States Pharmacopoeia or National Formulary . . . and (2) any substance or mixture of substances intended to be used for the cure, mitigation, or prevention of disease."[2]

Although tobacco had been listed in the 1890 *United States Pharmacopoeia*, the substance was conveniently removed from the *Pharmacopoeia* just before the passage of the 1906 statute. Some suggest removal was a price paid by pro-FDA forces to gain support for the FDA statute from tobacco states, but others disagree

(Fritschler 1969, 32; Pringle 1998, 102). Later, the tobacco companies' avoidance of substantive health claims in their marketing enabled the industry to escape FDA's authority by way of the statute's second condition. Until the 1990s, the FDA did not play an active role in tobacco regulation, although industry fear of FDA oversight lurked in the background and perhaps raised the price industry was willing to pay for political protection.

The Industry and the First Wave of Regulation

Tobacco's success was at least partly due to the power of seniority in the Senate, where long-serving senators from tobacco-producing states were able to block efforts by health interest groups to extend FDA jurisdiction to tobacco. Also, prior to the 1950s anti-tobacco groups were not politically savvy, consisting largely of "moralizing tub-thumpers who repeated, to no enduring effect, that tobacco was inherently dirty and ungodly and encouraged crime" (Pringle 1998, 122). For a time, cigarette manufacturers even advertised the purported weight control benefits of their brands with such catchphrases as "Reach for a Lucky instead of a sweet" (Parker-Pope 2001, 82–86).

In the 1950s, emerging scientific information on the health effects of smoking transformed the debate. The *New York Times* ran a lengthy series of articles on smoking and health during 1953–54 (Pringle 1998, 125). This inspired the FTC to target tobacco advertising claims, particularly those concerning tar (Kozlowski and O'Connor 2004, 39–41). But instead of seeking the moral high ground as a promoter of health, the FTC focused on another moral dimension: truth—and its enemy, deceptive advertising. Whether working to improve human health or truth in advertising, the FTC apparently served the interests of citizen Baptist groups.

Tobacco's political power remained a force to be reckoned with, however. The first serious proposal in Congress to regulate tobacco was a 1957 attempt to give the FTC powerful injunctive powers for deceptive tobacco advertising, including tar and nicotine content claims. The effort failed miserably. The House member who sponsored the legislation lost his subcommittee chair, and his subcommittee was abolished by the House leadership (Kluger 1996, 189).

But the failed attempt to regulate the industry brought out more Bootleggers and health care Baptists. With growing medical evidence on the Baptist side of the issue, and with the industry happy to cooperate, the FTC negotiated a ban on tar and nicotine advertising in 1960. The agency effort to eliminate low-tar and nicotine claims was based on the position that they lacked a scientific basis. Indeed, when the advertising was banned, the FTC chair called the ban "a landmark example of industry-government cooperation in solving a pressing problem" (Kluger 1996, 190). But what looked like industry-government cooperation to placate Baptist interests was really a Bootlegger success. The elimination of competitive health-related claims limited market entry, slowed the costly search for lower-tar cigarettes, and led to a market-share increase for unfiltered products. Polluters' profits soon followed. The briar patch beckoned one more time.

The ban also made it illegal to advertise which substances filters removed, though an advertisement could extol the virtues of the filter itself. In an effort to maintain taste while promoting filters, some of the brands introduced stronger tobacco, which in effect nullified the filter's original purpose (Kluger 1996, 188). When all was said and done, the tobacco cartel appeared to have won again, with the FTC now in control. Meanwhile, however, the Baptists were becoming better organized.

The Surgeon General's Report: The FTC Swings Again

In June 1961, several national organizations concerned with the health effects of smoking—the American Cancer Society, the American Heart Association, and the National Tuberculosis and Respiratory Disease Association—requested the appointment of a commission to examine tobacco's health hazards and propose solutions. Shortly afterward, Surgeon General Dr. Luther Terry announced that he was establishing an "expert committee to undertake a comprehensive review of all data on smoking and health" (Fritschler 1969, 37–38).

The resulting Surgeon General's report dramatically changed the political debate over tobacco. The 1964 report, which concluded that "cigarette smoking contributes substantially to mortality" from a wide range of diseases, including lung cancer, chronic bronchitis, and coronary disease, called for prompt regulatory action on smoking (U.S. Department of Health, Education, and Welfare 1964, 8–9, 31–32).

The report was just what the FTC needed. Four days after the report was published, the agency announced it would issue rules requiring health warnings on all cigarette packages and in all cigarette advertisements. The agency asserted that failure to warn consumers that smoking was dangerous was an unfair and deceptive trade practice and thus a violation of the FTC statute (Fritschler 1969, 83–84).

On July 2, 1964, the FTC issued the final version of its Trade Regulation Rule on Cigarette Labeling and Advertising, requiring all cigarette ads as of January 1, 1965, and all cigarette packages as of July 1, 1965, to carry a stern warning: "Cigarette Smoking Is Dangerous to Health and May Cause Death from Cancer and Other Diseases" (FTC 1964, 8324). Note that subsequently it took 46 years for death to reenter the picture with the FDA's 2011 abortive advertising rule.

The cigarette industry immediately mobilized, created a voluntary advertising code, and lobbied Congress for protection (Kluger 1996, 280). Following a pattern that would regularly characterize tobacco regulatory activities, Congress assessed the politics and intervened. On August 19, 1965, at the request of then chair of the House Committee on Interstate and Foreign Commerce Rep. Oren Harris (D-AR), the FTC delayed the effective dates of the Trade Regulation Rule to allow Congress to develop a regulatory package acceptable to the industry (Kluger 1996, 272, 286–87). The Senate acceded, and Congress passed the Federal Cigarette Labeling and Advertising Act.[3]

The statute gave the FTC specific authority to regulate cigarette advertising related to health claims and nicotine content, but it provided the tobacco industry much more and was called "a victory for cigarettes" (Fritschler 1969, 112–16). The "death" warning the FTC had proposed was watered down to read "Caution: Cigarette Smoking May Be Hazardous to Your Health" (FTC 1964). Even more important, the statute prohibited any further mandated warnings by the FTC or state or local governments on cigarette packages and prohibited any warning requirement in cigarette advertising until 1969.

The Fairness Doctrine: Enter the Federal Communications Commission

In June 1967, another agency joined the FTC in its lonely battle over cigarette advertising. The Federal Communications Commission (FCC), a second regulator working on behalf of the

Baptists, ruled that the "fairness doctrine" applied to cigarette commercials. Under this regulatory doctrine, the FCC required broadcasters to provide airtime for opposing viewpoints whenever they broadcast controversial opinions. As a result, health groups and the government Public Health Service were able to air announcements on the dangers of tobacco use on television and radio. In 1968 alone, the three major networks aired 1,300 anti-smoking messages (Kluger 1996, 309). The ads appear to have been effective: per capita cigarette sales dropped 5.7 percent between 1967 and 1970 (R. Jones 1997, 13).

When courts upheld the fairness doctrine's application to cigarettes, both the FCC and the FTC put forward additional proposals designed to restrict cigarette advertising and consumption. In February 1969, the FCC issued a notice of proposed rulemaking to completely prohibit cigarette advertising on television and radio. In May 1969, the FTC issued a proposal to require all cigarette advertising (both broadcast and print) to contain a more direct warning: "Cigarette Smoking Is Dangerous to Health and May Cause Death from Cancer, Coronary Heart Disease, Chronic Bronchitis, Pulmonary Emphysema, and Other Diseases." (FTC 1969, 7917). Once again, death was in the message. And once again, the industry mobilized.

Hearing the call of their Bootlegger buddies, Congress again intervened. In April 1969, representatives of tobacco-producing states introduced a series of bills in the House to prevent the stronger warning label and make permanent the temporary ban on state and federal regulation of cigarette advertising. But the political climate had changed, and some members now saw "that legislation backing consumer interests was becoming good politics," as Ralph Nader's consumer movement demonstrated (Kluger 1996, 331).

Following extensive negotiations, a compromise bill emerged that banned all cigarette advertising on electronic media beginning January 1, 1971, and mildly strengthened the package warning, requiring that all cigarette packages include the statement "Warning: The Surgeon General Has Determined That Cigarette Smoking Is Dangerous to Your Health."[4] Once again, "death" was deleted from the message.

Some may have seen this as a slam-dunk victory for anti-smoking groups, but the tobacco industry had even more to celebrate. First, banning TV ads eliminated the fairness doctrine–mandated public service announcements. Second, eliminating television ads saved the companies the more than $200 million they were spending annually on television in 1969—a necessary expenditure for each company as long as their competitors were buying TV ads, but not if all could be barred from the airwaves at once (R. Jones 1997, 13). Third, the TV ad ban enabled producers of existing brands to maintain market share and created substantial barriers to the entry of new firms by denying them an effective means of establishing a brand.

Sales figures support the interpretation that the bill helped tobacco: cigarette sales *increased* following the legislation. Total U.S. cigarette consumption rose steadily from 536.4 billion units in 1970 to 621.5 billion in 1979 (USDA 2005, table 1). Consumption per capita for the above-18 population rose from 3,985 in 1970 to 4,122 in 1975 and then began to decline somewhat (J. Nelson 2004, table 2). To put it mildly, the major tobacco firms, now ensconced in a cozy regulatory cartel, benefited from this lively Bootlegger/Baptist interaction.

The 1998 Master Settlement Agreement: The Ultimate and Final Cartel

With passage of legislation specifying marketing practices and the end of the FCC's oversight, the tobacco industry entered a some-what stable relationship with Congress and regulators. What the cigarette companies could not avoid was a renewed assault by private lawyers. A wave of tobacco litigation began in 1983. Armed with new evidence on smoking's health effects, entrepreneurial plaintiffs' attorneys pooled their resources in an effort to win their suits. Tobacco companies continued their all-out defense and won every case. The labeling regulation had bolstered their "assumption of risk" defense: not only were the dangerous health effects of smoking well established and publicly known, tobacco lawyers argued, but the tobacco companies even placed a warning label on their product to that effect.

Despite their victories in the courthouse, the suits weakened the tobacco companies by increasing public awareness of the companies' efforts to conceal tobacco's health hazards. Internal documents revealed at trial showed that industry executives were aware of smoking's hazards at a time when they were denying those very hazards publicly (Kluger 1996, 559–61; Roemer 2004, 688–89).

The incriminating documents, along with publicity surrounding high-profile whistleblower cases, yielded a public relations debacle that turned public opinion against the tobacco interests by the 1990s.

In a dramatic series of events that followed, a third Baptist-anointed regulator entered the fray when the EPA in 1992 issued a report declaring secondhand smoke to be a carcinogen (EPA 1992). Then, in 1996, the FDA asserted its authority to regulate tobacco products without congressional approval. After proposing regulations with the support of the Clinton White House, the FDA was sued by the industry, which claimed the FDA lacked jurisdiction. The FDA was sent back to its former regulatory territory in 2000, when the U.S. Supreme Court sided with the industry.[5]

Then, congressional hearings were held in conjunction with Medicaid legislation that put smoking-related illnesses in the spotlight. Anti-smoking interest groups, burned by their past support for regulation that turned out to favor the tobacco industry, seem to have wised up; they were no longer available as a Bootlegger/ Baptist coalition partner.

Meanwhile, tobacco imports were up, and production in the United States was headed to oblivion. The former tobacco states no longer relied significantly on tobacco as a money crop. The tobacco states' delegation in Congress turned its interest to other matters, including health care. As time passed, new civil suits were brought successfully against the tobacco companies by state attorneys general suing on behalf of state Medicaid reimbursement funds (Orey 1999). With secondhand smoke now accepted as causing harm, it was no longer crucial to prove cause-and-effect links or grapple with "assumption of risk" defenses. Successful actions in four states brought recovery of Medicaid funds and delivered huge payments for legal services to attorneys hired to assist in the state attorneys general actions.

As the number of Medicaid reimbursement suits increased, the tobacco companies found themselves facing not just a well-financed group of plaintiffs' counsel but a growing number of state government attorneys. By 1997, 22 state attorneys general had filed suit against the tobacco companies (Zegart 2000, 226). By the summer of 1997, 40 had done so. Instead of taking them on one at a time, the industry circled the wagons and called for settlement talks. The talks eventually produced an initial settlement agreement on June 20, 1997.

The tobacco companies were willing to concede a great deal but insisted on protection from future lawsuits and limits on regulation as the quid pro quo. The protections they sought required congressional action to approve those portions of the deal protecting the tobacco interests from future efforts by the FDA and health interest groups at the federal level. That relief was valuable. Three weeks after news of the settlement negotiations was announced, Philip Morris's stock market value had increased by more than $10 billion, a testament to the value of ending the liability problem (Mollenkamp et al. 1998, 98). The stock rose another 11 percent when the *Wall Street Journal* reported an outline of what became the resolution several weeks later.

For the states, the resolution provided an annual payment by the participating tobacco companies. Tobacco companies were to pay $10 billion to the states up front and to make inflation-adjusted annual payments to total $358.5 billion over 25 years, with payments of $15 billion per year in perpetuity thereafter. Although substantial, the payments were less onerous than the numbers suggest. Because of the relative price inelasticity of tobacco sales, companies would be able to pass along a good chunk of their payments to consumers as higher prices. Furthermore, tobacco companies would be able to deduct the annual payments as ordinary and necessary business expenses on their income tax returns, thus reducing their tax liabilities. The monetary payments envisioned by the resolution were thus primarily a promise of a transfer to the states from future smokers (through higher prices) and taxpayers generally (through the deductibility of the payments) rather than from the tobacco companies' shareholders.

For the FDA, the resolution offered authority to classify nicotine as a drug and cigarettes as a drug delivery device (albeit with some restrictions on agency action), the power to regulate health claim advertising, and the ability to treat tobacco product approvals in much the same way the agency treated new drug approvals. The resolution also contained detailed rules that affected marketing and advertising and underage tobacco restrictions. For example, the use of a human image to promote a product was banned: no more Joe Camel or Marlboro Man; no more outdoor advertising. Providing gifts based on proof of purchase of tobacco products was prohibited.

Congress began deliberations nearly a year after the resolution was signed; by that time, it was apparent that the general mood was for the industry to feel pain. As the legislation moved through the Senate Commerce Committee, the payments required from the tobacco companies were raised to $516 billion from $365 billion over 25 years, a $1.10 increase in the federal cigarette tax over five years was added, a higher level of FDA regulation was allowed, and litigation immunity was eliminated.[6] Eventually, the price apparently became too high. The tobacco companies rejected the revised proposal and launched a massive advertising campaign to kill the bill (Kelder 1998, 6). The bill died.

With the failure of the federal legislation in the Senate, the seven tobacco companies and the state attorneys general began discussions. A revised settlement agreement without the federal portion of the deal—what is now known as the Master Settlement Agreement—was signed on November 17, 1998. The revised deal did not address warning labels (where the FDA had exclusive jurisdiction), include any expansion of FDA authority, or provide the crucial national immunity provisions, which would have required congressional approval.

But the industry got a better price. The expected flow of payments from the industry to the states dropped from $365 billion to $200 billion. Within days of signing the MSA, two producers announced the largest price increase in history; the others soon followed (Capehart 2001). Over the next five years, 14 industry-wide price increases were announced. By 2001, the firms had more than doubled the per pack wholesale price of cigarettes.

Despite the collapse of the original deal in Congress, the federal government was not yet done with the tobacco industry. Unsuccessful efforts were made in Congress to drain some of the settlement funds headed to the states and to extract wealth from the industry by way of U.S. Justice Department suits. The MSA also alarmed U.S. tobacco growers. Fearful that their political protection was ebbing, farmers sought to cash out the value of their government-provided price supports and quotas. Joined by cigarette producers interested in seeing an end to government programs that kept a floor under tobacco prices, the farmers negotiated for redemption of their government-created tobacco growing quotas and compensation for the end of government price support programs (Womach 2005). Holders of tobacco quotas received some $6.7 billion to retire their rights. Tobacco farm operators (many of whom leased quotas) received $2.9 billion. The revenues to fund the retirement and buyouts came from government sources and, as might be expected, from the cigarette producers, who nudged cigarette prices upward again to generate a contribution of $5.5 billion toward buyouts.

In spite of numerous attacks on antitrust and other grounds, and despite competitive entry by small cigarette producers, the MSA cartel has thus far remained relatively durable—and for good reason. The MSA is a cash cow for the states and a source of funding for health interest groups. MSA cash flows are now woven inextricably into the finances of all 50 states, national interest groups, and private litigators who guard the gates, and these groups are not likely to allow their streams of funds to dry up.

Aftermath: Downhearted Baptists

One last question remains to be addressed. Did the MSA accomplish a public interest goal? The public interest inspiration for the initial deal was the aim of reducing smoking and recouping state Medicaid expenditures. By the time the deal had been made concrete in the MSA, however, much of that was lost. The promise that MSA revenues would be devoted to smoking reduction programs has not been met; the majority of the proceeds has been devoted to other activities. Only about one-third of the revenue has been spent on health enhancement or cancer prevention programs. Little has been spent on efforts to reduce teenage smoking, which had been one of the main public causes associated with the MSA (Campaign for Tobacco-Free Kids 2011). The Baptists were downhearted. Bruised but not beaten, the Bootleggers went to the bank.

Nuthin' But a "B&B" Thang: California Attempts to Legalize Marijuana Use

So far, we have discussed Bootlegger/Baptist interaction in the development of rules affecting marketing practices for alcohol and cigarettes. Alcohol is a mature consumer product, widely regulated at every level of government, and has been legal, on a restricted basis, since Prohibition ended in 1933. Cigarettes have never been banned by the federal government, but their marketing practices have been subject to a complex array of regulatory actions taken by colonies and states centuries ago, by the FTC and the FCC in modern times, and most recently by the FDA.

As we saw, Bootleggers and Baptists have interacted continually in the development of marketing practices for alcohol and cigarettes. Such is not the case for marijuana. There are Bootleggers—lots of them. But the Baptist side of the winning coalition has not fully emerged. In this section, we examine marijuana and one episode involving an attempt to legalize marijuana production and consumption in California. Here we meet some burgeoning Bootleggers and some conflicted Baptists.

A Product in Transition?

The marketing practices associated with marijuana, a product not legal since 1937 when the U.S. Congress passed the Cannabis Prohibition Act, are murky and very much an evolving story. Although federal law makes growing, selling, possessing, or using marijuana illegal, the plant is nonetheless grown widely, sold extensively, and used by a meaningful percentage of Americans. Important for our story, a growing market exists for medicinal marijuana, which can be sold in 18 states to consumers with a medical doctor's prescription, as of 2013. Some see the medicinal market as a precursor to marijuana legitimacy.

At least four factors help support the existence of a large, illicit marijuana market: (a) the weed can be grown in flowerpots, gardens, and larger plots so that detection costs are high; (b) small but valuable amounts of the product can be carried in pockets, purses, and other small containers, which means distribution costs are low; (c) as a high-value, low-weight product, marijuana can easily be exported from abroad to U.S. markets; and (d) Bootleggers want to maintain the market's illegal status, while Baptists, for the most part, are happy to assist them. Circumstances do change, however, especially during a Great Recession.

These strands came together on November 2, 2010, when California voters turned down Proposition 19, a highly publicized initiative known as the Regulate, Control and Tax Cannabis Act. The vote was close, with 54 percent opposing the action ("California Prop 19 and the Electoral Results" 2010). Had it passed, the act would have allowed an adult to possess one ounce of marijuana and to grow plants in an area no larger than 25 square feet. (Going to larger production would be too much for Bootleggers.) As part of a vanguard effort to relax laws that restrict marijuana production, sales, and personal use, California in 1996 was the first state to legalize marijuana's medicinal use (Klare 2011).

As doctors' permission became easier to obtain, marijuana shops began to grow like weeds in the Golden State. Moreover, as marijuana use became more acceptable, California reduced the penalty for possession to about the same fine charged for a speeding ticket. Governor Arnold Schwarzenegger signed a law reducing the penalty to $100 in October 2010, just a month before the November vote, some say in an effort to weaken support for the initiative (Neff and Wohlson 2010; Aaron Smith 2010).

How the Bootlegger/Baptist Coalition Formed and Reformed

An interesting array of Bootleggers and Baptists held forth during the prelude to the vote, with ample passion on both sides. But passion does not necessarily translate into campaign contributions and election-day votes. Our theory suggests that what matters most are dollars that go to the bottom line. Thus we should expect those who have a lot to gain (or a lot to lose) in concrete terms to be counted among the most vehement partisans in the struggle. Furthermore, groups that are already organized will have an advantage over masses of people who, however individually passionate about the cause, are not a part of a solidified interest group.

Let us now explore the potential winners and losers in the struggle to pass the law. First, consider the state itself. The California state government was practically bankrupt at the time and was engaged in the painful business of cutting programs, closing state parks, and laying off state employees. Some had projected that legalizing and taxing the sale of weed could bring in as much as $1.2 billion annually, if a state sales tax was imposed (Kennedy 2010). Later, as legislation developed, taxing authority was to be vested with local governments. Needless to say, $1.2 billion was a nontrivial amount for a nearly bankrupt state. There were also indications that legalization would make marijuana production, sale, and use an activity like any other in the legal marketplace. As a result, the crime associated with marijuana activity would be reduced, as would related law enforcement expenditures.

Nevertheless, the public-sector proceeds associated with these arguments, although large, would not be tagged for individuals who might convert the proceeds to bottom-line bank accounts. Because of this, only those swayed by public interest arguments would be inclined to offer financial support for the law. Billionaire George Soros was just such a person (Aaron Smith 2010). Putting forth the public interest arguments we just summarized, Soros gave $1 million to support the legalization effort.

For public-sector revenues to matter, real people with pocketbook interests in those revenues have to get involved. For Bootleggers to get interested, in other words, the profits must be appropriable as pork. Apparently, the state teachers' union liked the smell of money. Randi Weingarten, president of the American Federation of Teachers, and whom we might call a leading Baptist, endorsed the legislation. We might normally think that it takes a lot for public schoolteachers to endorse marijuana consumption, but saving one's job from budgetary cataclysm is no small thing. Indeed, when *Washington Post* writer Jonathan Capehart reacted to Weingarten's announcement by exclaiming, "Teacher approved!," Weingarten responded, "If it's legal" (Rush 2010). The shift on the issue demonstrates that incentives matter. The shift might also explain why opposition forces were successful in eliminating the state revenue component from the proposed legislation.

Just as some public employees hoped to see more cash in the coffers, others in law enforcement balked at the prospect of losing huge amounts of revenue from civil forfeiture actions involving the drug trade. Many law enforcement officials were dead set against the law's passage—not just locally. Marijuana-related law enforcement activity was so extensive that legalization would lead to serious cuts in police and prison employment. Harvard professor Jeffrey Miron estimated in 2005 that budget savings in those areas would amount to $981 million annually (Miron 2005). Opposition from leading law enforcement officers may have looked a lot like Baptist opposition, but these were Bootleggers in disguise. Put another way, drug dealers are not the only beneficiaries of illegal markets. Nevertheless, with police opposing and teachers favoring the measure, there were Baptists on both sides of the issue.

To complicate things even further, three groups favored legalization because of their belief that certain minority groups bore the brunt of drug law enforcement. The NAACP, the National Black Police

Association, and the League of United Latin American Citizens of California endorsed the act.

Literally hundreds of endorsements came on both sides of the issue, but the more interesting effort opposing legalization came from the literal Bootleggers in the situation, the illegal growers and sellers of the weed itself. California's Humboldt County prides itself as a major producer of high-quality marijuana. Humboldt State University economists estimated marijuana accounts for $500 million to $700 million of the county's $3.6 billion economy (Ammiano 2010). Concern for the county's future ran so deep that a Humboldt County radio host organized a community meeting labeled "What's after Pot?" (Ammiano 2010). Several other marijuana-rich counties followed with similar events. Whatever the exact amount of revenue at stake, the Humboldt growers were not going to go down without a fight. They even had a trade association, the Humboldt Growers Association (HGA). Here is how the HGA described itself:

> The HGA is a non-profit, member-based business associa-
> tion that promotes the sustainable cultivation of medical
> cannabis in Humboldt County. It is run by a committed
> volunteer board of directors. We work to develop programs
> and policies that promote safety and sustainability for the
> legal cultivation of medical cannabis. We know that regula-
> tion of medical cannabis is occurring—our county officials
> are already working on it—and we want the cannabis-
> growing community to have a voice in this process. The
> HGA represents cannabis growers not only locally, but also
> on a state-wide level, since that is where the most change in
> the industry needs to happen to keep our local farmers in
> business.[7]

As referendum time approaches, bumper stickers that read "Keep Pot Illegal" showed up in Humboldt County (Frauenfelder 2010).

It is easy to see why the Humboldt producers were so opposed. Legalization brought the prospects of expanded scope for marijuana production and the possibilities that the small Humboldt grow-ers would not be competitive in an open market. At the very least, opening up the market to greater competition would reduce their cur-rent profit margins. All kinds of rumors abounded; some suggested that the world-class tobacco companies would enter the industry, and there was the additional possibility that the U.S. Department of Agriculture would someday support marijuana production again, as the agency had done in 1915 (USDA 1915).

As the vote approached, the U.S. Department of Justice sent word that it would diligently enforce the 1937 federal cannabis prohibition statute. This move, which must have delighted the Humboldt growers, would jeopardize the newly opened market. Meanwhile, background preaching against legalization continued, and the Campaign for Children and Families led efforts to get out the opposition vote (Baptist Press 2010).

The final referendum vote suggests that a strange set of bedfellows joined forces to keep pot illegal in California: (a) the marijuana growers of California's marijuana counties; (b) local and state law enforcement officials; (c) religious and other leaders who saw marijuana consumption as an unmitigated evil; and (d) the U.S. Department of Justice, which threatened to steamroll California law enforcement if the state opened the market for a product deemed illegal under federal law (M. Hall 2010).

Reactions were mixed when the final tally was reported. Obama administration spokesman Gil Kerlikowske said in an e-mail:

> Today, Californians recognized that legalizing marijuana will not make our citizens healthier, solve California's budget crisis, or reduce drug related violence in Mexico. The Obama Administration has been clear in its opposition to marijuana legalization because research shows that marijuana use is associated with voluntary treatment admissions for addiction, fatal drugged driving accidents, mental illness, and emergency room admissions. (M. Hall 2010)

Alex Kreit, professor of law at Thomas Jefferson School of Law, and a supporter of Proposition 19, countered: "People are realizing that the war on marijuana and the war on drugs is a failed strategy. We've been pursuing it for 40 years and marijuana is just as available now as it was 40 years ago" (Hall 2010).

In sum, California's Proposition 19 was narrowly defeated by opposing Baptists who appear to have neutralized each other's influence; by California cannabis growers and their supporters who feared the loss of a major regional industry; by organized law enforcement officers who feared the loss of major sources of drug enforcement revenues; and by the U.S. Department of Justice, which made it clear that an open marijuana market would not be tolerated. In our opinion, the Department of Justice action was the coup de grâce.

Aftermath: The Secret Is in the B&B Sauce

Ah, but the story has a sequel. Since California's rejection of Proposition 19, two other states, Washington and Colorado, both held ballot measures in November 2012 to legalize possession of marijuana in small amounts. In a similar vein to California, Bootleggers and Baptists lined both sides of the fence. For example, in Washington, medical marijuana users rallied around an anti-legalization group called "No on I-502." This group claimed that legalization was flawed in that it threatened to prosecute those who drove under the influence, even if marijuana use had occurred days before (Johnson 2012).

Indeed, the lack of language regarding prosecution of driving under the influence was seen in hindsight as one factor that injured Proposition 19 in California. Initiative 502 was an attempt to buttress this criticism by explicitly establishing "a per se driving under-the-influence hold for marijuana of 5 nanograms of active THC metabolite per milliliter of blood." The initiative also provided for "annual distributions of $500,000 for the Washington State Health Youth survey; $200,000 for cost-benefit evaluations by the Washington State Institute for Public Policy; $20,000 for web-based public educational materials about the health and safety risks posed by marijuana use; and $5 million for LCB administration" (Washington State Senate Committee Services 2012).

These provisions marked a greater regard for public sentiment and helped turned the tide in the initiative's favor. Furthermore, they drew support from all of the various Bootlegger and Baptist organizations that directly benefitted from the financial support. Once the ballots were counted, Initiative 502, along with its counterpart in Colorado, had passed (Healy 2012).

Although these recent events in no way undermine the public's repugnance for sin, they do highlight the lesson that Baptist support is essential for successful legislative victory, particularly with popularly determined voting initiatives. As marijuana legalization advocates realized, the secret is in the B&B sauce.

Final Thoughts

It is no surprise that activities viewed as sinful would attract Bootlegger/Baptist interaction. Purveyors of sinful products are eager to serve their customers, especially in restricted markets. And guardians of moral high ground readily mobilize opposition when sin arrives on the political agenda. But we must look closely to see how the interaction occurs and what result obtains. We have examined three products that are sold in either heavily regulated or illegal markets.

The regulation of alcoholic beverages has matured in a cartelized industry where Bootleggers and Baptists openly cooperate to solidify favorable legislation. The resulting division of labor places the 50 states in the driver's seat, but Bootleggers are concerned about some competitive clouds on the horizon.

By comparison, tobacco products have been regulated for centuries with little in the way of open cooperation between Bootlegger and Baptist interests. But the pace of regulation has accelerated in recent decades. Indeed, tobacco-delivered nicotine as a consumer good may well be on the way to becoming illegal. Yet so far, industry profits have increased with each new restriction.

Finally, marijuana exists in a halfway house between being a regulated and an illegal consumer good. Pot's illegal status does not mean that no profit is to be made in the illegal market—just the opposite. Indeed, Bootleggers have fought to maintain the status quo, while some unexpected Baptists joined the movement to legalize the product.

We draw one general conclusion from the three case studies presented in this chapter. Bootlegger/Baptist interaction rises to a high level when changing voter attitudes threaten to upset the relative fortunes of Bootleggers—and open wide a door for Baptist influence. As lobbying becomes more intense, politicians become more important, and more valuable. Some members of an industry coalition may like things the way they are. Those who have achieved financial gain under the status quo prefer a stable, government-coordinated cartel. They like the briar patch.

Others in the industry, who never made it to their particular briar patch, are apt to be more eager for disruptive reform. Savvy politicians profit from both groups. Similarly, those who strive to make the world a better place but who have been walled out by government cartel managers also love it when the regulatory walls begin to crack and crumble.

Political power brokers become more important in times of flux. Regulatory turbulence brings brighter days to political entrepreneurs. The successful politician can craft regulatory reforms that serve both Bootleggers and Baptists, creating a new equilibrium. This may be observed when newly designed strictures enhance Bootlegger profits and generate large government revenues that can be spent to "serve the public interest," as we saw in the cases of alcohol and cigarette regulation. On other occasions, the new political balance seems to serve one group at the expense of the other, as when Congress intervened to counter the FTC's efforts to require stronger warning labels on cigarette packages.

When change is in the air, it is also time for Baptists to rethink their strategies and in some cases break off their support for past regulations. When change is sufficiently radical, as with marijuana, the Baptists must first identify themselves and decide which hymns to sing, as Bootleggers attempt to predict which briar patch they will prefer. When those positions are sorted, it is then possible for the politician-broker to make mutually beneficial deals. But as the marijuana case teaches us, uncertain Baptists and not-so-sure Bootleggers can lead to lost opportunities for regulatory reform. Moral appeals through the political process, without accompanying hidden financial beneficiaries, are like a sailboat without a breeze.

5. The Rocky Road to Climate Change Legislation

Environmental regulation provides a rich vein of gold for Bootleggers and Baptists to mine.[1] Fervent environmentalists make good Baptists.[2] In their view, uncaring polluters are willing to trade the last landscape for another shot of positive cash flow. To prevent such rampant greed, public-spirited defenders of the Earth must expand and enforce environmental laws to punish firms that put private profit over the public interest. Then there are the Bootleggers, industrialists who prefer polluter profits to no profit at all. Just the right form of government regulation can be a dream come true for profit-loving Bootleggers. Although perhaps never fully comfortable in a room of self-righteous Baptists, Bootleggers still welcome their religious counterparts when pious pleading can be parlayed into persistent profits.

This chapter focuses on a specific episode of this common phenomenon: climate change regulation inspired by the 1997 Kyoto Protocol. It established goals for reducing global greenhouse gas emissions, primarily in the form of carbon discharge.

Bootleggers require regulations that raise rivals' costs, block entry, impose differential costs across firms, cartelize entire industries, and in other ways favor successful seekers of pork. We show how producers of natural gas and nuclear energy, with a lot to gain by providing low- or zero-carbon fuels, joined forces with environmental groups in an effort to reduce carbon emissions. In response, the less-favored coal producers teamed with environmentalists to lobby for clean coal subsidies. Concurrently, corn producers harmonized with clean air advocates in an appeal for mandated and subsidized use of domestically produced ethanol as a gasoline supplement.

As Bootlegger/Baptist feeding frenzies go, the scramble for regulatory pork inspired by Kyoto takes the cake. By 2010, however, the banquet seemed to be coming to an end—at least temporarily.

That was when the Senate abandoned efforts to pass climate change legislation that, among other things, would have introduced a cap-and-trade program for reducing carbon emissions from major dischargers (Siddique 2010). Nevertheless, that Great Recession breather is more likely to represent a semicolon than a period in the long story of the political effort "to do something" about carbon emissions.

This interruption indicates how quickly even coordinated Bootlegger/Baptist coalitions may come unglued in the face of a major recession. Economists know that demand for environmental quality and a willingness to pay for environmental improvements are sensitive to income levels and growth—a fact equally well understood by policymakers (e.g., Grossman and Krueger 1991, 1995; Yandle, Vijayaraghavan, and Bhatarai 2002). What may not have been fully appreciated was how income differences between countries could erode coordinated international efforts to bring down carbon emissions (Lipford and Yandle 2010a, 2010b). Those income effects explain many of the bumps in the highway toward climate change regulation.

This chapter gives a Bootlegger/Baptist interpretation of what happened between the adoption of Kyoto in 1997 and the near-demise of climate change legislation in 2010. The next section provides some detail on the Kyoto Protocol and the differential support it received. We present a series of stories to illustrate how specific Bootlegging firms and industries sought "polluter profits" through a series of carbon-reduction cartels. We then focus on the formation and splintering of Kyoto coalitions and describe how Bootleggers covertly became Baptists—and then sometimes reverted to their former Bootlegger status. With coalitions coming unglued, the following section lays out the story of a failed final effort in Copenhagen to structure an international Kyoto cartel and then explains how the late 2000s Great Recession dealt a blow to the prospects for U.S. cap-and-trade legislation. We close with some final thoughts.

Kyoto, the Carbon Commons, and Its Repair

Whether or not climate change is caused systematically by human action—or proposed rules are likely to remedy it—is not central to our story. What matters for the economic analysis of climate regulation is that many people are convinced of the need to reduce carbon emissions globally. Yet they are wary of the cost—in the form of reduced economic growth—of doing so locally. This dichotomy creates political challenges because our atmosphere is a commons; one country's efforts to reduce emissions can be offset by the behavior of others who share the atmospheric commons (Anderson and Leal 2001; Hardin 1968). The problem is akin to two people in a leaking boat; one is diligently sealing cracks in the bottom and proclaiming progress while the other is drilling new holes.

Having embarked on a global effort to reduce the emission of greenhouse gases by way of the Kyoto Protocol in 1997, wealthy nations struggled to implement the terms of the action that set binding commitments to reduce greenhouse gas emissions to 1990 levels (UN 1997). The United States signed the 1997 agreement, but the agreement was not ratified by the U.S. Senate. In all some 37 industrialized countries and the European Union became parties to the agreement. The chief challenge was posed by developing countries, which according to the protocol were not required to reduce emissions but instead were to be subsidized by rich nations for making improvements in emission levels. In the post-1997 period, emission levels from the developing world rose markedly while industrialized nations showed some improvements. As it turned out, the developing nations were drilling holes in the boat about as fast as developed countries asserted they would seal up the leaks. Arguably, the greatest challenge to the Kyoto Protocol was that the United States was not then and is not now an official party.

Prior to the 1997 Kyoto discussions, the Senate voted overwhelmingly to instruct U.S. delegates not to sign the agreement unless it constrained all countries, including those in the developing world (Freedman 1997). The final word on this came in 2001 when the George W. Bush administration decided formally to reject Kyoto (Yandle and Buck 2002, 177). The Bush decision was widely supported by the U.S. Senate and by some important special interest groups, such as the AFL-CIO and the Teamsters Union, which were worried about jobs. Even so, the Bush administration became the target of vitriolic criticisms from our European cousins.[3] Although not one European country had ratified the agreement at the time, the United States was described by various European spokesmen as being "completely irresponsible" and "guilty of sabotage" (Andrews 2001, 1).

Two Competing Kyoto Viewpoints

The 1997 Kyoto Protocol can be viewed in two decidedly different ways. The popular view embraces the public interest theory of regulation and sees the protocol as an enlightened effort (by 84 countries initially and 193 eventually) to reduce greenhouse gas emissions to 1990 levels by 2012 (Sparber and O'Rourke 1998; UN 1997). For the protocol to become binding, at least 55 countries, collectively responsible for at least 55 percent of 1990 carbon emissions, had to ratify the agreement (UN Framework Convention on Climate Change 2011). This requirement was met on February 16, 2005, when Russia ratified the protocol (Pershing 2005).

The protocol allowed countries that reduced emissions below 1990 levels to bank those reductions and sell them in a future carbon offset market. Russia's willing endorsement was prompted partly by the prospect of earning $10 billion from the sale of carbon emission reductions that had accrued to the country by virtue of its recent economic collapse (Ferriter 2005). With Russia in the fold, the United States and Australia were the only industrialized countries that remained outside the Kyoto family.

When viewed through the public interest lens, the Kyoto plan looks a lot like an enlightened effort to save the planet from human harm.[4] But the fact that Kyoto set limits for higher-income industrialized nations while leaving the developing world unconstrained begs for a less benign interpretation. After all, the 1997 emissions from the developing world were almost equal to those of the richer world— and rising fast. Indeed, by 2011 developing economies accounted for 58 percent of total emissions, with China alone responsible for 23 percent of world emissions (Wilted Greenery 2011, 73). In December 2012, former World Bank chief economist and noted climate change analyst Nicholas Stern indicated that based on current calculations, by 2030 the developing world would be emitting 37 billion to 38 billion tons of carbon annually while the developed world's emissions would be about 11 billion to 14 billion tons (Harvey 2012). He went on to note that even if the developed world cut emissions to zero, world emission levels would still exceed 1990 levels.

The facts leave the public interest theory for parlor discussions and call for a special interest interpretation, a Bootlegger/Baptist explanation, to shed light on what really happened. Viewed through the Bootlegger/Baptist lens, Kyoto is about redistributing income from higher- to lower-income countries and creating a process that enables interest groups to build profitable cartels. Kyoto delivered a bright green invitation to a major-league pork cookout.

The Carbon Commons

As with most environmental issues, the problem Kyoto sought to address begins with a commons: an unfenced resource that tends to be overexploited. One way to avoid that undesirable outcome, often dubbed the "tragedy of the commons" (Hardin 1968), is to string regulatory barbed wire around the commons. We know that regulatory fences and other forms of rationing can convert tragedy into triumph by preserving vital resources. But we should also anticipate that pork-seeking efforts to influence regulatory strategies will help determine just how those fences are built (Buchanan and Tullock 1975).

Coordinated output restrictions are necessary to gain the support of Bootleggers in a Bootlegger/Baptist coalition: even the most public-spirited companies would be foolish to limit their own emissions unless they are assured their competitors will do the same. Better still, however, would be a restriction that generates extra profits—money that the Bootlegger can take to the bank. Regulators can reduce carbon dioxide emissions in at least five ways. Consider the following choices.

Choice 1: Performance standards

The simplest and perhaps most cost-effective way is to announce a reduction goal that applies to all emission sources along with penalties for failure to meet the goal. Then monitor what comes out of the smokestack and enforce the rule. This approach is called setting a performance standard. Emitters can accomplish the goal any way they wish. Competition will drive firms to discover low-cost ways to bring down emissions. Some firms may decide to switch fuels. Others may install new technologies. Still others may just shut down their dirtier plants. One way or another—assuming credible enforcement of the law—the goal will be met. But note that the regulated firms gain no pork. The best Bootleggers can hope for is avoiding penalties—not putting money in the bank. Baptists may like this approach, but no decent Bootlegger would lobby for it.

Choice 2: Taxing emissions

Instead of announcing a performance standard and leaving it to dischargers to find solutions, the regulator can experiment with taxing emissions. This can be done with a combination of performance standards and emission taxes. A goal is set, and any firm that emits more than its allocated share must pay a tax on each unit discharged. An even simpler approach just imposes taxes on each unit of emission. These can be raised and lowered as necessary to bring about the desired goal. To avoid paying taxes, dischargers will search for cleaner ways to operate their plants. Plant operators may change fuels, alter technologies, and shut down dirty plants.

Taxes induce companies to find efficient ways to meet environmental goals. Furthermore, emission taxes offer a special advantage to deficit-stricken nations eager for additional revenues. If deficits are not a problem, then emission tax revenues may be used to replace other more burdensome taxes, such as personal income and employment taxes, yielding what some call a "double dividend" (Carraro, Galeotti, and Gallo 1996; Green, Hayward, and Hassett 2007). The regulator would accomplish two things: emissions would be reduced, and the economy would be made more productive by the removal of less-efficient taxes.

So what's the problem? Well, for one, taxes rob Bootleggers of pork they might otherwise earn. Thus, special interest groups lobby aggressively against them. Even if these challengers can be defeated, the happy story sketched above makes a heroic assumption: that all-knowing regulators dedicated to finding the most efficient outcome are running the show. A more realistic alternative is that those regulators, or at least their bosses in Congress, end up captured by Bootleggers and assess a tax in the manner most favorable to influential industry players.

Choice 3: Adopting technologies

Taking a different approach, regulators might specify particular technologies that must be used in different plants and industries.

Then, providing proof that specified technologies are installed and operating is sufficient to satisfy the regulator. This approach, which is called the use of technology-based standards, is the approach found in U.S. clean water and clean air statutes. Once again, however, Bootleggers don't particularly like this approach unless (a) the Bootlegger happens to hold patents on the technology specified, (b) the Bootlegger already uses the technology but his competitors do not, and (c) stricter standards are required of new and expanding firms than for existing firms. It turns out that U.S. technology-based standards have set stricter standards for expanding firms, much to the Bootleggers' delight.

Choice 4: Cap and trade

Finally, the regulator may take a cap-and-trade approach. The "cap" part of this approach sets an overall output goal to be met by all polluters taken together—in this case, so many tons of carbon emissions annually. The "trade" part allows individual polluters to reduce more than the initial constraint and to sell the extra reductions to others who reduce less. In essence, cap-and-trade creates an asset: a tradable allowance that may be sold.

Now when the binding constraint is announced, provided the associated rights are assigned to polluters at no charge, Bootleggers who know how to clean up at low cost can dance all the way to the bank. They have gained a new source of earnings: profits from selling the rights to the emissions they've managed to cut. If the Bootleggers are forced to pay for the initial and future distribution, however, then all bets are off. There would be no money to take to the bank. Once again, no Bootlegger worth his salt would support paying for such a scheme.

From the standpoint of a viable Bootlegger/Baptist solution, the cap-and-trade approach to managing the environmental commons is hard to beat. The environmental Baptists like the "cap" part of the plan, and the Bootleggers like the "trade" part—as long as those initial permits are distributed free of charge.

Choice 5: Common law protection

In desperation, a regulator might take the approach of the old common law and assign property rights to unsullied air quality to parties downstream from carbon dioxide dischargers. Then if the polluters fail to reduce emissions, public defenders can organize public nuisance suits against the dischargers and seek court injunctions to shut them down as well as pay compensatory damages. Common law solutions may work so well that Bootleggers never support a common law regime (Meiners and Yandle 1999). Again, there is just no money in it for the Bootlegger.

Although a common law approach to reducing carbon emissions may seem far-fetched, just such an effort was mounted by attorneys general for eight northeastern states. The attorneys general brought a common law nuisance case against electric power generators whose emissions were received by those states. Arguing that environmental costs had been imposed on the affected populations against their will, they eventually made it to the U.S. Supreme Court. In June 2011, the Court ruled unanimously against the plaintiffs in *American Power v. Connecticut*. Speaking for the majority, in an opinion that must have made the Bootleggers and Baptists happy, Justice Ruth Bader Ginsburg wrote:

> [t]he Court remains mindful that it does not have creative power akin to that vested in Congress. . . . It is altogether fitting that Congress designated an expert agency, here, EPA, as best suited to serve as primary regulator of greenhouse gas emissions. The expert agency is surely better equipped to do the job than individual district judges issuing ad hoc, case-by-case injunctions. Federal judges lack the scientific, economic, and technological resources an agency can utilize in coping with issues of this order. (*American Electric Power Co. v. Connecticut*, 131 S. Ct. 2527 [2011], quoted in ". . . And the Climate Tort Cashiered" 2011)

Thus, the Court affirmed that EPA is the official climate change cartel manager.

The Struggle for Advantage and Breakup of Coalitions

The Bootlegger/Baptist theory calls attention to coalitions that seem to prevail when environmental and other social regulation is being formulated. In the post-Kyoto period, we find environmentalists playing the familiar Baptist role. The theory suggests that we should find allies among the Bootlegger population—countries, industries, and firms that foresee a "greener" bottom line resulting from their support for green policies. Accordingly, within such industries, we should find firms that have specialized assets or outputs favored by rules that raise the cost of competing assets and products.

Under Kyoto and cap-and-trade, countries such as the United Kingdom and Russia were positioned to exploit carbon reductions that had already occurred—and to raise the costs of competing economies that were burdened with large emission reduction targets. But unlike conventional regulatory arrangements that involve one national government regulating domestic industries, Kyoto presents us with the unusual situation of countries behaving like firms, strategically positioning themselves to benefit while gaining protection and credibility from international environmental groups. Within any given economy, polluting firms might become low-cost producers of carbon reductions if a cap-and-trade approach were taken. The trade in carbon reductions would then provide an opportunity for firms that operate exchanges in which reduction permits are bought and sold.

Bootleggers Hear the Call

Consider the following anecdote. Enron president Ken Lay was a widely celebrated supporter of the Kyoto Protocol. He was an even earlier supporter of international efforts to attack carbon emissions, especially when market-like approaches were being considered (Morgan 2002). Enron, a major natural gas producer and pipeline operator, had developed one of the world's leading trading floors for energy contracts and futures—one that could easily expand to include carbon emission contracts. Environmental groups had recognized Lay for his leadership.

Describing Enron's Kyoto stance, Dan Morgan (2002) writes:

> Enron officials later expressed elation at the results of the Kyoto conference. An internal memo said the Kyoto agreement, if implemented, would "do more to promote Enron's business than almost any other regulatory initiative outside of restructuring the energy and natural gas industries in Europe and the United States."

John Palmisano, Enron's chief Kyoto lobbyist, wrote that the Kyoto outcome "is exactly what I have been lobbying for and it seems like we won. The clean development fund will be a mechanism for funding renewable projects. Again we won. . . . The endorsement of emissions trading was another victory for us" (L. Solomon 2009).

In January 1997, Enron announced that it was forming the Enron Renewable Energy Corporation in an effort to "take advantage of the growing interest in environmentally sound alternatives of the $250 billion U.S. electricity market." Tom White, Enron Renewable Energy CEO, supported the Clinton administration's plan to fight global warming, which included $3.6 billion in tax credits to spur the production and purchase of renewable energy and related technologies (Salisbury 1998b).

Taxpayer subsidies can, of course, become habit-forming. On April 9, 1998, the National Corn Growers Association announced a major lobbying effort opposing congressional efforts to eliminate the 54-cent-per-gallon subsidy to producers of corn-based ethanol (National Corn Growers Association 1998). The association's newsletter claimed that "ethanol is good for the economy, good for the environment, good for America."

The celebration of ethanol did not mention that ethanol production may use more energy than it provides and causes significant collateral environmental damage or that the federal government's $6 billion annual ethanol subsidy assisted the production of beverage as well as industrial alcohol (Bandow 1997). But that did not seem to matter. The fuel additive was praised by EPA, by some leading environmental organizations, and especially by Vice President Al Gore, the nation's most prominent advocate for saving the planet.

On May 6, 1998, Republican leaders salvaged the subsidy, partly in the name of global warming prevention (Pianin 1998). Global climate change appeared to have saved the day for the corn producers—at least for a while. Following the corn producers' cue, U.S. soybean producers heralded the environmental benefits associated with blends of diesel fuel and soybean oil (National Biodiesel Board 1998). In efforts to gain regulatory approval of biodiesel as an "alternative fuel" to substitute for ordinary diesel—which would ensure the industry's participation in the Department of Energy's alternative fuel program—the lobbying organization argued that "biodiesel helps reduce the effects of global warming by directly displacing fossil hydrocarbons" (National Biodiesel Board 1998).

Yet the 1998 ethanol subsidy victory, like most political victories, was not without threats. In late 2011, Congress removed the highly visible ethanol subsidy from the budget (Llanos 2011) but offset the subsidy elsewhere in the corn bill by requiring a whopping increase in the amount of ethanol to be introduced annually into gasoline (Drum 2012). But there was more to the story. Ethanol champion Al Gore had recanted. He publicly disclaimed his previous celebration of ethanol's environmental benefits, calling his support a mistake and saying that his original enthusiastic support had no environmental basis at all ("Al Gore's Ethanol Epiphany" 2010).

It was strictly political. Gore described his situation this way, "One of the reasons I made that mistake is that I paid particular attention to the farmers in my home state of Tennessee, and I had a certain fondness for the farmers in the state of Iowa because I was about to run for President" ("Al Gore's Ethanol Epiphany" 2010). When Al Gore walked, the entire Baptist convention followed him out the door. All that was left were Bootleggers—and Bootleggers without Baptist cover look awfully naked.

As regulatory theory predicts, not every member of an industry could expect to benefit from the Kyoto restrictions. For example, Dean Kleckner, president of the 4.8 million-member American Farm Bureau Federation, opposed the protocol "because of its potential harm to U.S. farmers." Kleckner reflected the concerns of farmers who expected to see Kyoto-induced increases in the prices of food, fertilizer, and fuel ("Farm-State Senators Skeptical" 1998). The differential effects generated by regulation partly explain the formation and destruction of political coalitions.

Latent Bootleggers Energized

Energy action groups that had been around for years, some since the oil embargoes of the 1970s, were inspired by post-Kyoto legislation that called for new energy efficiency standards.[5] Others formed for the first time, with both industrial and environmental organizations on their membership rosters. These soon became Bootlegger cheerleaders for rules and subsidies that would favor their members. Among them were the American Council for an Energy-Efficient

Economy, the Alliance to Save Energy, the Business Council for Sustainable Energy, the American Wind Energy Association, and the Sustainable Energy Coalition.

In 2001, when newly elected President George W. Bush called for cuts in federal funding for energy efficiency and renewable energy—to the tune of $277 million—the cheerleaders scowled and howled (Holly 2001). Susanna Drayne, coordinator of the Sustainable Energy Coalition, which contained a mix of Bootleggers and Baptists, said, "To say we are disappointed by this budget is an understatement . . . [T]he Bush budget is patently irresponsible" (Sustainable Energy Coalition 2001).

Undaunted, other pro-Kyoto groups soon followed the Enron pattern. Kyoto provided regulatory opportunities to raise rivals' costs or to gain new revenues from increased demand for cleaner technology. For example, Cummins Inc., a producer of natural gas–fired diesel engines, joined forces with the Pew Center for Global Climate Change to support clean energy regulation. Pew Center president Eileen Claussen noted that the industrial firms joining the effort "recognize the best way to make money is to be there first" (Lavelle 2001, 38). The nuclear power industry unsuccessfully attempted to put on a green face worldwide—but did manage to receive government endorsements from the European Union, Germany, and Sweden as a necessary partner in meeting Kyoto's goals ("EU's De Palacio Says Nuclear Needed for Kyoto Targets" 1999).

The Breakup of Kyoto Coalitions

The Kyoto Protocol provided a setting where some Bootleggers heard the altar call and covertly converted to Baptists, only to backslide as the prospects of earthly rewards for the faithful dimmed. For example, one of the larger anti-Kyoto groups, the Global Climate Coalition (GCC), formed by major oil producers and hundreds of other firms, attempted to debunk Kyoto's weak scientific underpinnings and emphasized the expected economic costs of the protocol.

Over time, however, some GCC members began to see a silver lining in the Kyoto cloud. In June 1998, Shell Oil heard the Baptist call and announced its departure from the GCC. Friends of the Earth representative Anna Stanford claimed credit for Shell's green conversion, declaring, "We're delighted that our hard work has paid

120

off, that Shell has bowed to public pressure and seen that the future lies in . . . investing in green energy" ("Shell agm: FOE Urges Huge Increase in Green Energy Investment," 1988). Speaking the language of both a Bootlegger and a Baptist, Shell responded that "there are enough indications that CO_2 emissions are having an effect on climate change" and that the firm was "promoting the development of the gas industry particularly in countries with large coal reserves such as India and China" (Magada 1998).

Shell seemed to demonstrate that with Kyoto's help, firms with strategically located supplies of clean natural gas could improve their bottom lines while bolstering their green image. But Shell was not the first to see this possibility. The earlier decision of British Petroleum (BP) to part company with the GCC made Shell's departure a bit easier. Following serious discussions with leaders of the Environmental Defense Fund and the World Resources Institute, John Browne, CEO of BP (also touted to mean Beyond Petroleum), argued that firms such as BP should play a "positive and responsible part in identifying solutions" to the global warming problem ("British Petroleum to Take Action" 1997). Anticipating increased demand for oil as a cleaner coal substitute, BP also announced significantly increased investment in the development of solar and alternative energy technology.

Although the different anticipated effects of Kyoto-inspired regulations may explain the positions taken by members of the oil industry, the situation facing coal producers was more clear-cut. Coal producers and related unions were among the most vocal in their opposition to Kyoto. They succeeded in obtaining legislation in West Virginia to prohibit the state's division of environmental protection from "proposing or implementing rules regulating greenhouse gas emissions from industrial sites" ("Governor Signs Bill" 1998). When Governor Cecil Underwood signed the bill, however, he urged that the state "should continue to encourage the development and implementation of technologies that allow the clean burning of coal" ("Governor Signs Bill" 1998).

As time passed, even more Bootleggers heard the altar call. In November 1998, the American Automobile Manufacturers Association, speaking for General Motors, Ford, and Chrysler, refused to help pay for anti-Kyoto television ads produced by the Global Climate Information Project, another major coalition of firms,

121

labor unions, and farmers ("Look Who's Trying to Turn Green" 1998). Shortly thereafter, the World Resources Institute gathered executives from GM, BP, and Monsanto to pledge support for Kyoto. Bill Ford, the newly named president of Ford Motor Company, stated: "There is a rising tide of environmental awareness. Smart companies will get ahead of the wave. Those that don't are headed for a wipeout" ("Look Who's Trying to Turn Green" 1998).

Pure environmentalism might, of course, explain the behavior of firms leaving the anti-Kyoto club—but other incentives may be involved, too. In October 1998, Senate Bill 2617 was introduced, amending the Clean Air Act to provide regulatory relief for voluntary early action to mitigate greenhouse gas emissions. The proposed legislation, which received strong bipartisan support, was geared toward providing advance carbon-reduction credits for efforts already under way to reduce emissions.

If enacted, the rule change could have provided immediate and massive bottom-line benefits to carbon-emitting firms. For example, three years prior to the proposed rule change, Mobil Oil had cut carbon dioxide emissions by 1 million tons (Salisbury 1998a). At the then-estimated price of $300 per ton, the reduction was a potential asset worth $300 million. The U.S. electric utility industry had actions under way that would cut emissions by 47 million tons of carbon dioxide in two years. The potential side payments associated with this level of emission reductions were enough to make a firm revise its anti-Kyoto stance and push for a cap-and-trade system.

Following this rampant exodus of the converted, the GCC disbanded in 2002, stating that its initial purpose had been served. It was apparent that its coalition had splintered and that other industry groups were forming that would lend support to pending carbon emission reduction legislation.

Bootleggers and Baptists Unite and Then Split

In 2007, a Bootlegger/Baptist coalition replaced the anti-Kyoto GCC. Interestingly enough, some of the GCC defectors were leading members of the new U.S. Climate Action Partnership (USCAP), which quickly released a report calling for a cap-and-trade system for reducing carbon emissions (Odell 2007).

USCAP's strength was in its membership, which included a small but influential group of U.S. companies and environmental organizations. Its corporate members included Alcoa, BP America, Caterpillar, Duke Energy, DuPont, FPL Group, General Electric, Lehman Brothers, Pacific Gas & Electric (PG&E), and PNM Resources. Four nongovernmental organizations joined with these business leaders: the Environmental Defense Fund, the Natural Resources Defense Council, the Pew Center on Global Climate Change, and the World Resources Institute (Odell 2007).

Making reference to USCAP's inclusive membership, BP president Bob Malone said: "It is very important to interact with a wide group of stakeholders when you are trying to understand any complicated matter. The USCAP framework document is a great example of a diverse group working together to help progress an issue as complex as climate policy" (Odell 2007).

While lending strong support to cap-and-trade, key industrial members such as Duke Energy, PG&E, and BP stood to gain because either they would be sellers in a resulting permit market because of their position as clean energy producers, or they would become providers of low-carbon-content fuels that would command a higher price. Alternatively, they would execute trades for such transactions.

A fracture in the USCAP foundation occurred in late September 2009 when the U.S. Chamber of Commerce found itself shedding members over its opposition to climate change legislation. Exelon Corporation, a major electric utility, followed industry partners PG&E and PNM when it resigned from the chamber (Krauss and Galbraith 2009). The departures were understandable in a Bootlegger/Baptist world. The chamber opposed the Waxman–Markey climate change bill, which would sharply limit carbon emissions, raise the cost of power, and impose as much as a 15 percent tax increase on each U.S. household. Heavy nuclear power generators, Exelon, PG&E, and PNM favored the law.

Things began to unravel further in 2010 when details of proposed congressional legislation were unveiled. All along, USCAP key members hoped to gain profits in a world where carbon emissions would be restricted. Those cutting back would receive marketable permits at no cost that they could sell later. But then the worm turned. On February 16, 2010, BP, ConocoPhillips, and Caterpillar announced their departure from USCAP (Burnham 2010). In breaking the news, ConocoPhillips CEO John Mulva explained:

> House climate legislation and Senate proposals to date have disadvantaged the transportation sector and its consumers, left domestic refineries unfairly penalized versus international competition, and ignored the critical role that natural gas can play in reducing GHG [greenhouse gas] emissions. (Burnham 2010)

His story became more relevant to our theory when it was reported that the House bill would give the electric utility industry 35 percent of the newly created tradable permits, an amount roughly equal to the industry's emissions. In contrast, Mr. Mulva's refinery industry, which produced one-third of the nation's industrial emissions, received 2 percent of the permits. The industry would have to purchase the rest, with some coming from their competition, the electricity producers. In a moment of candor, perhaps born of desperation, Mr. Mulva explained, "We want to make sure refineries get protection" (Burnham 2010).

In an earlier comment on the USCAP fracturing, Environmental Defense Fund president Fred Krupp repeated a commonly held misconception about government regulation when he said: "It's very unusual for big corporations to raise their hands and say, 'We want to be regulated for something that we're not regulated for now. When the history . . . is written, it will show USCAP to have played a very constructive role'" (Power 2009). Fred Krupp had apparently not heard about the Bootlegger/Baptist theory of regulation.

With splits occurring right and left, some pro-Kyoto coalitions were losing their Bootleggers, and some anti-Kyoto groups were losing their Baptists. Although this was bad enough, more trouble was on the horizon. The Great Recession was on the way, and the recession's income-eroding effects would undermine basic support for the purchase of environmental quality.

Recession, Copenhagen, and the End of Cap-and-Trade

Bootleggers and Baptists are not immune to a recession's forces. The demand for regulation—as for any other good—depends on a nation's level of income and prosperity. In addition, when times

124

are tough, the politicians who organize the supply of favors often have more pressing problems on their minds. Consequently, when a recession is truly severe, such as the Great Recession of the late 2000s, environmental priorities get reshuffled.

The Great Recession became associated with massive federal deficits—and political struggles over what to do about them. It seemed the handwriting was on the wall: the United States was running short of money and credit and would not be able to tax and spend as it had in the past. The pork-seeking climate had changed just at the time when the environmental community was gearing up to push for carbon emissions control legislation. This push was motivated first by an April 2007 Supreme Court decision that instructed the EPA to determine whether carbon emissions endangered human health and well-being (Till 2008). If it found that they did, the EPA would be instructed to proceed with regulations authorized by the Clean Air Act for dealing with harmful emissions.

Paving the Way to Copenhagen

The Great Recession officially began in December 2007. With more than one hot potato to handle at the time, the George W. Bush White House—never especially enthusiastic about climate change legislation—took no action, leaving the matter for the Obama administration. As the EPA continued its "endangerment" deliberations, the next and final post-Kyoto international climate change gathering was scheduled to take place in Copenhagen, December 6–18, 2009.

Regarded as critical to the ultimate success of Kyoto, the Copenhagen gathering would be the last chance for climate change conferees to settle their differences before the Kyoto Protocol's 2012 expiration date. Two critical issues needed to be resolved at the meeting. The first was China's stance on joining the developed countries in taking meaningful actions to reduce greenhouse gas emissions; the second was the United States's continued failure to pass carbon control legislation. A refusal by China to take action would blunt congressional interest in imposing costly carbon control legislation on the American people. Furthermore, if Congress would not act, the climate change Bootleggers would walk away from the coalition.

On December 7, 2009, just one day before departing for the Copenhagen conference, EPA administrator Lisa Jackson announced that agency scientists, taking into account hundreds of thousands of comments, had determined that carbon and other greenhouse gas emissions endanger the health and safety of the U.S. population (EPA 2009). But Jackson's announcement noted the involvement of Bootleggers and Baptists along with the scientists:

> Business leaders, security experts, government officials, concerned citizens and the United States Supreme Court have called for enduring, pragmatic solutions to reduce the greenhouse gas pollution that is causing climate change. This continues our work towards clean energy reform that will cut GHGs [greenhouse gases] and reduce the dependence on foreign oil that threatens our national security and our economy. (EPA 2009)

To put pressure on Congress, Jackson also pointed out that the decision enabled the agency to move forward with draconian command-and-control regulation as dictated by the Clean Air Act. She expressed hope that Congress would pass the debated cap-and-trade legislation and therefore preclude EPA from moving forward with the regulatory process. It was as if the EPA administrator had cried, "Stop me before I regulate again!"

Meanwhile, the Great Recession was taking its toll on any willingness in Congress to place another burden on the U.S. economy. Even so, Jackson's announcement raised the Obama administration's bid to bring the Congress, kicking and screaming, to the Kyoto negotiating table. Commenting on the Jackson announcement, Massachusetts senator John Kerry, who was spearheading cap-and-trade in the U.S. Senate, had this to say: "The message to Congress is crystal clear: Get moving. Imposed regulations by definition will not include the job protections and investment incentives we are proposing in the Senate today. . . . Industry needs the certainty that comes with Congressional action on this vital issue" (Morford 2009).

The jaws of the vise were set to tighten. Legislate, or the EPA will regulate. Of course, there was still the matter of China continuing to poke holes in the leaky boat. Unfortunately for those seeking meaningful reductions in total greenhouse gas emissions, unilateral cuts taken by the United States could quickly be replaced by expanding emissions from China and other developing countries. With U.S. regulation or legislation in hand, however, the Obama administration could more credibly place pressure on China to join the carbon reduction cartel.

The EPA announcement was orchestrated perfectly to coincide with the start of the December 2009 Copenhagen Conference on climate change. The proclamation armed President Obama with much-needed rhetoric for his Copenhagen soliloquy, and Secretary of State Hillary Clinton was accordingly authorized to commit to an annual $100 billion fund that would pay off developing countries for supporting the Kyoto-inspired carbon emissions reduction effort (Gray and Mason 2009). But Secretary Clinton's offer came with strings: China and India would have to commit first and provide transparent monitoring of their emission reduction efforts.

The Demise of Cap-and-Trade

It was not to be. China's president Hu Jintao had earlier announced to the United Nations Assembly that his country would not be a party to a global commitment on greenhouse gas reduction (Carrington 2009). After a 31-hour negotiating session led by President Obama, Mr. Hu repeated his position in Copenhagen (Pilkington 2009). Instead of agreeing to a promise that China would not keep, Hu indicated that he would go forward with forest carbon sequestration and expanded clean energy production. Without apologizing, Hu indicated that China would not promote greenhouse gas reductions at the expense of GDP growth and that China's carbon emissions would continue to increase in the future, though at a reduced rate.

Mr. Obama's attempt to offset Hu's disappointing announcement left more than a few Copenhagen attendees frustrated (Goldenberg and Stratton 2009; Stone 2009). Many had come with high expectations that the president would announce a special commitment to pushing climate change legislation through Congress. This was not given. There had also been hopes that the president would make a generous offer of support to African leaders, who hoped to obtain transfers from the wealthier countries in exchange for their cooperation. They too were disappointed. Finally, there were those who wanted to hear an apology from Mr. Obama for U.S. failure to do more. This they received—but the combination of diminished U.S. wealth, dissolving previously coordinated Bootlegger and Baptist coalitions, and unfulfilled high expectations placed America's president in the position of being seen as an example of failed leadership in a foreign land.

However disappointing it may have proved to attendees, the failure of the Copenhagen conference had been predicted in the pages of the Cato Institute's *Regulation* magazine (see Lipford and Yandle 2009). Their empirical work on carbon emissions from a sample of industrialized and developing economies showed that China emits 2,173,000 metric tons of carbon to yield a $1 increase in per capita income, the United States emits 204,000 metric tons to get the same dollar, and France emits just 2,470 metric tons for each dollar increase. Mr. Hu's commitment to GDP growth was unambiguously a commitment to high levels of carbon emission.

The cap-and-trade climate change bill, which had passed the U.S. House but could not make it to the Senate, carried the equivalent of an annual tax on each household of between $450 and $1,531—or as much as a 15 percent tax increase. This paid for carbon reductions that would easily be offset by emissions growth in China and elsewhere (Chamberlain 2009). When the international parties seeking to extend Kyoto met in Durban, South Africa, in late 2011, China surprised attendees by suggesting the country would be willing to make a post-2020 commitment to carbon emission reduction (Conway-Smith 2011). Outwardly, China challenged the United States—the other large noncommitted emitter—to join the effort. However, a closer reading of China's position suggested that nothing had really changed other than the quality of the country's public relations messages.

Final Thoughts

Kyoto provides a prime illustration of how Bootlegger/Baptist coalitions form, transform, and ultimately dissolve. It also shows what happens when the forces of a major recession seriously erode the ability of politicians to dole out the rewards that hold those coalitions together. In a sense, the political market for Kyoto-based favors shut down. But it is not dead: new groups can always be formed when the time is right, after all. Most recently, when the EPA's contested decision to regulate greenhouse gases under the Clean Air Act was affirmed by the U.S. Court of Appeals for the District of Columbia Circuit, the struggle began anew (Volcovici 2012). As the economy recovers and new regulatory proposals surface, Bootlegger/Baptist coalitions are likely to prove renewable and sustainable.

6. TARP: A Bootlegger without a Baptist

Introduction

Until now, we have focused on cases in which groups figuratively waving banners of righteousness give cover to private parties seeking government-grounded profit. Profiteers pursuing preferred policy changes must normally appeal to some public interest or face a negative backlash; that is the essence of Bootlegger/Baptist theory. But what happens when no such moral appeal is forthcoming? Or if the appeal is found wanting? What if there are no Baptists? The simple answer is that such endeavors typically fail—and indeed, this is one reason failed political initiatives are more common than successful ones.

Sometimes Bootleggers just have to go it alone. Circumstances arise that compel Bootleggers to mount a very public campaign for political benefits without Baptist protection, relying wholly on sheer lobbying might. This is the story of the Troubled Asset Relief Program. TARP was a response to the financial crisis of 2008–10, which shook the political landscape with as much force as it did the economy. Following the collapse of financial markets in September 2008, President George W. Bush repeatedly warned that an immediate political response was necessary to avoid another Great Depression. "Too big to fail" became a rallying cry for firms hoping for government rescue. A high-level scramble for pork came in the wake of financial disasters, as executives lobbied for greater support through newly invigorated political channels (Smith, Wagner, and Yandle 2011). The result was the creation of TARP, which would quickly evolve into a multifaceted mechanism for delivering massive subsidies to politically blessed failing enterprises.

Yet a populist backlash against the bailouts soon marred the seemingly happy exchange between lawmakers and ailing industries. Companies such as American International Group (AIG) came under heavy fire from lawmakers and their constituents for passing out executive bonuses widely seen as being over the top. As it turned out, the very lawmakers who would become AIG's most vocal critics had approved the bailout contract that provided for those much-maligned bonuses. Knowing about such footnotes of history did not deter those same lawmakers from cheerfully proposing clawback legislation to cancel the bonuses in response to popular outrage.

With executive salaries at risk, many who had stood hat in hand hoping for Washington pork looked desperately for a TARP escape hatch. Requests for TARP monies, which previously showed no signs of abating, immediately slowed to a trickle—and among larger firms ceased completely. Suddenly, the very players who had been instrumental in creating this massive vehicle for pork couldn't escape it fast enough.

We begin by describing the events that led to TARP's creation. The subsequent section provides detail on the program's initial conception and its evolution into a subsidy mechanism for ailing firms. The narrative illustrates lawmakers' struggle to find political cover for a massively unpopular initiative tailored to benefit the same firms the public blamed for the economic crisis and show how TARP was increasingly used to benefit firms found palatable by more voters. We then document how the TARP mechanism was vilified as a result of AIG's executive compensation packages, ultimately leading to the collapse of TARP-supported political arrangements. The chapter concludes with a note on how lawmakers have sought cover from the TARP fallout in the shade of the newly formed Consumer Financial Protection Bureau (CFPB).

TARP to the Rescue

The worldwide financial crisis of 2008–10 bankrupted families, spurred runs on banks, ruined hoary financial institutions, and brought serious volatility to financial and political markets alike (Cohan 2009; Hall and Woodward 2008; Posner 2009; Sowell 2009; L. White 2008; Yandle 2010a). The crisis hit its American apex in September 2008, as the global financial services firm Lehman Brothers failed, major banks trembled, and liquidity markets suddenly froze.

The immediate cause of this catastrophe was a collapse in the value of securities known as credit default swaps, financial assets that served as insurance policies for a variety of mortgage debt obligations. These insured mortgage debt packages enabled investment banks to trade assets that had previously been regarded as too risky to own by effectively bundling and dispersing the risk. In particular, by purchasing credit default swaps to cover their riskier loans, mortgage lenders were able to extend homeowner-ship to less-affluent borrowers—a Baptist endeavor supported and celebrated by the Clinton and George W. Bush administrations. The credit expansion, which was also accommodated by federal housing finance programs, facilitated the inflation of an enormous housing bubble—one that eventually popped. The credit default swaps became essentially worthless as an epidemic of defaults in mortgage markets eradicated their underlying value (Diamond and Rajan 2009).

The first company to fall prey to this calamity was Bear Stearns, a global investment bank and securities trading and brokerage firm. On March 14, 2008, the Federal Reserve Bank of New York provided a $25 billion loan to avert a sudden failure of the well-connected invest-ment bank (Paulson 2010, 112–14). Government officials worked to find a buyer for the company to avoid contagion effects. Days later, the firm—valued at $20 billion as recently as January 2007—was pur-chased by J. P. Morgan for $236 million (Paulson 2010, 115).

The impending crisis, however, was not averted by these meas-ures, only delayed. In the fall of 2008, Lehman Brothers—a much larger investment firm with substantial holdings in subprime mort-gage securities, now on their way to becoming worthless—saw its stock value fall dramatically. At the time, Lehman Brothers was the fourth-largest investment bank in the United States and con-sequently of critical importance to the integrity of financial mar-kets. Despite efforts to facilitate a merger or acquisition with Bank of America and Barclays, Lehman Brothers filed for Chapter 11 bankruptcy protection on September 15, 2008 (Cohan 2009, 442–47; Paulson 2010, 188–233). With more than $600 billion in debt, it was the largest bankruptcy in U.S. history (Mamudi 2008).

These dramatic events put the entire financial system at risk of collapse. Fearful that another Great Depression was on the way, government officials scrambled to find a solution to the burgeon-ing crisis. The nation's top political leaders called for an immedi-ate emergency response by the federal government (Paulson 2010). After attempts were made to merge the weakest companies with stronger ones, officials decided that massive injections of liquidity into investment banks were necessary to avoid collapse of credit markets worldwide. Unfortunately, such injections were not feasible under the existing rules of operation of the Federal Reserve and Treasury Department

Thus, TARP was initially justified as a novel and critically important response to this development. The program would remove bad assets from the balance sheets of major investment banks—the so-called toxic assets—and, in exchange, provide much-needed capital to sustain ongoing lending services. Congress passed this initiative on its second attempt, on October 3, 2008, as part of the Emergency Economic Stabilization Act of 2008. The law, as summarized in its own preamble, was an effort "to provide authority for the Federal Government to purchase and insure certain types of troubled assets for the purposes of providing stability to and preventing disruption in the economy and financial system."[1]

Dealing with the Absent Baptist

Given the crisis atmosphere, government efforts initially met with public approval. After all, there were runs on banks and the public was concerned about the safety of their deposits. Only 11 percent of Americans polled by Gallup believed that the government should do nothing (Newport 2008a). Nevertheless, in the same poll, 56 percent of respondents wanted Congress to consider a different plan than the proposed TARP. Thus, as the TARP juggernaut took off, the broader electorate felt left behind.

Public officials were clearly worried about a backlash from voters and because of this took steps to limit TARP's objectives by constraining how TARP monies could be spent. This is perhaps why Bush administration officials insisted that TARP would not exceed its mandate—at least before the law passed. Just one week later, on October 14, 2008, the objectives of TARP took a dramatic turn from purchasing toxic assets to injecting capital directly into the balance sheets of ailing banks by way of government purchase of equity ownership. This shift in direction opened the door for a new means of securing capital by ailing firms: direct subsidy using taxpayer dollars.[2]

Several factors contributed to this shift in objectives. First, direct purchase of toxic assets in a contrived public securities exchange would be hampered by considerable logistical difficulties, imposing large transaction costs in a crisis when time was of the essence. These transaction costs included setting up and administering a viable auction market that all parties would deem credible, a task well beyond the capacity of a time-constrained bureaucracy. Second, and perhaps more serious, any public offer to purchase at discount failing mortgage-backed securities would immediately affect, if not determine, the offering price of the securities, which could not be sold elsewhere. Put another way, government entry into the toxic assets market would bring with it a serious moral hazard problem. The very presence of a buyer paying bargain-basement prices would tend to make the typical balance sheet problem even worse. Finally, and most important to our story, unlike the purchase of equity ownership, the purchase of toxic assets would give lawmakers limited leverage in the operations of the firms, whereas taking ownership shares would enhance their ability to deliver pork to preferred interest groups.

The absence of a credible Baptist counterpart to the investment banks and other TARP Bootleggers left lawmakers with limited cover for this arrangement. An outright purchase of toxic assets would have granted Treasury discretion over only those assets rather than the firms themselves. Direct capital injections, in contrast, would put Treasury in the driver's seat and come with the ability to specify how, and to what extent, profits would be distributed by the assisted firms. With an equity share and the power of the federal government, Treasury exercised a controlling interest in these firms.

In addition to these concerns, public officials needed to ensure that funds would not be allocated to politically disastrous outlets, such as executive bonuses. In anticipation of a public backlash against this perceived subsidy to Wall Street executives, participating companies reluctantly agreed to certain stipulations regarding executive compensation. These included:

> (1) ensuring that incentive compensation for senior executives does not encourage unnecessary and excessive risks that threaten the value of the financial institution; (2) required claw back of any bonus or incentive compensation paid to a senior executive based on statements of earnings, gains or other criteria that are later proven to be materially inaccurate; (3) prohibition on the financial institution from making any golden parachute payment to a senior executive based on

the Internal Revenue Code provision; and (4) agreement not to deduct for tax purposes executive compensation in excess of $500,000 for each senior executive. (http://www.treasury. gov/press-center/press-releases/Pages/2008101495019994. aspx)

These limitations would constitute a curious addition to the political contract if we did not recognize the dilemma inherent in a legislative bargain that had attracted so little Baptist sympathy. After all, no prior study had found an empirical link between executive pay and the excessive leveraging of risk responsible for the downturn. Fahlenbrach and Stulz (2011), in fact, report that not only was there no correlation between CEO compensation and negative stock performance (relative to average market return) in the wake of the crisis, but also that companies with CEOs whose incentives were more aligned with those of shareholders fared worse. Indeed, the inclusion of constraints on executive compensation was not necessary for stability in financial markets but represented an attempt to help legitimize an un-Baptized political transfer from taxpayers to Bootleggers.

Another stipulation geared toward limiting the amount of pork, thereby placating the electorate, involved insuring full recovery of taxpayer dollars. The Emergency Economic Stabilization Act ((H.R. 1424 2008), sec. 134) requires the president to submit "a legislative proposal that recoups from the financial industry an amount equal to the shortfall in order to ensure that the Troubled Asset Relief Program does not add to the deficit or national debt." The means by which these funds would be secured were not specified, though the language of the bill indicated that this would take place within five years of the initial TARP disbursements.

TARP was capable of providing enormous short-run benefit to Bootleggers, but in exchange, lawmakers demanded discretion over the market practices of participating companies. The lawmakers' demands were necessary, at least in part, because of the missing Baptist component. In effect, the lawmakers made themselves TARP nannies in an effort to mitigate public disapproval,[3] as reflected in the low polling figures cited previously. Playing to the public's rational ignorance, the nanny oversight signaled to the electorate that these Bootleggers could not simply take the money and run but would be held accountable in the public forum.

TARP Evolves into a Versatile Pork Barrel Mechanism

With TARP firmly established, the Treasury Department's first action was to distribute $250 billion in subsidies to nine large banks and financial institutions by purchasing preferred stock and warrants.[4] Government documents show that Treasury Secretary Henry Paulson had a closed meeting with CEOs from these nine institutions, most of which were financially strong and needed no government assistance. Paulson warned the assembled bankers that noncompliance with his plan "would leave you vulnerable and exposed" and threatened further regulation (CEO Talking Points 2008).[5]

This strong-arming of major financial institutions ostensibly occurred so that Paulson and his advisers would not have to identify to the public the weakest major banks in the financial system. By bundling the banks, he prevented a potential run on the few banks that actually needed the assistance. Furthermore, by setting up contracts with nine of the largest investment banks in the country, he paved the way for subsequent TARP disbursements.

Although this initial disbursement greatly benefited several cash-hungry firms, a case could be made that this Faustian bargain actually delivered pork not to the nominal recipients but to their creditors. Indeed, law professor J. W. Verret (2010) claims that the TARP mechanism represents an innovative type of extraction that indirectly funnels resources to companies tied to TARP-supported firms. Put another way, all the TARP recipients had debt on their books involving other financial institutions and transaction counterparties. Funds distributed to the TARP recipients could be extracted by anxious creditors, some of whom fully recouped their money.

This can be viewed as an instance of successful profit seeking by recipients converted to successful extraction by other far less visible parties. Suppliers, business partners, and large investors could all benefit indirectly from the continued solvency and liquidity provided to weak firms by TARP. Direct benefits to these Bootleggers in the form of transfers then became possible, because the TARP recipients were able to maintain payment schedules to their creditors and even generate new contracts with those Bootleggers indirectly favored by the much-celebrated political action.

As Verret demonstrates, the TARP mechanism created a complex arrangement with elements of pork generation, pork extraction, and indirect transfers all embedded within it. Consider, for example, the inclusion of special legislative language tailored to support the bank OneUnited, a constituent of the powerful Rep. Barney Frank (D-MA), then chair of the House Financial Services Committee. Paletta and Enrich (2009) report:

> Rep. Frank was intimately involved in crafting the legislation that created the $700 billion financial-system rescue plan. Mr. Frank says that in order to protect OneUnited bank, he inserted into the bill a provision to give special consideration to banks that had less than $1 billion of assets, had been well-capitalized as of June 30, served low- and moderate-income areas, and had taken a capital hit in the federal seizure of Fannie Mae and Freddie Mac. "I did feel that it was important to frankly try and save them since it was federal action that put them into the dumper," Mr. Frank says.

By serving as handmaidens to local companies, lawmakers gained political advantage from an otherwise unpopular program.

Following this initial disbursement, applications for TARP funds grew at a rapid pace. Just two months after the initial disbursement, 206 additional banks had received subsidies under TARP's Capital Purchase Program (Treasury Department 2009). In addition, the Treasury Department designed a new program for the sole purpose of accommodating the failing insurance giant AIG. This new program, called Systemically Significant Failing Institutions, allowed Treasury to consolidate previous obligations to AIG under the TARP initiative.

AIG, the world's largest insurance company, invested heavily in mortgage-backed securities and was the leading writer of the credit default swaps that protected subprime mortgage investors from default losses. AIG's operating losses rendered it technically bankrupt, but with financial linkages that reached across the entire financial community, AIG was viewed as too big to fail.

As a result, the federal government had become increasingly entangled with AIG even before TARP was established. The Federal Reserve Bank of New York had authorized a two-year loan of up to $85 billion for AIG to draw upon following the collapse of

Lehman Brothers and the dramatic fall in the value of AIG shares on September 16, 2008 (Federal Reserve 2008a). An additional loan of $37.5 billion was extended on October 8 (Federal Reserve 2008b). On November 10, the Treasury Department assumed some of the financial burden by issuing a $40 billion subsidy through the TARP to purchase senior preferred stock. This allowed the Federal Reserve Bank of New York to reduce its previous allocation of $85 billion to $60 billion.

In exchange for this subsidy, the Treasury Department (2008b) stipulated the following:

> Under the agreement AIG must be in compliance with the executive compensation and corporate governance requirements of Section 111 of the Emergency Economic Stabilization Act. AIG must comply with the most stringent limitations on executive compensation for its top five senior executive officers as required under the Emergency Economic Stabilization Act. Treasury is also requiring golden parachute limitations and a freeze on the size of the annual bonus pool for the top 70 company executives. Additionally, AIG must continue to maintain and enforce newly adopted restrictions put in place by the new management on corporate expenses and lobbying as well as corporate governance requirements, including formation of a risk management committee under the board of directors.

AIG thus had even more stipulations than other companies participating in TARP, given its special circumstances and previous financial assistance from the Federal Reserve Bank of New York.

Yet the public was split on whether AIG should be bailed out at all, with a Gallup poll showing 40 percent in favor of the rescue and 42 percent opposed (see Jacobe 2008). This lack of popular support further constrained the level of subsidy the Treasury Department could provide. Any bailout would need to come with hard constraints on what could be done with public dollars. In this sense, officials acted to tailor the TARP mechanism to individual cases when warranted, such as with AIG.

Using the disbursement of funds to AIG as a blueprint, three of the largest national insurance companies took steps to qualify themselves for TARP money. Lincoln National, Hartford Financial

Services Group, and Genworth Financial each acquired federally regulated financial institutions to make themselves eligible for TARP. Whereas Genworth was unable to secure TARP funding, Lincoln and Hartford both announced their preliminary approval for the disbursal of TARP funds on May 14, 2009 (McGee and Frye 2009). Many other companies, such as CIT Group Inc., GMAC, and IB Finance Holding Company LLC, also repositioned themselves to qualify for TARP loans and take advantage of this new pork-generating mechanism.

Perhaps the most glaring example of the growing Bootlegger contingent came when General Motors, Chrysler, and Ford appealed to Congress for TARP funding. In testimony before Congress, the three CEOs of these firms argued that their companies were being driven to insolvency by the combination of a weak economy, constrained credit institutions, and the legacy costs of health care and retirement benefits promised to United Auto Workers union members. GM and Chrysler were on the ropes. They asked for $25 billion in TARP money (Vlasic and Herszenhorn 2008). Ford Motor Company, on the other hand, was in better financial condition and asked for a line of credit, rather than a direct injection of TARP money.

Though this initial request was rebuffed, President George W. Bush broadened the domain of the TARP through an executive order to include essentially any program he personally deemed necessary to avert the financial crisis. This stunning power grab was used to distribute funds to the ailing automotive industry: $9.4 billion to General Motors and $4 billion to Chrysler.

The United Auto Workers stood to gain a significant amount from the auto bailout as well. As law professor Todd Zywicki (2008) explains, the alternative of bankruptcy would have forced unions to "take further pay cuts, reduce their gold-plated health and retirement benefits, and overcome their cumbersome union work rules." These ancillary benefits to blue-collar workers threatened with the loss of promised pensions might have introduced a much-needed Baptist element to the mix. If support for unions could increase popular support for TARP subsidies, then public officials and Bootleggers alike could rest a bit easier.

Yet in a Gallup poll taken in December 2008, respondents were critical not only of automotive executives but of labor unions as well, with 34 percent stating "labor unions that represent many

U.S. auto workers" deserved a "great deal of blame" (Newport 2008b). Another poll taken just nine months after the bailout exposed waning sympathy for the plight of unions: more than 50 percent of respondents claimed that unions did more harm than good, particularly toward nonunion workers (Saad 2009b). Hence, not only did unions fail to generate increased demand for TARP disbursements, they may have also damaged their wider Baptist image as a consequence. The bottom line is that as Baptists, unions fared poorly.

In most cases, recipients of TARP funds had some link to financial markets and investment in subprime mortgages, no matter how indirect. In other cases, the primary goal was to counter rising unemployment and regional decline, whether or not related to subprime debt. Although these factors had little to do with the financial crisis, they did resonate more strongly with the electorate and paved the way for lawmakers to consider subsidizing them using the TARP mechanism, regardless of the break with TARP's original objectives. Hearing the ring of the dinner bell, hungry Bootleggers began to arrive by the dozens.

TARP Runs Aground

Though recipients were initially pleased with their TARP funds, dark clouds of discontent soon loomed on the horizon. On January 15, 2009, just days before President Obama took office, Gallup reported that a majority of Americans (62 percent) believed Congress should block President Obama's expected request to release the second half of the TARP monies ($350 billion) until more details were provided about how it would be spent. The rationally ignorant had become at least a bit more informed and were increasingly wary of bailing out Bootleggers. Only 20 percent of Americans felt that the money should be released without further conditions, and 12 percent said it should be blocked entirely (Newport 2009b).

On February 17, 2009, perhaps fearful of this increasingly irate electorate, President Obama signed into law a broad stimulus package, enacted under the American Recovery and Reinvestment Act of 2009. The legislation was nominally geared toward reducing unemployment rates and halting economic decline, but an additional provision in the act imposed greater restrictions on executive compensation for firms under TARP. The law further detailed how firms could exit

TARP through buyback of preferred shares that had been sold to the Treasury Department, facilitating early departure for some firms, as we detail below. At least with respect to TARP, these restrictions were meant to further buttress the constraints on pork seeking, forcing companies to use taxpayer dollars in ways that would incur lower political costs.

Despite the greater attention to executive compensation practices generated by the Emergency Economic Stabilization Act, in mid-March 2009 AIG announced it would be handing out $165 million in bonuses to its top executives. A media firestorm ensued. Polls indicated strong disapproval of both AIG and the lawmakers involved in the bailout negotiations. A Gallup poll indicated that 55 percent of those polled described themselves as "outraged" by the bonuses, with 76 percent indicating they wanted the government to block them and recover those that had been issued (Morales 2009). A follow-up Gallup poll found that whereas participants were dissatisfied with Congress (65 percent); Treasury Secretary Timothy Geithner (54 percent), who had succeeded Paulson; and President Obama (39 percent), the greatest resentment was aimed at AIG itself, with 80 percent of those polled reporting dissatisfaction (see J. Jones 2009).

This result shows the danger for not only the political broker but also the Bootlegger when pork barreling draws public ire. AIG was contractually obligated to pay the bonuses, even before the financial crisis had hit its peak. Still, the use of taxpayer dollars to enrich those whose apparent blunders drove the financial turmoil was quite simply too much for voters and their political representatives.

This "populist outrage"—the reaction of an electorate now more rationally informed—spurred political actors to punish AIG along with other market enterprises connected to TARP, an acknowledgment that a greater supply of pork had been distributed than was politically palatable. As Phillips (2009) reports, Rep. Barney Frank admitted, "Clearly not enough was done in the beginning to put conditions on A.I.G." The AIG controversy had shown that the original TARP mandate would not rest within the constraints that public officials so desperately hoped would confine it—constraints that had been forced upon lawmakers by the absence of credible Baptist support. Instead, the affected firms would use funds for politically unpalatable practices such as paying executive bonuses.

Accordingly, officials were forced to reduce the level of subsidies in response to voter outrage. These reductions manifested themselves in several ways, including a direct tax on bonuses, the establishment of a Special Master for Executive Compensation, and a proposed special tax to recoup TARP losses assessed to companies that had already paid back TARP monies. We briefly summarize each of these efforts.

Taxation on Bonuses, the Rise of the Pay Czar

Lawmakers immediately reacted to the news of AIG's lavish bonuses by vilifying the company's actions. In one of the more widely covered and representative responses, President Obama voiced strong opposition:

> Under these circumstances, it's hard to understand how derivative traders at A.I.G. warranted any bonuses, much less $165 million in extra pay. How do they justify this outrage to the taxpayers who are keeping the company afloat? In the last six months, A.I.G. has received substantial sums from the U.S. Treasury. I've asked Secretary Geithner to use that leverage and pursue every legal avenue to block these bonuses and make the American taxpayers whole. (*New York Times* 2009)

On March 19, 2009, the House passed a bill specifically tailored to the AIG incident, which levied a 90 percent tax on all bonuses received by employees making more than $250,000 if they were currently employed by companies receiving more than $5 billion in TARP monies (Hulse and Herszenhorn 2009).[6] The Senate version reduced this tax to 70 percent. By taxing the bulk of these bonuses, Congress was attempting to reel back in previously distributed pork.

For some, however, the damage had already been done. Sen. Chris Dodd (D-CT), the lawmaker held responsible for the inclusion of the exemption for bonuses in the executive payments clause of the TARP bill, came under heavy fire from the electorate. Despite his contention that he had tried to prevent the exemption language from entering the bill—only to be warded off by Secretary of the Treasury

Geithner and White House officials—the controversy so damaged Dodd's reputation that he opted not to seek reelection following the end of his term (Solomon and Maremont 2009). The more immediate result of the threatened tax was the voluntary return of bonuses by most executives—and a withdrawal of top talent from many of the TARP-subsidized firms.

Special Master for TARP Executive Compensation

A second response to the public outcry against AIG came when the Treasury Department appointed an overseer to determine optimal compensation packages for seven of the largest firms receiving TARP funds (Labaton 2009).[7] Treasury later expanded this domain of responsibility to include all firms that received TARP monies (see Solomon and Lucchetti 2009).

The appointed overseer, Kenneth Feinberg, indicated that he viewed his role more as that of a broker. His efforts, while highly intrusive, were likely less constraining than what Congress would opt for. At a meeting with the AIG board of directors, according to one account:

> Mr. Feinberg told the board that AIG would suffer if he signed off on exorbitant pay packages. "You're looking to me to protect you," Mr. Feinberg said. "If I just give you whatever you want . . . they'll kill you up there," he said, referring to Capitol Hill, where anger over AIG pay had persisted. (Goldman and Katz 2010)

In other words, Feinberg was pledging to take back less pork than his counterparts in Congress.

The primary outcome of Feinberg's efforts was to replace bonus compensation in the form of cash with compensation in the form of stock options, reflecting the Obama administration's emphasis on tying compensation to performance. Yet the creation of the office alone indicates how rapidly—and sharply—lawmakers can respond when a legislative deal breaks down. This is why maintaining a viable Baptist component in any major policy initiative is critical for the long-term success of not only political brokers but Bootleggers as well. When political arrangements go awry, unexpected and detrimental interference in market practices often follow.

Efforts to Tax the Recovering Firms

Finally, President Obama proposed a recoupment tax on January 15, 2010, to charge TARP recipients who had bounced back after the crisis. The tax was intended to recoup losses from outlays to companies that, struggling as they were to regain solvent positions, seemed unlikely to pay back all monies borrowed, such as AIG, Freddie Mac, Fannie Mae, Chrysler, and General Motors (Calmes 2010). President Obama's proposed tax would be levied on large financial firms—regardless of their TARP participation—with more than $50 billion in assets and assessed at a flat rate of 0.15 percent of each firm's liabilities. Projections suggest the tax would accrue $90 billion in revenue over the next 10 years. Later, Secretary Geithner proposed a weighted assessment of the tax that applied more heavily to riskier liabilities on a firm's balance sheet as opposed to the flat tax approach. The ostensible purpose of this shift was to avoid discouraging these companies from purchasing Treasury securities (Vaughn 2010).

It is difficult to rationalize this proposal without appealing to political motivations. Like the tax on bonuses, the recoupment tax would reduce the pork appropriated by Bootleggers by taking it back. Though such a move might seem to follow from the recoupment clause in the Emergency Economic Stabilization Act described above, it was proposed several years before the five-year deadline indicated in the language of the bill and, indeed, before the budget report that was supposed to reveal the ultimate net loss of the TARP program.

Although ultimately the recoupment tax did not become law, along with the other two developments summarized above, it represented an unexpected shift in TARP policy, at least from the perspective of subsidized companies. Again, though the recoupment clause allows for reimbursement above the loans received by companies, such a tax would not likely have been proposed (at least this early) had the already shaky support for TARP not collapsed altogether.

Exodus from TARP, Interrupted Cash Flow, and the Aftermath

The immediate consequence of the AIG bonus controversy and sub-sequent political fallout shut down the call for more money from TARP. Not only did companies stop requesting the larger subsidies offered before this controversy, they also began to insist on paying TARP monies back to cut ties with federal overseers altogether. Bootleggers were now fleeing by the dozens.

The American Recovery and Reinvestment Act of 2009[8] lays out the procedures for repayment of TARP monies:

> Subject to consultation with the appropriate Federal banking agency (as that term is defined in section 3 of the Federal Deposit Insurance Act), if any, the Secretary shall permit a TARP recipient to repay any assistance previously provided under the TARP to such financial institution, without regard to whether the financial institution has replaced such funds from any other source or to any waiting period, and when such assistance is repaid, the Secretary shall liquidate warrants associated with such assistance at the current market price.

This provision indicates that the repayment of borrowed funds is not subject to scrutiny by the Treasury itself.

Nevertheless, Bootleggers hoping to exit the program found a recalcitrant lender waiting. Discussing the repayment of borrowed TARP funds on April 17, 2009, JP Morgan CEO James Dimon claimed: "We could pay it back tomorrow. We have the money" (Sidel 2009). Goldman Sachs Group Inc. likewise stated that its "duty" was to repay funds borrowed from the TARP (Wutkowski and Stempel 2009). However, these banks—now firmly solvent—were required to pass an exit program called the Supervisory Capital Assessment Program, designed as a sort of performance stress test.

The stress test measured each firm's capital ratio under a baseline macroeconomic scenario and a more adverse macroeconomic scenario. In effect, this showed the before and after balance sheet effects of various hypothetical severe economic downturns. After passing the stress test, banks would be able to buy back the preferred shares held by the Treasury Department. They would not, however, be able to buy back equity share ownership warrants issued under TARP. This latter entanglement guaranteed that government will hold leverage over these companies for the foreseeable future.

In recognition of this obstinate entanglement, the American Bankers Association lobbied Congress to erase the warrants held by the Treasury Department. The organization called the payments generated by the warrants an "onerous exit fee" in addition to the already formidable stress test. Bank representatives even cited the unexpected evolution of TARP, in the form of additional executive compensation rules, as a reason why expunging the warrants would be justified. The bankers argued that "it's fundamentally wrong and unfair for a contract to be changed that much" (Paletta and Solomon 2009).

By March 2011, $171 billion (83 percent) of the total $205 billion of the preferred stock, purchased from 707 firms, had been repaid (Congressional Budget Office 2011). Looking at exactly which firms were able to exit yields several important Bootlegger/Baptist insights. Wilson and Wu (2011) show how the first group of firms allowed to exit the TARP shared the following characteristics: (a) larger size, (b) high executive pay, (c) fewer problem assets, and (d) better earning performance pre-2009. The last two characteristics seem consistent with the reported objectives of the Supervisory Capital Assessment Program, that is, ensuring that banks that exit the TARP are sufficiently financially solvent to be able to withstand a significant negative macroeconomic shock. But the first two characteristics are curious, in that larger banks played the largest role in jeopardizing the systemic integrity of the financial system. Furthermore, the Obama administration singled out executive pay in particular as an important factor in these firms' handling of risk, thus ostensibly exacerbating the financial crisis, despite the lack of evidence tying compensation packages to stock performance during the crisis. As Wilson and Wu (2011, 2) point out:

> We cannot explain why banks often replaced cheap government capital with more expensive private capital. Thus, the decision by most banks to exit [various TARP programs] cannot be easily reconciled with standard investment analysis. It involved paying back capital with more expensive private capital.

Bootlegger/Baptist Theory and the Fate of TARP

This conundrum begins to unravel when we consider the arrangement in the broader context of Bootlegger/Baptist theory.

145

Firms faced significant pork extraction as a result of the AIG bonus controversy. Without a Baptist counterpart to deflect public outcry, the beleaguered firms were left to fend off accusations by both lawmakers and the public of malpractice, corruption, and corporate excess.

When we think of which firms faced the greatest outcry, the first two characteristics of firms exiting the TARP offer important clues. As Wilson and Wu (2011, 3) note, "Larger banks are particularly exposed to this stigma because they have much larger reputations. The largest banks generate international, national, and local media attention." Smaller banks only have to explain their TARP dealings to local media and customers who are generally pleased that their bank is still solvent. Wilson and Wu (2011, 3) go on to point out that "banks with higher paid CEOs will be more susceptible to social stigma as news stories, politicians, and blogs mention the CEO's compensation package in reference to the federal bailout."

The first two characteristics can be reconciled with early TARP exit when we consider the incentives of the Bootleggers left hanging in the wind. The AIG debacle forced lawmakers to constrain subsidies below the previously agreed-upon level. This would have the greatest impact on large firms with high executive compensation packages. Accordingly, firms that entered the TARP program after the AIG bonus controversy tended to be smaller. As Wilson and Wu (2011) also observe, smaller banks more easily fly under the public radar screen, and what media attention they do garner may not even be negative on net. Smaller banks were also less afflicted by the stigma clinging to big Wall Street banks, thereby allowing politicians to offer them pork barrel deals with less political baggage.

The Small Business Jobs Act

The recent Small Business Jobs Act further evidenced the shift in support toward smaller banks. On October 6, 2011, the *Wall Street Journal* published an item with the headline "Tale of Two Loan Programs" (Maltby and Loten 2011, C1). Complete with a triangular flow diagram, the story told how a federal program designed to jump-start community bank lending to small businesses became a way for the banks to pay off loans owed to the

Treasury Department under TARP. It was pretty close to robbing Peter to pay Paul, but not quite.

Although Congress had authorized $30 billion when the Small Business Jobs Act of 2010 was passed, only $4 billion made it through the Treasury's spigot to the banks. Of that, some $2 billion rolled right back in as payments on TARP loans. The nation's unemployment rate stood at 9.6 percent when President Obama signed the law in September 2010. With midterm elections in the offing, Mr. Obama cheerfully declared: "It's going to speed relief to small businesses across the country right away. We've got to keep moving forward. That's why I fought so hard to pass this bill, and that's why I'm going to continue to do everything in my power to help small businesses open up and hire and expand" (Obama 2010). The law had been endorsed by the U.S. Chamber of Commerce, the National Federation of Small Businesses, and the Small Business Administration (Mills 2010). Times were tough, and bringing jobs to struggling families sounded like the right thing to do—a Baptist theme emphasized in the president's comments.

We seriously doubt that Mr. Obama—or any other politician— would ever have lobbied directly and openly for an infusion of taxpayer money to enable banks to refinance their TARP loans: it is impossible to imagine a law called The TARP Refinance Act making it through Congress in the fall of 2010. By then, the public was sick of bank bailouts. But a bill called the Small Business Jobs Act, which could be praised for bringing jobs to the unemployed, was just what the major players needed. And the results? The Baptist language was the key to the vault, just what the doctor ordered for the banks that wanted to escape TARP.

Although the law delivered some loan relief to struggling small businesses, the primary benefit was to small banks, the new Bootleggers in our story. As John Schmidt, chief operating officer of a Dubuque, Iowa, bank, put it, "It's a bit of a shell game" (Maltby and Loten 2011, C2). Schmidt's bank received $81.7 million from the fund and used all of it to pay off TARP debt.

Recall that banks receiving TARP funds gave the government special shares of stock that pay a 5 percent dividend. By contrast, funds received from the Small Business Jobs Act loan program carried a maximum interest rate of 5 percent, which could fall to 1 percent if the banks that received the funds increased their small business lending by 10 percent. As a story in the *Wall Street Journal* explained, "Of 332 banks that received cash through the lending fund, 137 used at least a portion—totaling $2.2 billion—to pay off their TARP obligations" (Maltby and Loten 2011, C1). We note that a 2013 report by Treasury special inspector general Christy Romero basically agreed with the earlier-described shift of funds from supporting small business lending to paying off TARP debt (Sparshott 2013).

One might wonder why a bank would use government-provided small business loan money to pay back government-provided TARP money, especially if the interest rate to be paid was 5 percent in each case. But this is easily reconciled once we factor in the numerous costs associated with TARP, such as closer surveillance and the possibility of heavier regulation of executive pay. In other words, whereas TARP dollars were both a benefit and a burden, small business loan dollars were a pure benefit—especially when used to pay off TARP loans. Once again, the case illustrates that where there is moral cover in the form of Baptist-inflected political activity, there is a Bootlegger waiting in the wings. The devil, as the old adage says, is in the details—especially in the world of Bootleggers and Baptists.

The Dodd-Frank Financial Reform Act

Although the TARP is still collecting previously disbursed funds, its viability as a pork barrel mechanism is over. The Dodd-Frank Wall Street Reform and Consumer Protection Act,[9] signed into law on July 21, 2010, reduced TARP monies from $700 billion to $472 billion, permanently limiting the potential gains from the program. Furthermore, the act puts several restrictions on what can be purchased with remaining TARP disbursements and maintains Treasury's authority over TARP-subsidized companies, despite their repayment of TARP monies.[10]

The Dodd-Frank Act furthermore established a whole new set of Bootlegger/Baptist relationships. Though touted as a crackdown on Wall Street, the act reflected a shift into calmer waters for all involved. Witness, for example, recent measures to reduce interchange fees, which are collected by credit card companies from providers of merchant customer credit card services. The Durbin Amendment to the Dodd-Frank Act caps the maximum fee that can be charged, which lowers costs for merchants and (ostensibly) credit card users but deprives banks and other credit card issuers of revenue. But as Zywicki (2010) explains: "Interchange partially compensates the cardholder's bank for the cost and risk of offering payment cards to consumers. This includes clearing costs, billing and collection, fraud recovery, customer service, credit losses, and the resolution of any disputes that might arise from the transaction." Revenues from these fees are accordingly used as a means to extend credit.

The legitimacy of these fees has, rather unsurprisingly, been challenged by merchants, who must pay about 2 percent of each transaction that uses a credit card. Enter the Baptist in this little drama: the Merchants Payments Coalition. Here's how they describe themselves:

> The Merchants Payments Coalition . . . is a group of retailers, supermarkets, drug stores, convenience stores, fuel stations, on-line merchants and other businesses who are fighting against unfair credit card fees and fighting for a more competitive and transparent card system that works better for consumers and merchants alike." (Unfair Credit Card Fees.com 2012)

These businesses—though obviously profit-seeking enterprises with a vested interest in the regulation—covertly pose as Baptists by providing a moral argument for capping interchange fees. Of course, the immediate result of such a measure would be to reduce the credit flow to those who are most risky and accordingly most likely in need of credit.

That foreseeable side effect means there's another, less obvious Bootlegger lurking in the wings: lenders willing to take on risky consumers who stand to gain from the squeeze in credit—such as payday loan companies, pawn shops, loan sharks, and various underground lenders—will soon see their businesses grow as companies unable to escape regulation cede their clientele to these less reputable businesses. As Zywicki (2011) puts it:

> Regulators cannot wish away the need of low-income consumers for credit: If your car's transmission blows, you need $2,000 for repairs to get to work, whether or not you have it saved in the bank (and most low-income Americans

don't). If you can't get a credit card, you're going to have to get that money from a payday lender, pawn shop or loan shark.

After TARP, regulators may not wish to wish it away but instead embrace a measure that allows for greater levels of pork.

Another part of the Dodd-Frank statute buttresses this alliance between consumer advocacy groups and businesses that gain from encroaching regulation: the provision establishing the Consumer Financial Protection Bureau, an agency set up to regulate consumer financial products. Organized by Harvard University law professor (now senator) Elizabeth Warren, a long-standing "consumer advocate" and lightning rod for anti-business sentiment, the agency resides within the domain of the Federal Reserve Board but operates independently. It has far-reaching authority to regulate consumer financial products (Solomon 2011). Recognizing that Professor Warren could not gain Senate confirmation, President Obama nominated former Ohio attorney general Richard Cordray to be the director of the CFPB (HuffPost Politics 2011).

The inception of this bureau showcases the lessons lawmakers learned from TARP. Baptists quickly ventured into the playing field, with popular consumer groups such as the Consumer Federation of America voicing support for the new agency. Where TARP was unable to acquire suitable Baptist cover for its activities, the CFPB starts from a position of political popularity before transferring pork to special interests. Indeed, the CFPB constitutes a far more durable pork barrel mechanism than TARP.

As a final example, Dodd-Frank established a new oversight council to monitor systemic risk in the financial system. This has led to the unusual spectacle of firms going before various public administrators to explain how unimportant they are. These firms are attempting to avoid being designated as "systemically important," which would trigger greater regulation, diminishing their profits. Some firms are even unloading assets to avoid the designation (Dash and Creswell 2011). Such odd behavior—though perfectly reasonable from a Bootlegger/Baptist perspective—emerges because of the incentives in the system. Firms that were previously looking for pork are now attempting to escape pork-extraction measures. Still other firms, particularly small financial services firms, welcomed such regulation, being assured that they would not be designated systemically important.

These measures and the larger policy goals of the Dodd-Frank Reform Act represent a transition from the politically dysfunctional TARP mechanism to a viable means of providing some needed cover for Bootleggers. Though far more palatable to the voting public, the shift in mechanisms brings together an insidious coalition of Bootleggers and Baptists that will ensure pork barrel politics flourish in the world of finance for some time to come.

Final Thoughts

This chapter presented a case study where Bootleggers were caught out in the cold without Baptist support. Stung by the ensuing backlash, public officials sought to constrain the pork barrel mechanism they had created, TARP, so that only disbursements they favored would be made. Unfortunately for both officials and firms connected to TARP, this was not to be. The payment of bonuses, seen as unbelievably excessive by the public, exposed a greater supply of pork than voters—and in turn their representatives—were willing to support.

The results of this arrangement proved disastrous for firms caught in the public spotlight. Not only were they subject to public outcry, but lawmakers soon turned on their would-be beneficiaries by engaging in sweeping interference in their business practices. Lawmakers sought to taint the supply of pork with taxes on bonuses, unexpected compensation oversight, and a premature recoupment tax.

The consequence of this fallout was an early exit for larger companies and the end of TARP's viability as a pork barrel mechanism. Large firms especially were caught in a situation where they could no longer gain the pork they had originally been promised. This proved too much for these firms, and they took great strides to exit a "sticky" TARP mechanism. As the situation deteriorated for leading Bootleggers, requests for subsequent disbursements slowed to a trickle, with only truly desperate—and usually small—firms continuing the search for pork.

The broader lesson from TARP is that transactions within the political marketplace risk disastrous consequences for all involved when no Baptist cover is forthcoming for the deal—even when the purely economic rationale for it seems overwhelming. What initially appeared to be a bona fide bailout soon became an entanglement mechanism that transferred wealth away from company executives. Although the market participants may not have anticipated these outcomes, they are easily reconciled within our theory. When a docile electorate becomes energized by transfers that lack a moral—rather than purely pragmatic or economic—justification, pork generation ceases to occur, causing unexpected negative consequences for firms bellying up to the barbecue counter.

7. Obamacare: Too Big to Plan (or Stop!)

Introduction: Can Planners Even Plan?

We have saved the biggest and most extreme Bootlegger/Baptist tale for last. How else can one describe the passage of a health care bill that restructured an industry representing 17 percent of the economy, yet was opposed in court by 26 state attorneys general and regarded as a "bad thing" by 50 percent of Americans (Saad 2010)?

Whether one supports the policy or not, Obamacare's success showcases how a runaway piece of legislation comes to fruition through rampant Bootlegger/Baptist interaction, leaving some of its original constituents behind. Its passage illustrates a basic lesson of government planning—one widely understood in principle but rarely recognized in practice: there are limits to what government planners can plan, especially when Bootleggers and Baptists are at play. Recognition of these limits makes for better policy. The cavalier attitude taken by congressional leaders in 2009, when the original health care plan was passed, revealed a broad disregard for these limits. As this story shows, what is too big to plan can quickly become too big to stop.

In this chapter, we focus on Bootlegger/Baptist elements in the health care reform process. Obamacare provides a classic example of our coordinated mode of Bootlegger/Baptist interaction that focuses on top-down leadership: interest group coalition building, spearheaded by a president, that enables the formation of a national cartel. But the story is much more complex than this. The episode also contains elements of other cooperative modes where some Bootleggers directly and openly support Baptists to bring about a desired end—while other Bootleggers, who find themselves out in the cold, secretly subsidize their opponents. Ours is a chaotic story, indeed.

Coordinated cartelization came to fruition when the Patient Protection and Affordable Care Act, popularly known as Obamacare, became law on March 23, 2010.[1] The event marked the culmination of a yearlong struggle to push through one of President Obama's marquee agenda items. Mr. Obama was not the first president to push for expanded health care. It has long been one of the most regulated segments of the U.S. economy. Lyndon Johnson successfully pushed Medicare and Medicaid into law in 1965, and George W. Bush added coverage for pharmaceuticals to Medicare. Perhaps the most ambitious previous effort was that of First Couple Bill and Hillary Clinton, who unsuccessfully sought to bring health coverage to the entire U.S. population. In each of these efforts, a vast Baptist choir sang the praises of government-assisted health care. But lurking in the background—and sometimes in the back row of the choir—were pharmaceutical, insurance, and other health care Bootleggers ready to expand sales to the regulated sector.

In this case, the president himself constantly shaped and reshaped the initiative to garner Bootlegger support, even while heaping public scorn on big business elements in the health sector. Instead of expanding subsidies and requiring health care providers nationwide to open their doors to all who need their services or giving indigent citizens access to the Veterans Administration's hospitals, the president's plan was based on requiring all uninsured citizens to purchase health insurance or pay a stiff annual penalty.

Thus, the leading Bootlegger—the insurance industry—was identified from the outset, or so it seems. After all, how could any insurance company oppose a plan that would require every citizen to buy an expensive insurance product every year? Surely the insurance firms would be the happiest Bootleggers on the planet. But there is more to the story. Things did not ultimately turn out well for the insurance Bootleggers.

News coverage of Obamacare helps identify the key Baptist themes. In March 2010, *The Economist* came out in support of the president's project. While acknowledging some of the bill's flaws, the influential news weekly supported the package for two related reasons: the ethical imperative of universal health care coverage and the law's potential to lower health care costs ("Pass the Bill" 2010). Both elements made Obamacare an example of doing the right thing. Yet just one week later, without wavering from its Baptist position, *The Economist* lamented: "This newspaper supported the final version of Obamacare, but only because we have long maintained that a country as rich as America should provide decent health coverage to all its citizens. Because the bill does almost nothing to control costs, it was a huge missed opportunity" ("Now What?" 2010).

The abrupt shift in the newspaper's analysis reflects the difficulty supporters had in reconciling their Baptist vision of universal health coverage with the disappointing outcome actually delivered by the final bill. It is easy to see why many grew frustrated with the final law. As in the examples explored in our "sins" chapter, what the public desires (as proclaimed by Baptists) can quickly get distorted once Bootleggers enter the political process.

So how does such a cumbersome—and ultimately unpopular —initiative become law? A brief exploration of the passage of Obamacare is necessary to address this important question. In doing so, we focus on how Bootleggers and Baptists interacted with the legislative process—and ultimately denied White House planners their dream of achieving a rational political outcome.

We Love the Benefits, but Not the Costs

Placing health care at the forefront of his domestic agenda, President Obama wasted no time in publicizing his vision for reform. In his first State of the Union address, the president claimed "the cost of our health care has weighed down our economy and the con- science of our nation long enough. So let there be no doubt: health care reform cannot wait, it must not wait, and it will not wait another year" (Obama 2009). He followed up with a whirlwind campaign to drum up support for his keystone legislation. Town hall forums and campaign-style appearances were part of a broader effort to con- vince the American public that health care reform was not just desir- able but mandatory for a modern democracy in the 21st century. In an address to Congress he argued, "We are the only democracy —the only advanced democracy, the only wealthy nation—that allows such hardship for millions of its people" ("Obama's Health Care Address to Congress" 2009).

The president found plenty of Baptists (and even a few early Bootleggers) ready and willing to support his cause. A joint statement in January 2009 from the American Cancer Society, the American Medical Association, Families USA, the Pharmaceutical Research and Manufacturers of America, Regence BlueCross BlueShield, and

SEIU declared, "In order to fix the ailing economy, the nation needs health care reform that addresses the related problems of health care costs and people losing health coverage" ("Obama Health Reform Drive Gets Diverse Backing" 2009).

But the president faced a hard sell with the public at large. A Gallup poll showed nearly half the country disapproved of new government interventions in the private health care system. This disapproval increased as debate continued on the issue, from a low of 28 percent disapproving in 2007 to a high of 50 percent in mid-2009. We find a similar trend when respondents were asked whether they favored preserving the current system or overhauling it through government intervention. In November 2007, 41 percent of those polled favored replacing the current system; by November 2009, this number had dropped to 32 percent. As debate continued and the rationally ignorant became more informed, Americans were less inclined to approve of government intervention in the private health care system (Newport 2009c).

One reason for this increasing wariness on the part of voters may have been a fear of higher costs under a public health care system. Even though the United States was spending the largest share of GDP on health care across developed nations, the adjustment problem posed by Obamacare remained (OECD 2012). Firms in the health sector looked warily at the potential for rising costs caused by new coverage requirements and restrictions on pricing. Recall that in 2009, Americans were just waking up from the financial nightmare described in our last chapter and suffering the effects of the global recession that followed. Unsurprisingly, 70 percent of Americans described economic issues as the nation's top problem; only 16 percent cited health care (Newport 2009a). In September 2009, cost was seen as the biggest problem with health care by 38 percent of those polled. Only 15 percent saw too many uninsured persons as the biggest problem. In other words, more than twice as many respondents were chiefly concerned with costs compared with lack of coverage (Saad 2009a).

Responding to the conversation in Washington, an unlikely alliance of Bootleggers and Baptists emerged to guide the legislation. Under the umbrella of coalitions such as Health Economy Now, these groups lobbied to shape health care reform in their favor. This particular coalition included the Pharmaceutical Research and Manufacturers of America, the AARP, the American Medical Association, the Business Roundtable, Families USA, and SEIU, among others (Fox News 2009).

Although the aims of reform were widely agreed upon—expanding coverage, reducing costs, and improving the overall quality of the system—they were also vague enough to leave plenty of room for Bootleggers and Baptists to operate. As we discussed in regard to sinful substances, the fuzzier the ends of a reform campaign, the greater the opportunity for Bootleggers to fill in their desired fine print when choosing the means. And of course, with 17 percent of the economy weighing in the balance, suitably designed health care reform legislation could pump billions of dollars in the direction of the hard-working Bootleggers.

An early approach favored by an array of progressive wonks and policymakers was called the "public option." This meant the federal government would establish a publicly sponsored and funded insurance agency that would compete directly with private insurers. Supporters of the public option claimed that it would reduce costs by providing competitive pressure on private insurers. In the planners' ideal world, the public option would extend coverage to all who need it, insulated from the bottom-line pressures that prevent private insurers from extending money-losing coverage.

Although a public option appeared compatible with the broader goals of health care reform, it met fierce resistance from pork-loving lobbyists. Several hospital Bootleggers, such as the Federation of American Hospitals, opposed the policy, fearing it would result in a reduction of rates paid for services; they preferred higher-priced health care. These lobbyists met with key legislative leaders, such as Sen. Max Baucus (D-MT), chair of the Senate Committee on Finance, to quash the plans for such an option (Kirkpatrick 2009).

The insurance industry represented another major Bootlegger. With no love lost between Washington and the insurance industry, at least in public utterances, battle lines were drawn on particular fronts of health care reform. The industry pursued two major goals: (a) eliminating the public option and (b) expanding its market base through mandatory coverage.

Like hospitals, the insurance industry saw the public option as a direct threat to its bottom line, though for different reasons.

157

For private insurers, a public insurance agency would act as a government-subsidized competitor, able to draw customers away at prices below the competitive market rate, an unacceptable result. Their second goal represented potential pork that might be extracted from an otherwise potentially dangerous bill (Pickert 2009c).

Because of hospital and insurance company Bootlegger opposition, the public option soon lost its chief supporters. At one town hall meeting in August 2009, President Obama sought to downplay the centrality of the public option to his larger reform ambitions. "The public option, whether we have it or we don't have it, is not the entirety of health care reform. . . . This is just one sliver of it, one aspect of it" (quoted in Stolberg 2009). Later, he signaled through his Health and Human Services secretary, Kathleen Sebelius, that the public option could be dropped. By the end of the year, the option was off the table (Stolberg 2009).

But the insurance Bootleggers didn't stop there. They further attempted to massage the bill, primarily by seeking to reduce the new cost burdens the legislation would impose. In October 2009, America's Health Insurance Plans, the major health industry lobbying organization, released a report by PriceWaterhouseCoopers showing how the latest version of the bill would increase private insurance premiums. Although congressional leaders widely panned the report for a variety of supposed shortcomings, insiders reluctantly admitted the bill's ultimate effect on private plans was uncertain, with one congressional aide claiming, "It's impossible to figure out what the bottom-line impact is" (Pickert 2009b).

Though it received plenty of caustic public reprimands for focusing so insistently on profit, the insurance industry nevertheless struck a chord with the public. Popular concern about rising costs in the wake of the Great Recession translated into reluctance on the part of Congress—and not just among Republicans—who were united in opposition.

Many Democrats faced constituencies hostile to the idea of a federal health care mandate. Sen. Blanche Lincoln (D-AR), for example, attracted opposition from both sides of the political aisle by opposing the public option but subsequently voting for the reform once it had been removed (Weisenthal 2010). Rep. Betsy Markey (D-CO) encountered more one-sided hostility from her largely conservative district in Colorado (Villegas 2010). Pennsylvania senator Arlen Specter, fighting an uphill battle against his own party after pivoting to support the president's agenda, shed his Republican affiliation only to be defeated in a Democratic primary, in a state where polls showed a majority of voters opposed to government health care mandates (Philip Klein 2010). Legislators realized they ran the risk of shortening their political tenure as a result of their support for an increasingly unpopular initiative.

At a critical moment, one politician became a linchpin for the entire reform effort: Sen. Ben Nelson (D-NE) represented the key vote needed to push filibuster-proof legislation forward in the Senate. Nelson not only felt pressure from Obamacare supporters (Bender 2009) but also received direct assistance from a major Bootlegger. The lobbying group Pharmaceutical Research and Manufacturers of America spent $150 million on an advertising campaign in Nelson's home state of Nebraska. Their price for this service? Language would be inserted into the bill barring the importation (or reimportation) of cheaper drugs manufactured or sold abroad. Eliminating foreign competition was just what the doctor ordered ("ObamaCare's Secret History" 2012). In December 2009, with the importation ban in place, Senator Nelson announced his support for Obamacare (Jonsson 2009).

Pharmaceutical companies had in fact agreed to support reform in early 2009. In addition to the concession on imported drugs, the administration promised to not repeal an existing rule enacted during the George W. Bush administration. It prevented government from negotiating drug prices under Medicare and Medicaid, a restriction that generates hundreds of billions of dollars to the pharmaceutical industry ("Drug Deals: Big Pharma, White House Unlikely Partners" 2009).

Private insurers, in contrast, began to see reform as a losing deal. Although the insurance industry succeeded in killing the public option, ensuring mandated coverage, and generating public fear over costs, one measure threatened to overwhelm any Bootlegger gains. This was a provision establishing a minimum "medical loss ratio," specialist jargon for the percentage of insurance premiums spent on actual health care services. Insurance companies would have to reduce overhead costs, refunding premium dollars if they failed to meet the proposed 80 percent medical loss ratio threshold (Pickert

2009a). The amount to be rebated retroactively for 2011 transactions alone rose to a nontrivial $1.1 billion (Ungar 2012, 2).

The medical loss ratio devastated an already shaky alliance between the insurance industry and health care reform advocates. The October 2009 report from PriceWaterhouseCoopers was just the start of a protracted, largely secretive effort to block reform. America's Health Insurance Plans, the insurance industry's super-lobby firm, spent $102.4 million in just over 15 months, funneling dollars into negative advertisements run by the Chamber of Commerce (Ungar 2012). Clearly, the honeymoon between insurers and reform advocates was over.

"Cosmos" and "Taxis"

Let's now take a step back and take stock of the story so far. With such an eclectic ensemble of aims and interests represented in the bill's more than 2,000 pages, health care reform became something quite different from what any one of its champions had initially envisioned. For example, the public option had been considered an essential feature of any meaningful reform by many advocates. But intense opposition by Bootleggers succeeded in relegating it to the legislative dustbin. As it turns out, outcomes in politics, as is often true in the market, emerge not from any grand synoptic plan but as a spontaneous byproduct of the struggle among interdependent actors striving toward distinct and often conflicting ends.

Some wisdom on this dynamic was offered by F. A. Hayek in his classic treatise *Law, Legislation, and Liberty* (1978). Hayek contrasted two types of order that may emerge from social processes—including the democratic process of framing legislation. Order that emerges from conscious direction he labeled "taxis" (from the Greek word *tassain*, meaning to arrange). Taxis is centrally planned and in theory yields whatever outcomes the planners have rationally designed it to produce. Examples of taxis include architectural design, engineering, and even the orchestration of gala events.

Order that emerges from the interaction of a multitude of interdependent yet decentralized parts, Hayek dubbed "cosmos" (from the Greek word *kosmos*, meaning to adorn). This type of order is spontaneous and emergent, generating outcomes as the upshot of an uncontrolled process shaped by a multitude of factors that are often unknown—and perhaps even unknowable. Examples of cosmos include markets, evolutionary processes, and improvisational jazz jam sessions.

We typically think of legislation as falling into the category of taxis: a contrived and reasoned product of rigorous debate and strict procedure. Through discussion and deliberation, lawmakers debate and fine-tune legislation until a majority consensus emerges. Though this may be the ideal of democratic politics, its actual practice lies far from this romantic conception—as the chaotic story we've just recounted demonstrates.

Even the health care bill's biggest supporter, President Obama, was himself unsure of its ultimate contents. In a revealing March 2010 interview—just before Obamacare passed—the president was unable to confirm what final measures would be added to the bill to ensure its passage. Here is part of a telling exchange with interviewer Bret Baier:

> Bret Baier: "So . . . you don't know exactly what will be in the bill?"
>
> President Obama: "By the time the vote has taken place, not only will I know what's in it, you'll know what's in it, because it's going to be posted and everybody's going to be able to evaluate it on the merits. . . . The notion that this has been not transparent, that people don't know what's in the bill, everybody knows what's in the bill." . . .
>
> Bret Baier: "Mr. President, you couldn't tell me what the special deals are that are in or not today."
>
> President Obama: "I just told you what was in and what was not in."
>
> Bret Baier: "Is Connecticut in?" . . .
>
> President Obama: "Connecticut—what are you specifically referring to?"
>
> Bret Baier: "The $100 million for the hospital? Is Montana in for the asbestos program? Is—you know, listen, there are people—this is real money, people are worried about this stuff."

President Obama: "And as I said before, this—the final provisions are going to be posted for many days before this thing passes." (Noonan 2010)

This is striking for several reasons. First, few definitions of "transparency" would cover the 24-hour exposure of a 2,000-page bill that would transform a huge swath of the economy. Second, the fact that the bill remained in flux until its passage shows just how volatile political outcomes can be when Bootleggers and Baptists are involved. Appealing to the sympathies of the public while placating economic interests requires deft and speedy maneuvering by political operatives. So much for transparency.

Even President Obama's weak criterion for transparency was ultimately not met, because the bill was never publicly posted before passing. How could it be, with 11th-hour additions being made left and right? From the representative from Chicago who was promised support on immigration policy, to the anti-abortion executive order notoriously issued as payment for Rep. Bart Stupak's (D-MI) vote, universal health coverage was scarcely the only goal achieved in this bill (Noonan 2010).

Not all the deals were sealed with carrots, either. Threats of unionized opposition and reduced campaign funds from the central Democratic Party coffers in the upcoming 2010 election were among the sticks brandished against potential defectors (Strassel 2010). Even the method by which the Affordable Care Act was to be passed remained uncertain until a day before its enactment, as Speaker of the House Nancy Pelosi (D-CA) decided the use of procedural shortcuts to circumvent opposition would be too brazen for such an important bill. The legislative process itself became a Bootlegger/Baptist–influenced outcome, further denying that Obamacare was to be the result of a rational, centrally controlled process.

The many last-minute additions and corrections to the legislation should be no surprise given the importance ascribed to the measure by its proponents, not to mention pressure from eager Bootleggers. Unpopular political initiatives operate a bit like unpopular financial securities: greater yields are needed to entice investors. The difference is that in politics, these yields come in the form of pork. This last point is often ignored when the costs of new policies are tallied. When a firm calculates the cost of issuing a security, it includes not only the value of the principal asset but also the yield needed to secure funding. In politics, this basic financial premise is ignored. The cost of the bill is reckoned by adding up the expenditures needed to provide the services it explicitly includes—not any side deals struck to ensure its passage. And for a bill as massive and consequential as Obamacare, there were sure to be deals aplenty.

The magical day finally came on March 23, 2010: the president signed the Patient Protection and Affordable Care Act into law. Of course, as with TARP and Dodd-Frank financial reform, enactment is only the beginning. Implementation is where much of the action takes place. It is also where many of Obamacare's supporters, such as *The Economist*, began to grow disillusioned by the ever-evolving bill they had championed.

The biggest letdown for supporters was that the law failed to deal with the rising costs of health care. Recall that although Americans were sympathetic to the aim of expanding coverage, their primary concern was with costs. Yet it is here that the law most conspicuously fell short of its supporters' earlier, loftier rhetoric. In October 2011, long after Obamacare was passed, the administration announced it was cutting the Community Living Assistance Services and Supports (CLASS) component of the act from its overall health care program.

CLASS, which would have provided a voluntary, public, long-term care insurance option for employees, was unceremoniously expunged from the bill after it was passed. The official reason cited was that it would be unsustainable given the premiums beneficiaries would need to pay. Because only those who could find no assistance elsewhere would voluntarily sign up for the program, adverse selection effects would ensure that only those with the highest medical costs joined the risk pool, jeopardizing the project altogether.

Obamacare has, of course, thundered on without this dysfunctional component. The outcome is telling, however, because CLASS was one of the key components that the Obama administration used to justify health care reform to a cost-conscious audience. It had greatly alleviated the official budgetary impact of the overall bill ($70 billion by Congressional Budget Office estimates) because it would ostensibly reduce the expenditures of Medicaid, by transferring benefits to the overall Obamacare program. In addition, even if the program was unsustainable in the long run, premiums were projected to exceed benefits over its first decade (Wayne and Armstrong

2011). Though the administration was skeptical of CLASS all along, the illusion of cost savings it provided greatly enhanced Obamacare's prospects for passage, making it too important to give up before the bill had been signed.

The story behind the CLASS component's inclusion in Obamacare illustrates Hayek's lesson that political outcomes are often a form of emergent cosmos, not planned taxis. Indeed, according to John McDonough's book *Inside National Health Reform* (2011), the CLASS Act would likely have died in committee but for a curious last-minute development, orchestrated (ironically enough) by a one of the bill's Republican opponents. As Ezra Klein (2011) of the *Washington Post* reported:

> Sen. Judd Gregg, a Republican, proposed to weaken the program by replacing its premium with instructions for the Secretary of Health and Human Services to develop an "actuarially-sound premium" at a later date. Much to Gregg's surprise—much to everyone's surprise—Dodd accepted the amendment. Gregg's attempt to underscore the financial weakness of the program led to its inclusion in the bill. After that point, removing it would have required 60 votes and a willingness to effectively betray Kennedy. CLASS was in.

Senator Gregg's proposed amendment to the health reform bill had the unintended consequence, at least from his perspective, of moving it out of committee. The amendment insulated CLASS from opposition, even though the ultimate fate of CLASS after enactment was now in question. Only in politics can greater uncertainty serve as a guarantor of fiscal soundness, at least through the magic of Congressional Budget Office accounting.

The CLASS element only disguised some of the hidden costs of Obamacare. The story of the law's passage is interwoven with future deals and trades made between its most vehement backers and their more reticent, moderate allies. These are a necessary part of the opportunity cost of passing the law, because they represent benefits that would not have been rendered if health care had failed to pass.

In addition, the law's implementation depends upon a future Congress enacting (or at least not preventing) additional taxes on Medicare. That implicitly assumes a Congress more willing to deal with these tough decisions than the legislators who enacted the law.

Obamacare assumes that Medicare costs will not continue to grow, which will require a future Congress to be aggressive in curtailing entitlement expenditures. Medicare's own actuary has recognized the implausibility of this assumption: "It is doubtful that Medicare providers can take steps to keep their cost growth within the bounds imposed by these price limitations, year after year, indefinitely" (Shatto and Clemens 2011).

Government outlays are scarcely the only costs of Obamacare, of course: new costs are imposed upon businesses and insurance providers. Smaller businesses will likely pay the bulk of the health insurance fees levied on companies that do not provide their own health plans and must document all business-to-business transactions of $600 or more. Such new burdens upon small business are supposedly offset by a tax credit, but the process of applying for this credit is complex, and it only applies to a narrow subset of the businesses affected by the new provisions.

In part because of these burdens, the National Federation of Independent Business, along with 26 U.S. states, brought suit against the new health care law. In the spring of 2012, their landmark case was heard by the Supreme Court, which ultimately rejected their arguments. But the story did not end there. Because of growing small business outrage over Obamacare's undefined complexities, unknown costs, and their effect on hiring decisions, the Obama administration unceremoniously delayed implementation of the business mandate, previously to take place in 2014, for another year (Kliff 2013).

What remains of Obamacare's promise to tackle the rising health care costs that so worried the public? The law's most economically rational feature may be a weak provision—deliberately diluted to ensure needed votes—that taxes expensive health care packages. These so-called Cadillac plans emerge as a result of the tax shelters afforded to companies that provide their employees with greater insurance benefits.

Payments to employees in the form of insurance benefits serve as a tax-free substitute for payments in income. Doctors in turn price their services in accordance with their patients' plans, meaning prices are invariably driven up by the prevalence of these premium plans. Health care professionals have long understood the inflationary pressures that such tax shelters place on health care prices.

If these insurance benefits were taxed at the same rate as any other payroll expenditure, then these price distortions would cease.

Unfortunately, this aspect of the law was watered down because of pressure from unions and their representatives in the House (Herszenhorn 2010). Organized labor won a big victory when it secured an exemption from the tax until 2018 (Campanile 2010). In total, the Joint Committee on Taxation estimated that only 14 percent of family health policies and 19 percent of individual policies would be affected by the time the legislation began to go into effect in 2013 (Beam 2009). That's hardly enough to "bend the curve" of health care costs downward.

Indeed, once the costs of the future pork, new revenue streams, and continuing tax shelters needed to ensure the bill's passage are added to the Congressional Budget Office's estimated price tag of $940 billion, we are looking at a staggering bill even by Washington standards.

Final Thoughts

This is ultimately how Americans ended up with a "reform" package that seems highly unlikely to achieve its twin purposes: reducing health care costs while expanding health care coverage. Obamacare became too big to stop because its supporters were able to garner votes through logrolling, which itself was a consequence of congressional flexibility on the bill's ultimate contents. This flexibility was enabled by a politically determined budget-scoring process that bears little resemblance to the cost-benefit analysis practiced by sound financial planners.

The resulting legislative Frankenstein's monster demonstrates that political outcomes are more accurately viewed as the upshot of a chaotic spontaneous order than the controlled and deliberative design process familiar from civics class. What causes politics to proceed so erratically? We submit that the twin demands of winning Baptist sympathy while placating Bootlegger economic interests played a decisive role in determining the final shape of Obamacare.

If politics resembles an unpredictable and emergent cosmos more than a rationally planned taxis, then lawmakers simply cannot credibly commit to a particular political outcome before the fact. They can promise to try but not to deliver. Nor, perhaps, should they want to: the flexibility inherent to cosmos allows policy to evolve as needed to ensure passage when rigid adherence to a rationally predetermined plan might yield only failure. Such flexibility enables the wise politician to placate important Bootlegger interests (such as the pharmaceutical industry) who provide indispensable support for the lawmaker's policy objectives—amorphous as these may prove to be.

In the case of Obamacare, attending to the emergent process of politics helps us explain just how a chaotic Congress ultimately ignored the cost considerations that 38 percent of the population believed to be the biggest problem with health care. Just as it is fruitless to insist that a debtor continue making mortgage payments he simply cannot afford, we cannot hold politicians to their stated policy goals: the political process does not operate predictably or rationally enough to make such promises credible. Of course, banks compensate for the risk of a debtor's default by charging interest rates and insisting on collateral. What comparable provisions exist in the public sector?

The answer is not much, at least nothing comparable to what we find in the market. Politicians do not have to account for the indirect and unintended consequences of their initiatives. For large-scale changes, these effects are inherently unknowable at the time legislation is crafted and so difficult to debate in the public forum. At worst, our representatives face the prospect of losing future elections—a fate several Obamacare supporters encountered. But as the saga of health care reform shows, this is ultimately not enough of a deterrent to curb the excesses of a legislative agenda that has grown too big to fail.

8. What Have We Learned? When Will It End?

And now, dear reader, we bring to a close our tale of Bootleggers and Baptists, at least for now. It is a story that explains why so many government regulations exist of a peculiar kind that constrain productive economic activity. It is a story of how key elements of society can form winning coalitions to achieve or influence regulatory outcomes. It is a story about a political dynamic that, in increasingly complex ways, connects interest groups who, for very different reasons, are prepared to spend time and resources seeking government favors. At its very root, it is a story about the demand for and supply of politically provided pork.

In this concluding chapter, we first summarize what we have we learned about the whys and hows of regulation. We then examine the Bootlegger/Baptist dynamic: Is it here to stay? Has it been running faster or slower? What does the evidence tell us? We close with thoughts about the future prospects of Baptists and Bootleggers. But first, a brief summary of our project.

Bootlegger/Baptist Theory in a Nutshell

The scale and pace of Bootlegger/Baptist activity rises and falls with the scale and pace of regulations that offer the prospects for achieving the moral goals of Baptists and enhanced profits for the Bootleggers. This means that Bootlegger/Baptist theory offers more light for explaining the characteristics of social regulation than for economic regulatory activity, although on some occasions Bootleggers and Baptists interact in that sphere as well. Social regulation tends to attract public interest groups that can speak from the moral high ground when endorsing—if not originating—new rules and restrictions. Bootlegger/Baptist coalitions succeed by driving down the cost of pork production. Politicians shielded by Baptist cover when

169

acting at the behest of Bootleggers are less likely to be challenged in the public forum. Because of this, successful politicians must send signals that demonstrate a regard for the public interest. Doing so lowers the cost of organizing delivery of legislative favors.

A Quick Review

As we explained in the preface and chapter 1, the Baptist action reinforces Bootlegger efforts to obtain political pork. When the pork is delivered, both groups win: the Baptists may get limits imposed on sin and their values validated, while the Bootleggers walk away with the cash. If regulatory activity subsides, Bootlegger/Baptist activity declines with it. When the pace of regulation accelerates, Bootleggers and Baptists are sure to barbecue while the political fire pits are hot. While they're gathered around the grill, they reinforce the ties that bind them to each other and to the congressional cooks who supply the pork.

Chapter 1 explained that Bootlegger/Baptist interactions can be grouped into four modes of interaction. In order of increasing complexity—the first three driven by the Bootleggers and Baptists themselves, and the fourth by political actors—these are (a) covert interaction, which involves the use of Baptist rhetoric by Bootleggers; (b) noncooperation with respect to the two groups, where each group independently pursues a shared policy goal; (c) cooperation with direct Bootlegger support for Baptist groups; and (d) coordination from the top with government-led coalition building that organizes Bootleggers and Baptists in support of large-scale cartels encompassing entire economic sectors and the regulatory agencies governing them.

The fourth strategic mode of interaction, in which political leaders coordinate the formation of an all-encompassing industry cartel, is the most costly of all to the overall economy, as we saw with Obamacare. This interaction mode is often driven by emergencies, national crises, sudden changes in the relative prices of important commodities, and canny politicians who spot opportunities to achieve long-standing national desires. In economic terms, these actions occur when major markets are in disequilibrium or when older regulation is being revised. Examples include setting new, higher fuel-economy standards, buffering rapidly changing energy prices, energizing national housing programs when interest rates are unusually low, and nationalizing requirements for personal health care.

The theory can also help predict the composition of interest groups as Bootlegger/Baptist activity moves through the four categories we outlined. As layers of regulation are imposed on different sectors of the economy, related Bootlegger/Baptist activities have cumulative effects on wealth creation. Thick layers of rigid rules reduce the economy's flexibility in an ever-changing world—the political equivalent of hardening arteries. And the layers themselves may interact, as when environmental regulation shapes the rules governing international trade, which may in turn generate demand for labor and food safety standards.

As Bootlegger/Baptist interaction becomes more prevalent and sophisticated, specialized lobbyists emerge to seek even more pork from the political process. As interest group lobbyists build larger fixed-cost enterprises, operating costs fall as lobbyists expand their political portfolios. At times the bonds linking special interest groups to political agents will seem to slacken, but at the right moment—when a large enough helping of pork is available—tethers tied over a shared history will draw both to the barbecue counter.

We detailed in chapter 2 how Bootlegger/Baptist theory is a part of the larger public choice theory that seeks to explain human action in the public domain through the use of economic logic. Assumptions about political reality, borrowed from the canons of public choice, establish the ideal conditions for flourishing Bootlegger/Baptist activity.

First, rational ignorance on the part of the general voting population enables key players to operate without fear of being held accountable for their pursuits, especially if they establish moral cover. For while rational ignorance applies to the details of policy, the body politic still insists on being assured that government is doing the "right" thing.

Second, voters are most likely to remain rationally ignorant—and pork most easily extracted—when lobbying yields concentrated benefits for coalition members while spreading the cost of providing those benefits across a vast pool of taxpayers and citizens at small cost to each.

Third, the scale and frequency of Bootlegger/Baptist interaction imposes a real deadweight loss on society. In the scramble for pork, the paired interest groups may nearly exhaust the gains obtained from their political struggle. Once Bootleggers and Baptists are locked into a successful coalition, their structural incentives change, making political wealth extraction more attractive than private wealth generation—to society's detriment. In other words, scarce resources that might be allocated to the production of valuable goods and services become obligated to the task of maintaining the supply of pork provided by politicians.

Bootlegger/Baptist coalitions succeed by driving down the cost of pork production. Politicians shielded by Baptist cover when acting at the behest of Bootleggers are less likely to be challenged in the public forum. Because of this, successful politicians must send signals that demonstrate a regard for the public interest. Doing so lowers the cost of organizing delivery of legislative favors.

But why Baptists? Why the need for moral justification? Why not patriotism? Why not wealth creation? We describe in chapter 3 how the Baptist element in the theory is best understood against the backdrop of our evolved disposition toward cooperation, which in turn supports religious practices that encourage order and community survival. The long history of close interaction between religious and political leaders helps explain why politicians in a secular state still tend to employ moral or religious rhetoric when justifying their actions, and why members of society respond favorably to those justifications.

Use of the political apparatus to impose social norms and achieve moral goals, however, entices Bootleggers to capture pork through the same mechanism. For Bootleggers, piety is a prelude to plenty. Politicians who deliver pork to the Bootleggers can justify their actions by appealing to higher Baptist morality. Those who fail to make the Bootlegger/Baptist connection disappear from the political domain. As poor political players perish and expert players flourish, pork distribution becomes more competitive. Expanding Bootlegger/Baptist activity leads to further specialization in the provision of pork.

Because moral credibility is hard to manufacture, the most valuable Baptists are those with broad bases of support, long institutional histories, and an ability to communicate with the larger public by invoking widely shared social values. Gifted political leaders—and sometimes even Bootleggers themselves—can deploy Baptist rhetoric as well, but being your own Baptist is risky business. The most durable deals require genuine Baptists to raise their voices in support of the outcomes that diligent Bootleggers prefer.

In our applied chapters, we have provided detailed stories about alcohol, marijuana, and tobacco regulation and about climate change, TARP, and Obamacare. We emphasize again that in telling these stories, we have shown how Bootlegger/Baptist theory is most useful in explaining why the details of regulations take the form they do rather than why regulation exists in the first place. The theory can predict that environmental regulation will tend to impose higher standards on new sources of pollution than old ones and that tobacco regulation will eliminate competition and cartelize the industry while providing interest groups preferred marketing restrictions. Lack of Bootlegger/Baptist interaction helps us understand the strange gyrations of TARP, and in contrast, the heavy interaction sheds light on how Obamacare, the political prize unwanted by the public at large, became the law of the land.

Bootlegger/Baptist Regulatory Opportunities, Consequences, and Prospects

Bootleggers and Baptists make their influence felt as both legislators and regulatory agencies are developing regulations. Common Bootlegger goals include raising the costs of competitors, gaining subsidies, cartelizing industries (in whole or in part), and building protective regulatory walls around their sectors of the economy. The more new rules are issued, the more opportunities Bootleggers have to benefit—and the evidence suggests the stakes are only getting higher: the number of "economically significant" regulations, those whose effect on the economy is estimated at $100 million or more for each year the rules are in force, is growing steadily.

If the number of such rules is rising, we may reasonably infer that Bootlegger/Baptist specialization among lobbyists and accommodating politicians is increasing in tandem, and vice versa. In recent years, the tally of new rules produced by regulatory agencies has risen significantly. In 2001, the number of those economically significant rules stood at 149. The figure then dropped slightly, ranging between 127 and 141 from 2003 to 2006 (Crews 2013, 21–23). In 2007, the number of "significant" rules rose to 160 and kept rising steadily through 2010, when 224 such rules were in the works. In 2011, the count stood at 212. For 2012, the most recent year for which we have data, the count recovered to 224.

Let's make some back-of-the-envelope calculations. If we assume that each of those 224 rules imposes a cost of "only" $100 million annually, which is the minimum threshold for being called significant, then the 2012 pipeline is loaded with more than $22 billion of projected annual economic impact. By comparison, similar calculations for 2001 yield not quite $15 billion. That would mean we've seen a 40 percent increase in annual cost imposed by large new rules, and this is just for the larger impact rules. Separate cost estimates that attempt to take account of the entire regulatory burden show the annual cost riding in the range of $1.7 trillion to $1.8 trillion, or $14,768 for each U.S. household (Crews 2013, 1). Although all such estimates are subject to debate, one thing is certain. The pace and burden of U.S. regulation is rising and large. Almost endless opportunities exist for Bootlegger/Baptist interaction.

The list of leading agencies that are issuing rules—large and small—gives a clue to where the Bootleggers and Baptists seem to be working hardest and tells us which economic sectors are most subject to regulatory artery hardening. In 2012, the Department of Treasury was king of the mountain—no surprise in the wake of TARP, Dodd-Frank financial reform, and other banking-related regulation. Treasury was followed by the departments of Commerce, Interior, Agriculture, and Transportation (Crews 2013, 24).

When it comes to production of higher impact, economically significant rules, EPA leads the pack, followed by the Department of Labor, the Department of Transportation, and the Department of Homeland Security (Crews 2013, 26). Based on these measures of activity, it seems certain that opportunities for Bootlegger/Baptist interaction stand at a very healthy level across the gamut of government activity.

The budgets of federal regulatory agencies provide another metric for assessing the incentives for Bootlegger/Baptist activity. What is happening with social regulation, as opposed to economic regulation, provides the more sensitive metric. Included in this category are rules affecting consumer safety and health, homeland security, transportation safety, the workplace, the environment, and energy. Using data from a recent report by Susan Dudley and Melinda Warren (2012, 5), we find that the ratio of budgeted expenditures on social versus economic regulation surged from 2.25 in 1970 to 4.90 in 1980 and rested at 4.37 in 1990. The ratio stood at 4.53 in the 2013 budget. Between 1970 and 2013, total budgets for both categories rose from $2.86 billion to $50.45 billion in constant 2005 dollars (Dudley and Warren 2012, 22).

These dry numbers are nevertheless significant to our story. First, social regulation is prime territory for Baptist lobbying that yields Bootlegger benefits—as illustrated in the chapters on the environment, "sin" substances, and health care. (We note that economic regulation is hardly devoid of Bootlegger/Baptist opportunities, especially during times of national crisis, as we saw in the discussion of TARP.) Second, regulatory activity for both categories as measured by budgeted expenditures has grown apace, rising more than 17-fold over the last 43 years. Obviously, not all of that growth is attributable to the machinations of Bootlegger/Baptist coalitions. But we would argue that such tag-team operations have been running in overdrive since 1970, contributing to the growth and burden of regulation in the United States. We note that even if there were consistent, all-inclusive estimates of the regulatory burden imposed by federal rules, we believe one major element of cost would not be—and perhaps could not be—quantified and included. This is the cost of the potential for wealth creation that is lost as special interest groups, firms, industries, organizations, and politicians discover that the pursuit of regulatory pork pays better than production—and allocate their resources accordingly.

Our Final Thought

We close with one final thought: no matter how blatant Bootlegger/Baptist practices may become, and no matter how heavy the associated economic burden, there is no foreseeable end to the story of Bootleggers and Baptists. The Bootlegger/Baptist phenomenon is driven by forces rooted deeply in the human psyche. Self-interest is the driver for both Bootleggers and Baptists—and in a deeper sense for the society that fosters these interest groups.

175

It is a safe bet that people will always seek better, safer, and more comfortable lives for themselves and those they love. It is an equally safe bet that there will always be individuals and groups whose happiness comes from envisioning a morally better world—and striving mightily to get there. Any recognizably human community will have a body politic, and within the political institutions that exist there, people with power will need to satisfy constituencies of some kind to maintain their positions. The ingredients for Bootlegger/Baptist interaction will always be present.

On the upside, given that there will be Bootlegger/Baptist interaction as far as the eye can see, we in the United States or others who enjoy similar freedoms can rejoice quietly in the fact that the greater the level of freedom, the higher the costs imposed on those wishing to grab power for themselves without going through the rigors of open political competition. Winning coalitions do expire and new ones are formed, but open political and economic competition does limit the loss that will be imposed in a Bootlegger/Baptist infected society.

So how might the activity be constrained? As mentioned at the outset, Bootlegger/Baptist activity is conditioned by the pace and extent of federal regulatory activity. Structural changes that constrain the production of federal regulation—for example, by shifting it to the states—would also shift the incentives driving Bootlegger/Baptist interaction and raise their operating costs. It is far more costly to lobby 50 state legislative bodies, for example, than one national government. Furthermore, states that adopt particularly pernicious regulations will suffer by being less competitive compared with their neighbors that are less responsive to assorted special interests. People more readily vote with their feet when comparing the relative benefits of living in one state versus another, as compared to moving from one country to another.

Steps taken to expose the Bootleggers—and embarrass Baptists for supporting them—could similarly slow their activity. Changing communications technology may help as well: as the ordinary citizens who ultimately pay the cost of all that pork become increasingly and more thoroughly networked, their costs of becoming informed and organized fall apace—which may make ignorance, and apathy, a bit less rational—especially when, as the Occupy movement reminded us, collective action itself can be a source of Baptist satisfaction.

The scope of lobbying and pork hunting may expand or contract in response to changes in political structures, public attitudes, or communication technologies, but the essence of the Bootlegger/Baptist dynamic is too tightly woven into our DNA to be easily eliminated. We are all each at least a little bit Bootlegger, a little bit Baptist—which means as long as we remain human, the story of Bootleggers and Baptists will continue.

Appendix: Bootleggers and Baptists—The Education of a Regulatory Economist*

Bruce Yandle

The search for regulatory relief is as young as the Reagan administration, and as old as man. When the American Medical Association chafes under Federal Trade Commission oversight, it feels the same frustration Adam must have felt at the menu regulations he faced in Eden. But often people want relief not from regulation but through the protections regulation can provide. Today, some airline executives want succor from the uncertainties they confront in a world without regulated (uniform) pricing. The London weavers felt that same way about their trade in the 13th century and obtained relief through a provision in the Magna Carta requiring all cloth woven in the realm to be of uniform dimensions—conforming to the London standard. Nothing is new under the sun.

Regulation and Murphy's Law

In my studies of the relationships between governments and business, my attention was first attracted to the unbelievably costly things that governments do when attempting to control businesses. It seemed, as Murphy might have said, that if there was a wrong way of doing something, the regulators would adopt it. I found countless cases where rules and regulations imposed tremendous costs while delivering little if any benefit.

- Freight rates for one class of shippers were subsidized by another class of shippers. As a result, factories were located on the basis of false signals, real costs were hidden, and goods were shipped great distances at lower fares to be processed in higher-cost plants.

*Reprinted from *Regulation: AEI Journal on Government and Society*, May/June 1983, pp. 12–16.

- Catalytic converters were installed on automobiles for the purpose of reducing emissions. But, for the converters to operate properly, unleaded gas had to be used—and it is more expensive than regular. So cost-conscious drivers put leaded gas in their tanks, which turned the converters into so much junk and added more emissions to the environment than there would have been had engines been even slightly modified or some other plan introduced.

- Petrochemical plants were required to reduce emissions at each and every stack by the same percentage. If instead managers had been given plant-wide targets and left free to attain them efficiently, the same degree of pollution control could have been achieved at much lower cost.

- Petroleum companies that found oil on Alaska's North Slope and sought to bring it to the lower 48 states by way of the West Coast were barred from doing so by complex environmental rules. Logic would then have dictated that the oil be shipped to Japanese refineries, which could have returned the refined product to the United States. But that was against federal law too. Instead, the crude oil is being shipped from Alaska to Texas, where it is unloaded and refined, all at considerable extra cost.

- Precise fuel economy standards were prescribed for automakers, to prod them into building the kind of cars that probably would have been produced and purchased voluntarily if the price of gasoline had been higher. But the price of gasoline was regulated so it could not rise; and the automakers had to ration their larger cars, which U.S. buyers wanted, while forcing smaller cars into the market. Eventually, the price of gasoline was deregulated and the effects of the mandated fuel-economy scheme tended to evaporate—for the time being, at least.

The list could go on and on. Not only does government rarely accomplish its stated goals at lowest cost, but often its regulators seem dedicated to choosing the highest-cost approach they can find. Because of all this, I and other in academia became convinced years ago that a massive program in economic education was needed to save the world from regulation. If we economists could just teach the regulators a little supply and demand, countless billions of dollars would be saved.

Bootleggers and Baptists

My views began to change after I joined the Council on Wage and Price Stability in 1976. There my assignment was to review proposed regulations from the Environmental Protection Agency (EPA), the Federal Trade Commission (FTC), the Department of Transportation (DOT), and parts of the Department of Health, Education, and Welfare (HEW). The field was "white unto the harvest," and I was ready to educate the regulators. But then I began to talk with some of them, and I began to hear from people in the industries affected by the rules. To my surprise, many regulators knew quite a bit about economics. Even more surprising was that industry representatives were not always opposed to the costly rules and occasionally were even fearful that we would succeed in getting rid of some of them. It was in considerable confusion that I returned later to my university post, still unable to explain what I had observed and square it with the economics I thought I understood.

That marked the beginning of a new approach to my research on regulation. First, instead of assuming that regulators really intended to minimize costs but somehow proceeded to make crazy mistakes, I began to assume that they were not trying to minimize costs at all—at least not the costs I had been concerned with. They were trying to minimize *their* costs, just as most sensible people do. And what are some of those costs that keep regulators from choosing efficient ways of, say, reducing emissions of hydrocarbons?

- *The cost of making a mistake.* Simple rules applied across the board require fewer decisions where mistakes can be made.
- *The cost of enforcement.* Again, simple rules requiring uniform behavior are easier to monitor and enforce than complex ones, and they also have a false ring of fairness.
- *Political costs.* A legislator is likely to be unhappy with regulators who fail to behave in politically prudent ways—who fail, in the legislator's view, to remember the industries and the workers in his area.

181

Second, I asked myself, what do industry and labor want from the regulators? They want protection from competition, from technological change, and from losses that threaten profits and jobs. A carefully constructed regulation can accomplish all kinds of anticompetitive goals of this sort, while giving the citizenry the impression that the only goal is to serve the public interest.

Indeed, the pages of history are full of episodes best explained by a theory of regulation I call "bootleggers and Baptists." Bootleggers, you will remember, support Sunday closing laws that shut down all the local bars and liquor stores. Baptists support the same laws and lobby vigorously for them. Both parties gain, while the regulators are content because the law is easy to administer. Of course, this theory is not new. In a democratic society, economic forces will always play through the political mechanism in ways determined by the voting mechanism employed. Politicians need resources in order to get elected. Selected members of the public can gain resources through the political process, and highly organized groups can do that quite handily. The most successful ventures of this sort occur whenever there is an overarching public concern to be addressed (like the problem of alcohol) whose "solution" allows resources to be distributed from the public purse to particular groups or from one group to another (as from bartenders to bootleggers).

What all this implies is that the challenges of regulatory reform are institutional. Regulation is relief for some and a burden for others, so that reform is a burden for some and a relief for others. The fact that a regulation has come into being as a result of a costly political exchange means that reform can hardly be gained easily. This is not to suggest that all is for naught, that there are no opportunities for reducing net (overall) regulatory costs or removing the protective regulatory cocoons woven so tightly and carefully around this activity and that. But it is to say that we can scarcely expect full-scale deregulation to occur often. Not when the Baptists and the bootleggers vote together.

Shocking the System: Pareto-Paperwork

Let us accept for the moment the proposition that all regulation produced in a given period has value at least sufficient to justify the direct costs borne by those supporting it. Since those who opposed a given regulation most probably fought it, rather than allowing it to proceed by default, we will not assume that the value of the regulation exceeds the total costs incurred by the winners, losers, and regulators.

Now consider an equilibrium state in which the political-economic market has produced a given quantity of regulation and will continue to maintain it unless there is an outside shock to the system. Imagine that you are regulatory czar, subject to all the economic forces at play in the system (other activities and actions being held constant) and with a free rein to reform the regulatory process. Finally, to make the situation more interesting (and more illuminating), imagine also that you are a long-suffering student of the regulatory system, with a long list of regulations you are convinced cannot be justified at all, or at least not in their present form. What would you do?

Regulatory paperwork would likely be your best candidate for reform—for it is an area where you might be able to reduce costs for both the regulated and the regulators (making both better off, no one worse off, in a kind of Pareto move), without disturbing the equilibrium state established by the interplay of rules and regulations. Of course, reducing paperwork is not nearly so dramatic as deregulating the airlines, speeding up new drug approvals, or removing import quotas (supposing any of these appealed to you). Still, it would not be a minor accomplishment. The cumulative savings from paperwork reduction for the years 1981 through 1983 are expected to reach 300 million hours. If you managed that as czar, we might well rise up and call your name blessed.

Unfortunately, other reforms would be much more difficult. Remember that you must act within the existing political forces, that the actors in the drama are all well-informed, and that the existing equilibrium is the product of a massive struggle.

Changes in the Demand for Regulation. So, let us ask, how might you upset that equilibrium by creating new players or causing the current players to acquire an interest in deregulation. Put differently, what factors might shift the demand for regulation?

- *Technological change.* A technology protected or even induced by regulation can nonetheless become obsolete, and the regulated businesses can find themselves hamstrung by the very rules that protected them.

- *Demographic change.* With migration and population growth, patterns of production and distribution supported by regulation can become so costly over time that the producer chooses to throw back the protective blanket.

- *Significant changes in factor costs.* Regulated firms generally seek regulations that fit production arrangements based on predicted prices for labor, materials, and capital—which means that unpredicted changes in those prices can alter the amount and incidence of the benefits of regulation.

- *New information.* With increasing scholarly and press attention to regulatory issues, voter/taxpayer/consumer groups might discover that their benefits from regulation are less than their costs.

Looking down the roster of successful regulatory reforms, it is not difficult to find cases that can be explained in part or as a whole by some combination of the above factors. For example, take the impact of technological change on the AT&T monopoly. Microwave, computer, and satellite technology outstripped the basic "hard-wire" systems used in Bell's telephone operations, creating competitive opportunities and weakening the demand for monopoly privilege. The field of action that had been created partly by inventions of the major telephone companies, yet barred to them, came to offer greater opportunities for growth and profit than the older regulated field. Technological change was also a crucial factor in banking and finance. The electronic transmission of funds, coupled with the Federal Reserve Board's dominant position in the check-clearing process, contributed significantly to a new technical base for financial institutions. This development, along with the unexpectedly high interest rates that commercial banks and savings and loans were barred from paying, made the old regulatory structure obsolete.

Changes in two other demand factors arguably undermined the traditional regulatory framework in trucking and other surface transportation. The unexpected increase in the price of energy magnified the costs associated with circuitous routes and empty backhauls, and changing population patterns made old route structures less desirable. Both developments fueled the demand for reform.

184

Finally, take airline deregulation. In this case, it was rising energy prices, changing patterns of equipment utilization, and population shifts—combined with the development of new aircraft and intensive reporting of research on the effects of these changes—that shifted the demand for regulation.

As for future reforms, what might we predict on this same basis? Two come to mind. First, like AT&T, the U.S. Postal Service has stuck to an obsolete technology. With electronic transmission of messages, arguments about natural monopoly status have lost any credibility they may have once had and, for that reason among others, the statutes barring competition in the delivery of first class mail are under increasing fire. Energy regulation is another likely candidate for reform. Technical change and rapidly shifting relative prices have placed enormous pressures on existing regulatory structures, so that producers and consumers are now seeking greater flexibility than the present "public utility" status of much of the industry will allow. For example, the need for appropriate incentives to increase the amount of natural gas delivered to the market is widely recognized, and alternative systems for pricing and arranging the distribution of electricity are being explored. (Here, at least, we may have found one beneficial aftereffect of OPEC and its works.)

Changes in the Supply of Regulation. The supply side of regulation, like the demand side, helps determine the quantity of regulation produced in political-economic markets. Among the variables here are the bureaucracy and the electoral and legislative process.

- *Bureaucratic incentives and structure*. If lawyers and economists can improve their expected lifetime earnings by filing enforcement actions against specific industries, for example, those actions will tend to be filed. More broadly, how agencies are organized (whether they are independent commissions or headed by a single administrator), what voting rules are applied in making decisions, to what extent the agency specializes in an industry or product, and whether there is competition from other agencies for jurisdiction are traditionally thought to affect the supply of regulation.

- *Congressional oversight*. The legislative component of the supply side is closely related to demand, since elected officials also represent special interests who seek regulatory benefits. But, even so, the competition among legislators, their voting rules, and their committee organization are supply characteristics.

Assuming that demand is held constant, to what extent will changes in these supply-side characteristics affect the quantity or quality of regulations produced? For example, will a reduction in the number of commissioners (as is happening now at the FCC), or a shift in the party mix of agency oversight committees, cause regulation to change?

Empirical research suggests strongly that the supply side matters. For example, Barry Weingast and Mark Moran report that, contrary to some opinions, the FTC's regulatory behavior mirrors the conservative-liberal makeup of the agency's key congressional committees: in other words, the agency is hardly ever "out of control" (*Regulation*, May/June 1982). Roger Faith, Donald R. Leavens, and Robert Tollison find that the FTC has been less likely to take actions against firms headquartered in the districts of congressmen who sit on the FTC's congressional committees than against firms not so favorably situated (*Journal of Law and Economics*, October 1982). My recent research on the FTC suggests that the agency's behavior is influenced not only by shifts in the chairmanship from a Democrat to Republican and vice versa, but also by shifts in how the chairman is chosen (in 1950 the method was changed from rotation to presidential designation).

Putting all this together, we may say that there are strong possibilities for regulatory reform when the institutions involved are changing for other reasons anyway. Such changes would help explain the flurry of deregulation initiatives at the FCC, especially those dealing with broadcasting, as well as the shift away from industry-wide rulemaking and structural antitrust investigations at the FTC. Moreover, the cautious attitude now shown by the Justice Department and the FTC when considering price discrimination, resale price maintenance, and vertical combinations, along with the probing economic analysis applied in such investigations, reflect new learning in law and economics and changes in the structure of the two agencies. Indeed, the significant overall reduction in new regulatory initiatives across the entire federal government reflects a coordinated effort that draws on each of the items mentioned.

Other Agents of Change

So far I have hardly mentioned yet another interest group: those who gain special satisfaction from participating in the regulatory process in ways that will improve economic efficiency. While some might conclude that students of the process can only observe, record, and analyze, I have a more sanguine view: simply put, people and their ideas do make a difference.

Some individuals, for example, make a difference by continuing to raise questions about grand principles—overall social efficiency, the appropriate role of government, economic freedom, the virtues of the price system. The more articulate and informed of these point out the compromises being made by the rest of us. Of equal importance are those whose goal is to understand how the regulatory process works, what interests are driving it, and how its outcome might be predicted. These are the academic researchers, the public policy analysts, the economists with private firms and in government, who struggle to bring about marginal adjustments. Their task is the creative application of economic logic. At yet a third level, there is active participation in decisionmaking itself. When I observed the effect of an Alfred Kahn at the CAB, a Darius Gaskins at the ICC, and a James Miller at the FTC—to say nothing of the less visible but nonetheless significant work performed by scores of others in the arena where decisions are made—I must believe they make a difference, a very great difference.

Finally, one should not expect to see sudden and widespread transformation in regulation. Like all market processes, the market for regulation is relatively stable, the result of thousands of transactions and years of institutional development. Yet, also like other markets, the forces of supply and demand do change, and the agents for change can and do have a marginal but significant impact on political demand and regulatory supply. Bootleggers and Baptists may have been agitating for a century or more, but the saloon is still with us—and usually on Sundays, too.

Notes

Preface

1. A copy of the 1983 publication is in the appendix.

Chapter 1

1. We note that the resulting Sunday drinking cartel may be profitless for the bootleggers unless some way exists to restrict the entry of new bootleggers. Selective law enforcement may accomplish this. Alternatively, bootlegger wars over territory may arise, as happened during Prohibition, and as drug cartels war among themselves today.

2. Accordingly, we denote this group of people as a category with a capital B (i.e., Bootleggers). Any specific reference to actual bootleggers engaged in selling illegal booze is denoted with a lowercase b.

3. The most exhaustive estimates of regulation's effects on productivity for the entire economy were done in the late 1970s and early 1980s. These identified highly significant reductions in productivity growth in association with the growth and character of regulation. On this see Denison 1979; Christainsen and Haveman 1981; and for a survey, Christainsen and Haveman 1984.

4. http://www.saferoads.org/.

Chapter 2

1. Part of the material in this chapter is drawn from Morriss, Yandle, and Dorchak (2009). We express appreciation to Yale University Press for permission to use this material.

2. Gary S. Becker (1983) makes the fundamental theoretical point that the political process is competitive in the sense that actions taken, no matter how costly, are still accomplished at the lowest possible cost, given the associated constitutional rules and political costs. We consider Bootleggers and Baptists to be a component of Becker's politically competitive process. But we also note that Mancur Olson (1982) described the limits of interest group action, which might have been taken competitively through time, as causing a kind of hardening of economic arteries such that innovation and economic growth become stifled. Somewhere between Becker's one regulation at a time competition and Olson's locked-down economy, Bootleggers and Baptists work at the margin to gain another increment of rent.

3. On this point, Pigou laments in a footnote that, "In Germany the town-planning schemes of most cities render anti-social action of this kind impossible; but in America individual site-owners appear to be entirely free, and in England to be largely free, to do what they will with their land." Pigou's view that the freedom of site owners is

the source of "anti-social action," may offer some insight into his mindset regarding external effects (see Pigou [1932] 2009, 186).

4. Pigou later recognized that private interest lobbying would stand in the way of effectively applying his public interest theory. However, even though Pigou may have recognized this, his modern-day disciples disregard his warning and regularly promote the basic idea that government has a heavy public interest role to play (Yandle 2010b).

5. We note that the "as is" or warranty sticker seen on used cars today, a low-cost solution to the congressional effort, is the result of the Used Car Rule.

Chapter 3

1. Or as President George W. Bush's equally appropriate malapropism explained, "Fool me once shame on you . . . but you're not gonna fool me again!"

2. We thank David Rose for alerting us to this angle of our theory.

Chapter 4

1. Family Smoking Prevention and Tobacco Control and Federal Retirement Reform, Pub. L. No. 111-31, 123 Stat. 1776 (2009), http://www.gpo.gov/fdsys/pkg/PLAW-111publ31/pdf/PLAW-111publ31.pdf.

2. Pure Food and Drug Act of 1906, Pub. L. No. 59-384, 34 Stat. 768, 768–72 (1906) (repealed 1938).

3. Federal Cigarette Labeling and Advertising Act, 15 U.S.C. §§ 1331–1340.

4. Public Health Cigarette Smoking Act of 1969, Pub. L. No. 91-222, 84 Stat. 87 (1970).

5. Coyne Beahm, Inc. v. FDA, 966 F.Supp. 1374, 1388 (M.D.N.C. 1997), *rev'd* Brown and Williamson Tobacco Corp. v. FDA, 153 F.3d 155 (4th Cir. 1998), *aff'd* FDA v. Brown and Williamson, 529 U.S. 120, 160–61 (2000).

6. Universal Tobacco Settlement Act, S. 1415, 105th Congress (1998); Kelder (1998, 5–6). Senate Majority Leader Trent Lott, brother-in-law of attorney Richard Scruggs, had asked Sen. John McCain in early 1998 to craft in the Commerce Committee a bill that embodied the tobacco settlement. "The committee consulted Wall Street analysts who calculated Congress could extract that much without any of the tobacco companies going bankrupt" (Bierbauer 1998). See also O'Brien (2000).

7. http://humboldtmedicalcannabis.com/cannabis/humboldt_growers_association/.

Chapter 5

1. Sections of this chapter are reprinted with permission from the publisher of *The Independent Review: A Journal of Political Economy* (Summer 1999, Volume 4, no. 1, pp. 19–40). © 1999, The Independent Institute, 100 Swan Way, Oakland, CA 94621-1428 USA; mailto:info@independent.org; www.independent.org.

2. This is a loaded sentence. Volumes have been written that describe environmentalism as a religious movement. Robert H. Nelson (2010) leads this scholarly interpretation.

3. See Teamsters, General Executive Board Resolution on the Kyoto Protocol (January 2001), available at http://www.ujae.org/NewsRes/Teamster%20resolution%20on%20Kyoto%20Protocol.pdf, and AFL-CIO Executive Council, The Kyoto Protocol

(January 30, 1998), available at http://perc.org/sites/default/files/Yandle.Buck.Harvard.pdf.

4. This idea, discussed formally at Toronto in June 1988 and considered by Congress in 1989 in a proposed bill, the Global Warming Prevention Act, was fundamental to pre-Kyoto commitments reached in 1992, when representatives of 160 nations attended the Rio de Janeiro Conference on Environment and Development (Manne and Richels 1991, 88).

5. Anecdotes in this section are drawn from Yandle and Buck (2002).

Chapter 6

1. Emergency Economic Stabilization Act of 2008, Pub. L. No. 110-343, 122 Stat. 3765 (2008), http://frwebgate.access.gpo.gov/cgi-bin/getdoc.cgi?dbname=110_cong_public_laws&docid=f:publ343.110.pdf.

2. The terms of this appropriation were as follows. TARP would purchase senior preferred shares, which qualify as Tier 1 capital, ranking senior to common stock. These shares would yield 5 percent per annum for the first five years and reset to 9 percent thereafter. In addition, the Treasury would "receive warrants to purchase common stock with an aggregate market price equal to 15 percent of the senior preferred investment. The exercise price on the warrants will be the market price of the participating institution's common stock at the time of issuance, calculated on a 20-trading day trailing average" (Treasury Department 2008a, 4).

3. One possible exception was the Federal Deposit Insurance Corporation's increasing of its deposit coverage insurance from $100,000 to $250,000 (see FDIC 2008).

4. The represented banks were Bank of America Corp., Citigroup Inc., Goldman Sachs Group Inc., JPMorgan Chase & Co., Merrill Lynch & Co., Bank of New York Mellon Corp., State Street Corp., Morgan Stanley, and Wells Fargo & Co.

5. This comes from documents that reveal a list of talking points at the October 13 meeting. The points of relevance are (a) We don't believe it is tenable to opt out because doing so would leave you vulnerable and exposed, and (b) If a capital infusion is not appealing, you should be aware that your regulator will require it in any circumstance.

6. The companies that fit these parameters at the time the bill was proposed were AIG, Bank of America, Citigroup, General Motors, GMAC Financial Services, Goldman Sachs, JP Morgan Chase, Morgan Stanley, PNC Financial Services Group, U.S. Bancorp, and Wells Fargo.

7. These initial firms were AIG, Citigroup, Bank of America, General Motors, GMAC, Chrysler, and Chrysler Financial.

8. Pub. L. No. 111-5, 123 Stat. 115, 520 (2009), http://www.gpo.gov/fdsys/pkg/PLAW-111publ5/pdf/PLAW-111publ5.pdf.

9. Pub. L. No. 111-203, 124 Stat. 1376 (2010).

10. See Public Law 110–343. 2008. Emergency Economic Stabilization Act of 2008. http://frwebgate.access.gpo.gov/cgi-bin/getdoc.cgi?dbname=110_cong_public_laws&docid=f:publ343.110.pdf. Accessed December. 27, 2011.

Chapter 7

1. Pub. L. No. 111-148, 124 Stat. 119 (2010).

References

Adamy, Janey, and Ann Zimmerman. 2009. "Wal-Mart Backs Drive to Make Companies Pay for Health Coverage." *Wall Street Journal*, July 1, p. A1.

Adcox, Seanna. 2011. "SC House Rejects Sales Tax Break for Amazon." *Forbes.com*, April 28. http://www.forbes.com/feeds/ap/2011/04/27/general-sc-amazon-sales-tax_8438523.html. *Ventura County Star*, April 27. http://www.vcstar.com/news/2011/apr/27/sc-house-rejects-sales-tax-break-for-amazon/?print=1.

Affordable Mortgage Depression, The (blog). 2010. "Origin of the Housing Bubble: The National Homeownership Strategy." http://theaffordablemortgagedepression.com/2010/03/11/origin-of-the-housing-bubble-the-national-homeownership-strategy.aspx.

"Al Gore's Ethanol Epiphany." 2010. *Wall Street Journal*, November 27. http://online.wsj.com/article/SB10001424052748703572404575634753486416076.html.

Alter, Jonathan. 2006. *The Defining Moment: FDR's Hundred Days and the Triumph of Hope*. New York: Simon and Schuster.

Ammiano, Tom. 2010. "Legalizing Pot Frightens California County." *Cannabis News*, April 12. http://www.cannabisnews.org/united-states-cannabis-news/legalizing-pot-frightens-california-county/.

". . . And the Climate Tort Cashiered." 2011. *Wall Street Journal*, June 21. http://online.wsj.com/article/SB10001424052702303936704576397673915105838.html.

Anderson, Lloyd. 2004. "Direct Shipment of Wine, the Commerce Clause and the Twenty-First Amendment: A Call for Legislative Reform." *Akron Law Review* 37 (1): 1–40.

Anderson, Terry L., and Donald R. Leal. 2001. *Free Market Environmentalism, Revised Edition*. New York: Palgrave Macmillan.

Andrews, Edmund L. 2001. "Bush Angers Europe by Eroding Pact on Warming." *New York Times*, April 1, p. 1.

Aranson, P. H., and P. C. Ordeshook. 1981. "Regulation, Redistribution, and Public Choice." *Public Choice* 37:69–100.

Axelrod, Robert. 1984. *The Evolution of Cooperation*. New York: Basic Books.

Bandow, Doug. 1997. "Ethanol Keeps ADM Drunk on Tax Dollars." Cato Institute Commentary, October 2. http://www.cato.org/publications/commentary/ethanol-keeps-adm-drunk-tax-dollars.

Baptist Press. 2010. "Gov. Arnold Schwarzenegger Opposes Prop 19 Marijuana Initiative." *Opposing Views*, September 28. http://www.opposingviews.com/i/gov-arnold-schwarzenegger-opposes-prop-19-marijuana-initiative.

Beam, Christopher. 2009. "Do I Have a 'Cadillac Plan'?" *Slate*, October 14. http://www.slate.com/articles/news_and_politics/explainer/2009/10/do_i_have_a_cadillac_plan.html.

Becker, Gary S. 1983. "A Theory of Competition among Pressure Groups for Political Influence." *Quarterly Journal of Economics* 98 (3): 371–400.

Bender, Michael. 2009. "Health Care Reform Advocates to Pressure Nelson." Post on Politics blog, *Palm Beach Post*, July 23. http://www.postonpolitics.com/2009/07/health-care-reform-advocates-to-pressure-nelson/.

Berg, Joyce, John Dickhaut, and Kevin McCabe. 1995. "Trust, Reciprocity, and Social History." *Games and Economic Behavior* 10: 122–42.

Bierbauer, Charles. 1998. "Smoke 'Em, If You Got 'Em." CNN AllPolitics, June 19. http://www.cnn.com/ALLPOLITICS/1998/06/19/bierbauer/index.html.

Borders, Max. 2012. "How About a Cronyism Mitigation Index?" The Motley Fool (blog), August 2. http://beta.fool.com /maxborders/2012/08/02/how-about-a-cronyism-mitigation-index/8593/.

"British Petroleum to Take Action on Climate Change." 1997. *EDF Letter*, Vol. XXVIII, no. 4, September. http://www.edf.org/sites/default/files/175_Sep97.pdf.

Britton, Charles, Richard Ford, and David Gay. 2001. "The United States Wine Industry: Restraint of Trade and the Religious Right." *International Journal of Wine Marketing* 13 (2): 43–58.

Buchanan, James M. 1994. *Ethics and Economic Progress*. Norman: University of Oklahoma Press.

———. 2003. "Public Choice: Politics without Romance." *Policy* 19 (3): 13–18. http://www.cis.org.au/publications/policy-magazine/article/2379.

Buchanan, James M., and Gordon Tullock. 1962. *The Calculus of Consent*. Ann Arbor: University of Michigan Press.

———. 1975. "Polluters' Profits and Political Response: Direct Controls versus Taxes." *American Economic Review* 65 (1): 139–47.

Burnham, Michael. 2010. "Conoco, BP, Caterpillar Leave Climate Coalition." *New York Times*, February 16. http://www.nytimes.com/gwire/2010/02/16/16greenwire-conoco-bp-caterpillar-leave-climate-coalition-73582.html.

Calhoun, John C. (1810) 1992. "A Disquisition on Government." In *Union and Liberty: The Political Philosophy of John C. Calhoun,* edited by Ross M. Lence. Indianapolis: Liberty Fund, http://oll.libertyfund.org/title/683/107113.

"California Prop 19 and the Electoral Results." 2010. *Daily Political.com*, November 8. http://www.dailypolitical.com/politics/california-prop-19-and-the-electoral-results.htm.

Calmes, Jackie. 2010. "Taxing Banks for the Bailout." *New York Times*, January 15, p. B1.

Campaign for Tobacco-Free Kids. 2011. Tobacco Prevention Spending vs. State Tobacco Revenues. http://www.tobaccofreekids.org/research/factsheets/pdf/0219.pdf.

Campanile, Carl. 2010. "Unions Will Dodge O's Health Tax." *New York Post*, January 15. http://www.nypost.com/p/news/national/unions_get_pecial_treatment_in_health_AB053CwqPIJlIxXAm37DOM.

Capehart, Thomas C., Jr. 2001. "Trends in the Cigarette Industry after the Master Settlement Agreement." Electronic Outlook Report from the Economic Research Service, TBS-250-01, U.S. Department of Agriculture, October. http://www.ers.usda.gov/publications/tbs/oct01/tbs250-01/tbs250-01.pdf.

Caplan, Bryan. 2001. "Rational Irrationality and the Microfoundations of Political Failure." *Public Choice* 107: 311–31.

———. 2008. *The Myth of the Rational Voter*. Princeton, NJ: Princeton University Press.

Carraro, Carlo, Marzio Galeotti, and Massimo Gallo. 1996. "Environmental Taxation and Unemployment: Some Evidence on the 'Double Dividend Hypothesis' in Europe." *Journal of Public Economics* 62 (1–2): 141–81.

Carrington, Damian. 2009. "China Makes Its First Commitment to Climate Change Targets." *theguardian.com*, September 22. http://www.guardian.co.uk/environment/2009/sep/22/hu-jintao-new-york1.

CBS/AP. 2009. "U.S. Takes Over Ailing Mortgage Lenders." CBSNews.com Money Watch, February 11. http://www.cbsnews.com/2100-500395_162-4423279.html.

CEO Talking Points. 2008. Records obtained by Judicial Watch, Inc. http://www.judicialwatch.org/files/documents/2009/Treasury-CEO-TalkingPoints.pdf.

Chaloupka, Frank J., Melanie Wakefield, and Christina Czart. 2001. "Taxing Tobacco: The Impact of Tobacco Taxes on Cigarette Smoking and Other Tobacco Use."

In *Regulating Tobacco*, edited by Robert L. Rabin and Stephen D. Sugarman, pp. 39–71. Oxford: Oxford University Press.

Chamberlain, Andrew. 2009. "Who Benefits from Free Emission Allowances? An Economic Analysis of the Waxman-Markey Cap-and-Trade Program." Chamberlain Economics Policy Study No. 2009-007, Chamberlain Economics, Seattle, WA. http://www.instituteforenergyresearch.org/pdf/FINAL%20Waxman-Markey%20 Study%2009-28-2009.pdf.

Christainsen, Gregory, and Robert Haveman. 1981. "Public Regulations and the Slowdown in Productivity Growth." *American Economic Review* 71 (2): 320–25.

———. 1984. "The Reagan Administration's Regulatory Relief Effort: A Mid-Term Assessment." In *The Reagan Regulatory Strategy: An Assessment*, edited by George C. Eads and Michael Fix, pp. 49–80. Washington, D.C.: Urban Institute.

Clinton, William J. 1995. "Remarks on the National Homeownership Strategy." American Presidency Project, June 5. Online by Gerhard Peters and John T. Woolley, *The American Presidency Project*. http://www.presidency.ucsb.edu/ws/?pid=51448.

Cohan, William D. 2009. *House of Cards*. New York: Doubleday.

Congressional Budget Office. 2011. "Report on the Troubled Asset Relief Program—March 2011." Congressional Budget Office, Washington, D.C., March 29. http://www.cbo.gov/ftpdocs/121xx/doc12118/03-29-TARP.pdf.

Conway-Smith, Erin. 2011. "China Is Surprise Good Guy at Durban Climate Conference." *Global Post*, December 6. http://www.globalpost.com/dispatch/news/ regions/africa/south-africa/111205/china-surprise-good-guy-at-durban-climate-conference.

Crews, Clyde Wayne. 2012. *Ten Thousand Commandments*. Washington: Competitive Enterprise Institute.

Dash, Eric, and Julie Creswell. 2011. "Too Big to Fail, or Too Trifling for Oversight?" *New York Times*, June 12, p. A1.

Dawkins, Richard. 1976. *The Selfish Gene*. New York: Oxford University Press.

Denison, Edward. 1979. *Accounting for Slower Economic Growth*. Washington, D.C.: Brookings Institution.

Diamond, Douglas, and Raghuram Rajan. 2009. "The Credit Crisis: Conjectures about Causes and Remedies." *American Economic Review* 99 (2): 606–10.

Dooren, Jennifer Corbett. 2012. "Court Strikes Graphic Labels." *Wall Street Journal*, August 25–26, pp. B1–B2.

Driscoll, Julie. 2011. Occupy Wall Street: "It doesn't matter what you are protesting . . . just protest." *Politics Anonymous*, October 3. http://politicsanonymous.com/?p=4164.

"Drug Deals: Big Pharma, White House Unlikely Partners." 2009. *Houston Chronicle*, August 12. http://www.chron.com/opinion/editorials/article/Drug-deals-Big-pharma-White-House-unlikely-1617119.php.

Drum, Kevin. 2012. "Ethanol Subsidies: Not Gone, Just Hidden a Little Better." *Mother Jones*, January 5. http://www.motherjones.com/kevin-drum/2012/01/ethanol-subsidies-not-gone-just-hidden-little-better.

Dudley, Susan, and Melinda Warren. 2011. "Fiscal Stalemate Reflected in Regulators' Budget: An Analysis of the U.S. Budget for Fiscal Years 2011 and 2012." Washington, D.C.: Regulatory Studies Program, George Washington University, and St. Louis, MO: Weidenbaum Center, Washington University in St. Louis. http://wc.wustl.edu/files/wc/imce/2012regreport.pdf.

———. 2012. "Growth in Regulators' Budget Slowed by Fiscal Stalemate: An Analysis of the U.S. Budget for Fiscal Years 2012 and 2013." Washington, D.C.: Regulatory Studies Program, George Washington University, and St. Louis, MO: Weidenbaum Center, Washington University in St. Louis. http://wc.wustl.edu/files/wc/imce/2013regreport.pdf.

Duggan, Juanita, President, Wine and Spirits Wholesalers of America, Inc. 2003. Testimony before the Subcommittee on Commerce, Trade, and Consumer Protection of the House Committee on Energy and Commerce. *E-Commerce: The Case of Online Wine Sales and Direct Shipment.* 108th Congress, 1st session, October 30. http://www.gpo.gov/fdsys/pkg/CHRG-108hhrg90726/html/CHRG-108hhrg90726.htm.

Eads, George C., and Michael Fix. 1984. *The Reagan Regulatory Strategy: An Assessment.* Washington, D.C.: Urban Institute.

Economic Report of the President, Transmitted to the Congress January 1965. 1965. Washington, D.C.: Government Printing Office.

Economic Report of the President, Transmitted to the Congress January 1966. 1966. Washington, D.C.: Government Printing Office.

Economic Report of the President, Transmitted to the Congress January 1978. 1978. Washington, D.C.: Government Printing Office.

Economic Report of the President, Transmitted to the Congress January 1981. 1981. Washington, D.C.: Government Printing Office.

Economic Report of the President, Transmitted to the Congress January 1989. 1989. Washington, D.C.: Government Printing Office.

Economic Report of the President, Transmitted to the Congress February 1990. 1990. Washington, D.C.: Government Printing Office.

Economic Report of the President, Transmitted to the Congress February 1992. 1992. Washington, D.C.: Government Printing Office.

Economic Report of the President, Transmitted to the Congress January 1993. 1993. Washington, D.C.: Government Printing Office.

Economic Report of the President, Transmitted to the Congress February 2002. 2002. Washington, D.C.: Government Printing Office.

Economic Report of the President, Transmitted to the Congress February 2003. 2003. Washington, D.C.: Government Printing Office.

EPA (U.S. Environmental Protection Agency). 1992. *Respiratory Health Effects of Passive Smoking: Lung Cancer and Other Disorders.* Washington, D.C.: Environmental Protection Agency.

————. 2009. EPA: "Greenhouse Gases Threaten Public Health and the Environment." News Releases issued by the Office of Air and Radiation, December 7. http://yosemite.epa.gov/opa/admpress.nsf/7ebdf4d0b217978b852573590040443a/08d11a451131bca585257685005bf252!OpenDocument.

"EU's De Palacio Says Nuclear Needed for Kyoto Targets." 1999. Reuters News Service, October 15. http://www.planetark.org/dailynewstory.cfm?newsid=10679.

Fahlenbrach, Rudiger, and Rene Stulz. 2011. "Bank CEO Incentives and the Credit Crisis." *Journal of Financial Economics* 99 (1): 11–26.

"Farm-State Senators Skeptical of Climate Plan." 1998. Reuters. http://www.yahoo.com.

FDA (U.S. Food and Drug Administration). 2011. Cigarette Health Warnings. U.S. Department of Health and Human Services website. http://www.fda.gov/TobaccoProducts/Labeling/ Labeling/CigaretteWarningLabels/default.htm.

FDIC (Federal Deposit Insurance Corporation). 2008. "Emergency Economic Stabilization Act of 2008 Temporarily Increases Basic FDIC Insurance Coverage from $100,000 to $250,000 Per Depositor." News Release, October 7. http://www.fdic.gov/news/news/press/2008/pr08093.html.

Federal Reserve. 2008a. News Release, September 16. http://www.federalreserve.gov/newsevents/press/other/20080916a.htm.

————. 2008b. News Release, October 8. http://www.federalreserve.gov/newsevents/press/other/20081008a.htm.

Felton, John R., and Dale G. Anderson. 1989. *Regulation and Deregulation of the Motor Carrier Industry.* Ames: Iowa State University.

Ferriter, Sarah. 2005. "Russian Ratification of Kyoto Could Spark Large-Scale Renewable Energy Development. Climate Institute." Climate Institute, Washington, D.C. http://www.climate.org/topics/international-action/russian-ratification-kyoto.html.

Fox News. 2009. "Strange Bedfellows? Industry Groups Join in Effort to Push Health Care Reform." FoxNews.com, August 12. http://www.foxnews.com/politics/2009/08/12/strange-bedfellows-industry-groups-join-effort-push-health-care-reform/.

Frauenfelder, Mark. 2010. "'Keep Pot Illegal!' Say Humboldt Dope Farmers." *Boing-Boing*, April 9. http://www.boingboing.net/2010/04/09/keep-pot-illegal-say.html.

Freedman, Alix, and John Emshwiller. 1999. "Vintage System: Big Liquor Wholesaler Finds Change Stalking Its Very Private World; Southern Wine & Spirits Is a Mandated Middleman under Increasing Attack; A Vineyard Breaks the Mold. *Wall Street Journal*, October 4, p. A1.

Freedman, Allan. 1997. "Senate Sends Signal to Clinton on Global Warming Treaty." *Congressional Quarterly* 28 (July 26): 4.

Fritschler, A. Lee. 1969. *Smoking and Politics: Policymaking and the Federal Bureaucracy.* New York: Appleton-Century-Crofts.

FTC (Federal Trade Commission). 1964. "Unfair or Deceptive Advertising and Labeling of Cigarettes in Relation to the Health Hazards of Smoking." 29 *Federal Register* 8324–8375, July 2.

———. 1969. "Cigarettes in Relation to the Health Hazards of Smoking: Unfair and Deceptive Advertising and Labeling." 34 *Federal Register* 7917–18.

Gallup. 2010. Healthcare System poll. Gallup.com, June 8. http://www.gallup.com/poll/4708/Healthcare-System.aspx.

Gascoigne, Bamber. 2001, ongoing. "History of Loathsome Custom." *HistoryWorld.* http://www.historyworld.net/wrldhis/PlainTextHistories.asp?historyid=331.

Goldenberg, Suzanne, and Allegra Stratton. 2009. "Barack Obama's Speech Disappoints and Fuels Frustration at Copenhagen." *theguardian.com*, December 18. http://www.theguardian.com/environment/2009/dec/18/obama-speech-copenhagen.

Goldman, Julianna, and Ian Katz. 2010. "Obama Doesn't 'Begrudge' Bonuses for Blankfein, Dimon (Update 1)." *Bloomberg*, February 10. http://www.bloomberg.com/apps/news?pid=newsarchive&sid=aKGZkktzkAlA&pos=1.

Gordon, Peter. 2012. "Just Another 'Bootleggers and Baptists' Moment." Peter Gordon's Blog, July 7. http://www.petergordonsblog.com/2012/07/just-another-bootleggers-and-baptists.html.

"Governor Signs Bill Critical of Kyoto Protocol." 1998. http://www.state.wv.us.

Graham, Michael. 2011. "Occupy Elsewhere!" *BostonHerald.com*, October 12. http://www.bostonherald.com/new/opinion/op_ed/view.bg?articleid=1372685&srvc=rss.

Gray, Louise, and Rowena Mason. 2009. "Copenhagen Climate Conference: Hillary Clinton Attempts to Break Deadlock with $100bn Offer." *The* (London) *Telegraph*, December 17. http://www.telegraph.co.uk/earth/copenhagen-climate-change-confe/6833072/Copenhagen-climate-conference-Hillary-Clinton-attempts-to-break-deadlock-with-100bn-offer.html.

Green, Kenneth P., Steven F. Hayward, and Kevin A. Hassett. 2007. "Climate Change: Caps vs. Taxes." Environmental Policy Outlook no. 2, American Enterprise Institute, Washington, D.C., June 1. http://www.aei.org/outlook/26286.

Greenfieldboyce, Nell. 2011. "Indie Truckers: Keep Big Brother out of My Cab." *NPR*, April 20. http://m.npr.org/story/135507979.

Grossman, Gene, and Alan B. Krueger. 1991. "Environmental Impacts of a North American Free Trade Agreement." NBER Working Paper 3914, National Bureau of Economics, Cambridge, MA.

———. 1995. "Economic Growth and the Environment." *Quarterly Journal of Economics* 110 (2): 352–77.

Hall, Matthew T. 2010. "Proposition 19 Loses in California." *Signon San Diego*, November 2. http://www.signonsandiego.com/news/2010/nov/02/proposition-19-in-early-returns/.

Hall, Robert E., and Susan E. Woodward. 2008. "The Financial Crisis and Its Causes: What Is Happening and What the Government Should Do." November 29. http://sites.google.com.site/woodwardhall.

Hardin, Garrett. 1968. "The Tragedy of the Commons." *Science* 162: 1243–48.

Harvey, Fiona. 2012. "Lord Stern: Developing Countries Must Make Deeper Emissions Cuts." *The Guardian*, December 3. http://www.guardian.co.uk/environment/2012/dec/04/lord-stern-developing-countries-deeper-emissions-cuts.

Hattersley, Roy. 1999. *Blood and Fire*. New York: Doubleday.

Hayek, F. A. 1978. *Law, Legislation, and Liberty*. Vol. 1, *Rules and Order*. Chicago: University of Chicago Press.

Healy, Jack. 2012. "Voters Ease Marijuana Laws in 2 States, but Legal Questions Remain." *New York Times*, November 8, p. P15.

Hedler, Ken. 2011. "Occupy Prescott Protesters Call for More Infrastructure Investment." *Daily Courier* (Prescott, AZ), November 17. http://www.dcourier.com/main.asp?SectionID=1&SubSectionID=1&ArticleID=100176.

Henry, Mary Kay. 2011. "Why Labor Backs 'Occupy Wall Street.'" *Wall Street Journal*, October 8–9, p. A15.

Herszenhorn, David. 2010. "Obama Urges Excise Tax on High-Cost Insurance." *New York Times*, January 6. http://www.nytimes.com/2010/01/07/health/policy/07 health.html.

Hiltzik, Michael. 2011. "Occupy Wall Street Shifts from Protest to Policy Phase." *Los Angeles Times*, April 12. http://www.latimes.com/business/la-fi-hiltzik-20111012,0,114761.column.

Holly, Chris. 2001. "DOE Whacks Renewables, Efficiency Programs." *Energy Daily*, April 10.

H.R. 1424. 2008. Emergency Economic Stabilization Act of 2008. 110th Congress, October 3. http://www.govtrack.us/congress/bills/110/hr1424.

H.R. 1161. 2011. To reaffirm state-based alcohol regulation, and for other purposes. 112th Congress, 1st session, March 17. http://www.gpo.gov/fdsys/pkg/BILLS-112hr1161ih/pdf/BILLS-112hr1161ih.pdf.

HUD (U.S. Department of Housing and Urban Development). 2003. "Bush Signs American Dream Downpayment Act." HUD Archives: News Releases, HUD No. 03–140, December 16. U.S. Department of Housing and Urban Development, Washington, D.C. http://archives.hud.gov/news/2003/pr03-140.cfm.

HuffPost Politics. 2011. "Richard Cordray to Lead Consumer Protection Bureau." http://www.huffingtonpost.com/2011/07/17/richard-cordray-cfpb-elizabeth-warren_n_900967.html.

Hughes, John, and Kim Chipman. 2009. "Obama Speeds Fuel-Economy Standard, Sets Carbon Limit (Update1)." *Bloomberg*, May 19. http://www.bloomberg.com/apps/news?pid=newsarchive&sid=aKUXiuTCkyhw.

Hulse, Carl, and David M. Herszenhorn. 2009. "House Approves 90% Tax on Bonuses after Bailouts." *New York Times*, March 19, p. A1.

Hume, David. 2000. *A Treatise of Human Nature*. Oxford: Oxford University Press.

Interlaboratory Working Group on Energy-Efficient and Low-Carbon Technologies. 1997. *Scenarios of U.S. Carbon Reductions*. Washington, D.C.: Office of Energy Efficiency and Renewable Energy, U.S. Department of Energy.

Isidore, Chris. 2011. "Obama, Cantor Spar over Occupy Wall Street." *CNN Money*, October 7. http://money.cnn.com/2011/10/07/news/economy/occupy_wall_street/index.htm.

Jacobe, David. 2008. "Americans Split on AIG Bailout." *Gallup Economy*, September 19. http://www.gallup.com/poll/110494/public-split-aig-bailout.aspx.

Johnson, Kirk. 2012. "Marijuana Referendum Divides Both Sides." *New York Times*, October 14, p. A18.

Jones, Jeffrey. 2009. "AIG, Congress, Geithner Target of Bonus Backlash." *Gallup*, March 24. http://www.gallup.com/poll/117061/AIG-Congress-Geithner-Target-Bonus-Backlash.aspx.

Jones, Raymond M. 1997. *Strategic Management in a Hostile Environment: Lessons from the Tobacco Industry*. Westport, CT: Quorum Books.

Jonsson, Patrik. 2009. "Ben Nelson Backs Healthcare Reform Bill, Dems See Finish Line." *Christian Science Monitor*, December 19. http://www.csmonitor.com/USA/Politics/2009/1219/Ben-Nelson-backs-healthcare-reform-bill-Dems-see-finish-line.

Kane, Paul. 2012. "SOPA, PIPA Votes to Be Delayed in House and Senate." *Washington Post*, January 20. http://www.washingtonpost.com/blogs/2chambers/post/sopa-senate-vote-to-be-delayed-reid-announces/2012/01/20/gIQApRWVDQ_blog.html.

Kang, Cecilia. 2011. "Lawmakers Exchange Barbs in Hearing on Stop On-line Piracy Act." *Washington Post*, December 15. http://www.washingtonpost.com/business/economy/lawmakers-trade-barbs-in-hearing-on-stop-online-piracy-act/2011/12/15/gIQAqDnwwO_story.html.

Kelder, Graham. 1998. Fight the Future; or Everything You Always Wanted to Know about how the Tobacco Industry (a.k.a. the cigarette men) Killed the McCain Bill but Were Afraid to Ask. *Tobacco Control Update* 2(3-4): 5-21.

Kelder, Graham, Patricia Davidson, Alfred Gal, et al. 1997. The Proposed Tobacco Settlement. *Tobacco Control Update* 1 (304). http://www.tobaccocontrol.neu.edu/TCU/tcuo1.3,4/Contents/ settlement.html. Accessed July 6, 2011.

Kennedy, Bruce. 2010. "California's Prop 19: The First Step toward a National Marijuana Industry?" *Daily Finance*, November 2. http://www.dailyfinance.com/2010/11/02/californias-prop-19-the-first-step-towards-a-national-marijuan/.

Kirkpatrick, David. 2009. "Obama Is Taking an Active Role in Talks on Health Care Plan." *New York Times*, August 12. http://www.nytimes.com/2009/08/13/health/policy/13health.html?pagewanted=1&_r=2.

Klare, Joe. 2011. "Delaware Becomes 16th Medical Marijuana State." *420 Times,* May 25. http://the420times.com/2011/05/delaware-becomes-16th-medical-marijuana-state/.

Klein, Benjamin. 1995. "The Economics of Franchise Contracts." *Journal of Corporate Finance* 2 (1): 9–37.

Klein, Ezra. 2011. "What the CLASS Act Says about Health-Care Reform." Wonkblog, *Washington Post,* October 17. http://www.washingtonpost.com/blogs/ezra-klein/post/what-the-class-act-says-about-health-care-reform/2011/08/25/gIQA8cL0rL_blog.html.

Klein, Peter. 2011. "Bootlegger-and-Baptist Alert." The Beacon: The Blog of the Independent Institute, April 20. http://blog.independent.org/2011/04/20/bootlegger-and-baptist-alert-2/.

Klein, Philip. 2010. "Toomey Leads Specter, Obamacare Remains Unpopular in Pennsylvania." The Spectacle Blog, *American Spectator,* April 8. http://spectator.org/blog/2010/04/08/toomey-leads-specter-obamacare.

Kliff, Sarah. 2013. "White House Delays Employer Mandate Requirement until 2015." Wonkblog, *Washington Post,* July 2. http://www.washingtonpost.com/blogs/wonkblog/wp/2013/07/02/white-house-delays-employer-mandate-requirement-until-2015/.

Kluger, Richard. 1996. *Ashes to Ashes: America's Hundred-Year Cigarette War, the Public Health, and the Unabashed Triumph of Philip Morris.* New York: Alfred A. Knopf.

Kopytoff, Verne G. 2011. "Amazon Pressured on Sales Tax." *New York Times,* March 14.

Kozlowski, Lynn T., and Richard J. O'Connor. 2004. "Dealing with Health Fears: Cigarette Advertising in the United States in the Twentieth Century." In *Tobacco: Science, Policy and Public Health,* edited by Peter Boyle, Nigel Gray, Jack Henningfield, et al., pp. 37–50. Oxford: Oxford University Press.

Krauss, Clifford, and Kate Galbraith. 2009. "Climate Bill Splits Exelon and U.S. Chamber." *New York Times,* September 28. http://www.nytimes.com/2009/09/29/business/energy-environment/29chamber.html.

Labaton, Steven. 2009. "Treasury to Set Executives' Pay at 7 Ailing Firms." *New York Times,* June 11, p. A1.

Lallanilla, Mark. 2011. "Occupy Wall Street: An Environmental Protest?" *About.com,* October 8. http://greenlivingabout.com/od/greenprograms/a/Occupy-Wall-Street-Environemental-Protest.htm.

Lavelle, Marianne. 2001. "A Shift in the Wind on Global Warming." *U.S. News & World Report,* March 19, p. 38.

Leonnig, Carol. 2008. "How HUD Mortgage Policy Fed the Crisis." *Washington Post*, June 10.

Lipford, Jody, and Bruce Yandle. 2009. "Not the Time for Cap and Trade." *Regulation*, Winter 2010.

Lipford, Jody, and Bruce Yandle. 2010. "Environmental Kuznets Curves, Carbon Emissions, and Public Choice." *Environment and Development Economics* 15 (4): 417–38.

Llanos, Miguel. 2011. "$6 Billion-a-Year Subsidy Dies—but Wait There's More." U.S. News on MSNBC.com, December 29. http://usnews.msnbc.msn.com_news/ 2011/12/29/9804028-6-billion-a-year-ethanol-dies-but-wait-there's-more?lite.

"Look Who's Trying to Turn Green." 1998. *Time*, November 9, p. 30.

Magada, Dominique. 1998. "Focus: Shell Revamps Image." Reuters, April 21. http:// www.infoseek.com.

Maltby, Emily, and Angus Loten. 2011. "Tale of Two Loan Programs." *Wall Street Journal*, October 6, pp. C1–C2.

Mamudi, Sam. 2008. "Lehman Folds with Record $613 Billion Debt." Marketwatch. com, *Wall Street Journal*, September 15. http://www.marketwatch.com/story/leh-man-folds-with-record-613-billion-debt.

Manheim, Frank. 2009. *The Conflict over Environmental Regulation in the United States*. New York: Springer.

Manne, Allan S., and Richard G. Richels. 1991. "Global CO2 Emission Reductions: The Impacts of Rising Energy Costs." *Energy Journal* 12 (1): 87–107.

Marcus, Kim. 2005. "Bizarre Coalition Opposes Direct Shipment of Wine." *Wine Spectator*, February 14. http://www.winespectator.com/webfeature/show/id/Bizarre-Coalition-Opposes-Direct-Shipment-of-Wine_2398.

Martosko, David. 2012. "Sierra Club Took $26 Million from Natural Gas Lobby to Battle Coal Industry." *Daily Caller*, February 4. http://dailycaller.com/2012/02/04/ sierra-club-took-26-million-from-natural-gas-lobby-to-battle-coal-industry.

Marvel, Howard P. 1977. "Factory Regulation: A Reinterpretation of Early English Experience." *Journal of Law & Economics* 20 (2): 379–402.

McChesney, Fred S. 1987. "Rent Extraction and Rent Creation in the Economic Theory of Regulation." *Journal of Legal Studies* 16 (1): 101–18.

McDonough, John. 2011. *Inside National Health Reform*. Berkeley and Los Angeles: University of California Press.

McGee, James, and Andrew Frye. 2009. "Lincoln Takes TARP; Prudential Declines Aid: Timeline (Update1)." *Bloomberg*, June 17. http://www.bloomberg.com/apps/ne ws?pid=20601208&sid=attbD0r7Nr70.

McGrew, Jane Lang. 1972. "History of Tobacco Regulation." In National Commission on Marihuana and Drug Abuse, *Marihuana: A Signal of Misunderstanding: Appendix*. Vol. I, pp. 513–30. Washington, D.C.: Government Printing Office. http://legacy.library. ucsf.edu/tid/nhc92a00;jsessionid=B956991DBDA9546B241A445B3BABE036. tobacco03.

McKay, Betsy, and David Kesmodel. 2011. "Labels Give Cigarette Packs a Ghoulish Makeover." *Wall Street Journal*, June 22. http://online.wsj.com/article/ SB10001424052702303936 704576399320327189158.html

McKechnie, William S. 1914. *Magna Carta*. 2nd ed. New York: Burt Franklin.

Meier, Kenneth. 1994. *The Politics of Sin: Drugs, Alcohol, and Public Policy*. Armonk, NY: M.E. Sharpe.

Meiners, Roger E., and Bruce Yandle. 1999. "The Conceit of Environmental Law." *George Mason University Law Review* 7 (4): 923–63.

Melzer, Marc. 2004. "A Vintage Conflict Uncorked: The 21st Amendment, the Commerce Clause, and the Fully-Ripened Fight over Interstate Wine and Liquor Sales." *University of Pennsylvania Journal of Constitutional Law* 7: 279–309.

Micklethwait, John, and Adrian Wooldridge. 2009. *God Is Back*. New York: Penguin Press.

Mills, Karen. 2010. "Small Business Jobs Bill: No 'Itty Bitty' Thing." The White House Blog, September 3. http://www.whitehouse.gov/blog/2010/09/03/small-business-jobs-bill-no-itty-bitty-thing.

Miron, Jeffrey. 2005. *The Budgetary Implications of Marijuana Prohibition*. Washington, D.C.: Marijuana Policy Project. http://www.prohibitioncosts.org/mironreport.html.

Mollenkamp, Carrick, Joseph Karl Menn, Adam Levy, and Joseph Menn. 1998. *The People vs. Big Tobacco*. Princeton, NJ: Bloomberg Press.

Montanye, James A. 2011. "Property Rights and the Limits of Religious Liberty." *The Independent Review* 16 (1): 27–52.

Morales, Lymari. 2009. Outraged Americans Want AIG Bonus Money Recovered. *Gallup*, March 18. http://www.gallup.com/poll/116941/Outraged-Americans-AIG-Bonus-Money-Recovered.aspx.

Morath, Eric, and Jeffrey A. Fowler. 2012. "Congress Tosses Antipiracy Act." *Wall Street Journal*, January 21. http://online.wsj.com/article/SB10001424052970204301404577172703397383034.html.

Morford, Stacy. 2009. "US Declares Greenhouse Gases a Danger to Public Health and Welfare." *InsideClimate News*, December 7. http://insideclimatenews.org/news/20091207/us-declares-greenhouse-gases-danger-public-health-and-welfare.

Morgan, Dan. 2002. "Enron Also Courted Democrats." *Washington Post*, January 13, p. 1. http://www.washingtonpost.com/ac2/wp-dyn?pagename=article&node=&contentId=A37287-2002Jan12&notFound=true.

Morriss, Andrew P., Bruce Yandle, and Andrew Dorchak. 2009. *Regulation by Litigation*. New Haven: Yale University Press.

Moyers, Bill. 2012. "David Stockman on Crony Capitalism." *Moyers & Company*, March 9. Public Affairs Television Inc. http://billmoyers.com/segment/david-stockman-on-crony-capitalism.

Murphy, Kevin M., Andrei Schleifer, and Robert W. Vichny. 2003. "Why Is Rent Seeking So Costly to Growth?" *American Economic Review* 83 (2): 409–14.

Nasar, Silvia. 2011. *Grand Pursuit*. New York: Simon & Schuster.

National Biodiesel Board. 1998. "Agricultural Products Are Key to National Energy Security." February 24. http://biz.yahoo.com.

National Corn Growers Association. 1998. http://www.ncga.com.

Neff, Lisa, and Marcus Wohlson. 2010. "Proposition 19 Supporters Vow to Push Legalization in 2012." Huffpost Politics, November 3. http://www.huffingtonpost.com/2010/11/03/prop-19-results-marijuana_n_778050.html.

Nelson, Jon P. 2004. "Advertising Bans in the United States." In *EH.Net Encyclopedia*, edited by Robert Whaples, May 2. http://eh.net/encyclopedia/?article=Nelson.AdBans.

Nelson, Phillip J., and Kenneth Greene. 2003. *Signaling Goodness: Social Rules and Public Choice*. Ann Arbor: University of Michigan Press.

Nelson, Robert H. 2010. *The New Holy Wars: Economic Religion vs. Environmental Religion in Contemporary America*. Oakland, CA: The Independent Institute.

New York Times. 2009. "Obama's Statement on A.I.G." The Caucus blog, March 16. http://thecaucus.blogs.nytimes.com/2009/03/16/obamas-statement-on-aig/.

Newport, Frank. 2008a. "Americans Favor Congressional Action on Crisis." *Gallup Economy*, September 26. http://www.gallup.com/poll/110746/Americans-Favor-Congressional-Action-Crisis.aspx.

———. 2008b. "Americans Blame Car Company Execs for U.S. Auto Crisis." *Gallup Economy*, December 9. http://www.gallup.com/poll/112999/Americans-Blame-Car-Company-Execs-US-Auto-Crisis.aspx.

———. 2009a. "Americans on Healthcare Reform: Top 10 Takeaways." *Gallup Politics*, July 13. http://www.gallup.com/poll/121997/Americans-Healthcare-Reform-Top-Takeaways.aspx.

———. 2009b. "Americans Want Details before Release of More TARP Funds." *Gallup*, January 15. http://www.gallup.com/poll/113788/Americans-Want-Details-Before-Release-More-TARP-Funds.aspx.

———. 2009c. "More in U.S. Say Health Coverage Is Not Gov't. Responsibility." Gallup.com, November 13. http://www.gallup.com/poll/124253/Say-Health-Coverage-Not-Gov-Responsibility.aspx.

Noonan, Peggy. 2010. "Now for the Slaughter." *Wall Street Journal*, March 20. http://online.wsj.com/article/SB10001424052748704207504575130081383279888.html?KEYWORDS=noonan.

"Now What?" 2010. *The Economist*. March 25.

Nowak, Martin A. 2011. *Super Cooperators*. New York: Free Press.

Obama, Barack. 2009. "Remarks of President Barack Obama—As Prepared for Delivery, Address to Joint Session of Congress, Tuesday, February 24, 2009." White House, Briefing Room, Speeches and Remarks. http://www.whitehouse.gov/the_press_office/Remarks-of-President-Barack-Obama-Address-to-Joint-Session-of-Congress.

———. 2010. "Remarks by the President at the Signing of the Small Business Jobs Act." White House, Office of the Press Secretary, September 27. http://www.whitehouse.gov/the-press-office/2010/09/27/remarks-president-signing-small-business-jobs-act.

"Obama Health Reform Drive Gets Diverse Backing." 2009. Reuters, January 8. http://www.reuters.com/article/2009/01/08/us-usa-obama-healthcare-groups-s-idUSTRE50766N20090108.

"ObamaCare's Secret History." 2012. *Wall Street Journal*, June 11. http://online.wsj.com/article/SB10001424052702303883020457744647001584382.html.

"Obama's Health Care Address to Congress." 2009. *New York Times*, September 10. http://www.nytimes.com/interactive/2009/09/10/us/politics/20090910-obama-health.html.

O'Brien, Thomas C. 2000. "Constitutional and Antitrust Violations of the Multistate Tobacco Settlement." *Cato Institute Policy Analysis* no. 317, May 18.

O'Connor, John. 2011. "South Carolina Baptists Oppose Amazon Tax Break." *State* (Columbia, SC), April 22. http://222.thestate.com/2011/04/22/1788340/baptists-target-proposed-amazon.html.

Odell, Ann. 2007. "Top CEOs Address Climate Change." *ClimateBiz*, February 6. http://www.greenbiz.com/news/2007/02/06/top-ceos-address-climate-change.

OECD (Organisation for Economic Co-operation and Development). 2012. "OECD Health Data 2012: How Does the United States Compare?" http://organicconnect-mag.com/wp/wp-content/uploads/2013/05/BriefingNoteUSA2012.pdf.

Officer, Lawrence H., and Samuel H. Williamson. 2011. "Annualized Growth Rate and Graphics of Various Historical Economic Series." Measuring Worth. http://www.measuringworth.com/growth/.

Okrent, Daniel. 2011. *Last Call: The Rise and Fall of Prohibition*. New York: Scribner.

Olson, Mancur. 1982. *The Rise and Decline of Nations: Economic Growth, Stagflation, and Social Rigidities*. New Haven: Yale University Press.

OMB (Office of Management and Budget). 2010. *Fiscal Year 2012 Historical Tables, Budget of the United States*. Washington, D.C.: Government Printing Office. http://www.whitehouse.gov/sites/default/files/omb/budget/fy2012/assets/hist.pdf.

Orey, Michael. 1999. *Assuming the Risk: The Mavericks, the Lawyers, and the Whistleblowers Who Beat Big Tobacco*. Boston: Little, Brown & Company.

Paletta, Damian, and David Enrich. 2009. "Political Interference Seen in Bank Bailout Decisions." *Wall Street Journal*, January 22, p. A1.

Paletta, Damian, and Deborah Solomon. 2009. "Financial Firms to Cut Cost of TARP Exit." *Wall Street Journal*, April 22, p. A2.

Parker-Pope, Tara. 2001. *Cigarettes: Anatomy of an Industry from Seed to Smoke*. New York: New Press.

"Pass the Bill." 2010. *The Economist*, March 18.

Paulson, Henry, Jr. 2010. *On the Brink*. New York: Business Plus.

Pepitone, Julianne. 2011. "Thousands of Protesters to 'Occupy Wall Street' on Saturday." *CNNMoney*, September 16. http://money.cnn.com/2011/09/16/technology/occupy_wall_street/index.htm.

Pershing, Jonathan. 2005. "The Climate of a Post-Kyoto World." News, World Resources Institute, Washington, D.C., March 28. http://www.wri.org/stories/2005/03/the-climate-a-post-kyoto-world.

Phillips, Kate. 2009. "Frank Joins Chorus on A.I.G. Bonus Outrage." The Caucus blog, *New York Times*, March 16. http://thecaucus.blogs.nytimes.com/2009/03/16/rep-frank-joins-chorus-on-aig-bonus-outrage/?dbk.

Pianin, Eric. 1998. "Gingrich Halts Move to End Ethanol Subsidy." *Greenville News,* May 7, p. 6D.

Pickert, Kate. 2009a. "Forcing Insurers to Spend Enough on Health Care." *Time,* December 22. http://www.time.com/time/nation/article/0,8599,1949390,00.html.

———. 2009b. "How Valid Is the Insurers' Attack on Health Reform?" *Time,* October 13. http://www.time.com/time/politics/article/0,8599,1929930,00.html.

———. 2009c. "What Insurers Are Trying to Get Out of Health Reform." *Time,* August 6. http://www.time.com/time/world/article/0,8599,1914876,00.html.

Pigou, Arthur C. 1920. *Economics of Welfare.* London: Macmillan and Company.

———. (1932) 2009. *Economics of Welfare.* Brunswick, NJ: Transaction Publishers.

Pilkington, Ed. 2009. "A Great Step Forward: Obama's Verdict on Climate Change Pact." (Manchester) *Guardian,* December 20. http://www.guardian.co.uk/environment/2009/dec/20/copenhagen-summit-pact-obama-verdict.

Podesta, John, Andrew L. Stern, and Mike Duke. 2009. Letter to President Barack Obama, dated June 30. http://online.wsj.com/public/resources/documents/walmart_letter_063009t.pdf.

Posner, Richard A. *A Failure of Capitalism.* 2009. Cambridge, MA: Harvard University Press.

Power, Stephen. 2009. "Climate Bill Splits Industry Coalition." *Wall Street Journal,* July 12. http://online.wsj.com/article/SB124744273187130105.html.

Pringle, Peter. 1998. *Cornered: Big Tobacco at the Bar of Justice.* New York: Henry Holt.

Ridley, Matt. 1997. *The Origins of Virtue.* New York: Penguin Books.

Robert, Joseph C. 1967. *The History of Tobacco in America.* Chapel Hill: University of North Carolina Press.

Roemer, Ruth. 2004. "A Brief History of Legislation to Control the Tobacco Epidemic." In *Tobacco: Science, Policy and Public Health,* edited by Peter Boyle, Nigel Gray, Jack Henningfield, et al., pp. 677–94. Oxford: Oxford University Press.

Rose, David C. 2011. *The Moral Foundation of Economic Behavior.* New York: Oxford University Press.

Rubin, Paul H. 2002. *Darwinian Politics.* New Brunswick, NJ: Rutgers University Press.

Rush, George. 2010. "Head of American Federation of Teachers Randi Weingarten Supports Legalizing Pot." *NYDailyNews.com,* April 11. http://articles.nydailynews.com/2010-04-11/local/27061377_1_marijuana-pot-smoking-drug-free-america.

Saad, Lydia. 2009a. "Cost Is Foremost Healthcare Issue for Americans." *Gallup Politics*, September 23. http://www.gallup.com/poll/123149/Cost-Is-Foremost-Health-care-Issue-for-Americans.aspx.

———. 2009b. "Labor Unions See Sharp Slide in U.S. Public Support." *Gallup*, September 3. http://www.gallup.com/poll/122744/Labor-Unions-Sharp-Slide-Public-Support.aspx.

———. 2010. "One Week Later, Americans Divided on Healthcare." *Gallup Politics*, March 29. http://www.gallup.com/poll/127025/One-Week-Later-Americans-Divided-Healthcare.aspx.

Salisbury, Laney. 1998a. "Anti-Kyoto Group Disappointed by Shell Pullout." Infoseek: The News Channel. http://www.infoseek.com.

———. 1998b. "Enron Exec Wants Clean Energy Tax Break." Reuters, February 26.

Salop, Steven C., and David T. Scheffman. 1983. "Raising Rivals' Costs." *American Economic Review* 73 (2): 267–71.

Salvation Army, The. 2011. International Heritage Centre. http://www.salvationarmy.org.uk/uki/aboutus.

———. 2013. "History of The Salvation Army." http://www.salvationarmyusa.org/usn/www_usn_2.nsf/0/816DE20E46B88B2685257435005070FA?Opendocument.

Schatz, Amy. 2012. "What Is SOPA Anyway? A Guide to Understanding the Online Piracy Act." *Wall Street Journal*, January 18. http://online.wsj.com/article/SB10001424052970203735304577167261853938938.html.

Shatto, John, and M. Kent Clemens. 2011. Memo dated May 13 on Projected Medicare Expenditures under an Illustrative Scenario with Alternative Payment Updates to Medicare Providers. Office of the Actuary, Centers for Medicare & Medicaid Services, Department of Health & Human Services. https://www.cms.gov/Reports-TrustFunds/Downloads/2011TRAlternativeScenario.pdf.

"Shell agm: FOE Urges Huge Increase in Green Energy Investment." 1998. May 8. http://www.foe.co.uk/resources/press_releases/0508shel.html.

Shlaes, Amity. 2007. *The Forgotten Man*. New York: Harper.

Siddique, Haroon. 2010. "US Senate Drops Bill to Cap Carbon Emissions." *theguardian.com*, July 23. http://www.guardian.co.uk/environment/2010/jul/23/us-senate-climate-change-bill.

Sidel, Robin. 2009. "Profit Solid, J.P. Morgan Aims to Repay TARP Funds." *Wall Street Journal*, April 17, p. C1.

Simmons, Randy T., Ryan M. Yonk, and Diana W. Thomas. 2011. "Bootleggers, Baptists, and Political Entrepreneurs." *The Independent Review* 3 (15): 367–81.

Smith, Aaron. 2010. "Soros Banks Prop 19 for Marijuana Legalization." *CNNMoney*, October 26. http://money.cnn.com/2010/10/26/news/economy/soros_marijuana/index.htm.

Smith, Adam. (1759) 1982. *The Theory of Moral Sentiments,* edited by. D. D. Raphael and A. L. Macfie. Vol. 1 of *The Glasgow Edition of the Works and Correspondence of Adam Smith.* Indianapolis: Liberty Fund.

———. (1776) 1827. *An Inquiry into the Nature and Causes of the Wealth of Nations.* Edinburgh: University Press.

Smith, Adam C., Richard E. Wagner, and Bruce Yandle. 2011. "A Theory of Entangled Political Economy with Application to TARP and NRA." *Public Choice* 148 (1–2): 45–66.

Smith, Morgan. 2002. "Alcohol Distribution Laws Bottle Up Options for Consumers and Retailers." Georgia Public Policy Foundation, posted October 16, p. 8. http://www.georgiapolicy.org/alcohol-distribution-laws-bottle-up-options-for-consumers-and-retailers/.

Smith, Vernon. 1998. "The Two Faces of Adam Smith." *Southern Economic Journal* 65 (1): 1–19.

Solomon, Deborah. 2011. "Consumer Job Remains Vacant." *Wall Street Journal*, April 13. http://online.wsj.com/article/SB10001424052748704336504576258770479635708.html?KEYWORDS=advocate+consumer+protection.

Solomon, Deborah, and Aaron Lucchetti. 2009. "Feinberg to Review Pay at Bailed-Out Firms." *Wall Street Journal*, March 23. http://online.wsj.com/article/SB10001424052748704841304575137784246308728.html?KEYWORDS=kenneth+feinberg.

Solomon, Deborah, and Mark Maremont. 2009. "Bankers Face Strict New Pay Cap." *Wall Street Journal*, February 14, p. A1.

Solomon, Lawrence. 2009. "Enron's Other Secret." FP Comment (blog), May 30. http://network.nationalpost.com/np/blogs/fpcomment/archive/2009/05/30/lawrence-solomon-enron-s-other-secret.aspx.

Sowell, Thomas. 2009. *The Housing Boom and Bust.* New York: Basic Books.

Sparber, Peter G., and Peter E. O'Rourke. 1998. *Understanding the Kyoto Protocol.* Washington, D.C.: National Legal Center for the Public Interest.

Sparshott, Jeffrey. 2013. "Lenders Used Aid to Repay TARP." *Wall Street Journal*, April 10, p. C1.

Stolberg, Sheryl Gay. 2009. "'Public Option' in Health Plan May Be Dropped." *New York Times*, August 17. http://www.nytimes.com/2009/08/18/health/policy/18talkshows.html?_r=3&pagewanted=all.

Stone, Daniel. 2009. "Grading Obama's Copenhagen Speech." *Newsweek/The Daily Beast*, December 18. http://www.thedailybeast.com/newsweek/blogs/the-gaggle/2009/12/18/grading-obama-s-copenhagen-speech.html.

Strassel, Kimberley. 2010. "Inside the Pelosi Sausage Factory." *Wall Street Journal*, March 21. http://online.wsj.com/article/SB10001424052748703775504575136133814210008.html?KEYWORDS=inside+the+pelosi.

Strauss, Gary. 2011. "Graphic Cigarette Labels, Will They Work?" *USA Today*, June 22. http://yourlife.usatoday.com/health/story/2011/06/FDA-issues-graphic-cigarette-labels/48676990/1.

Sustainable Energy Coalition. 2001. "Bush Budget Plan Turns Its Back on a Sensible Energy Policy." News Release, April 9. http://www.sustainablenergy.org/press/coalition_pr/budget_request.htm.

Swindler, William F. 1965. *Magna Carta; Legend and Legacy*. Indianapolis: Bobbs-Merrill.

Thompson, Faith. 1948. *Magna Carta*. Minneapolis: University of Minnesota Press.

Thornton, Mark. 2007. *The Economics of Prohibition*. Auburn, AL: Ludwig von Mises Institute.

Till, Dustin. 2008. "EPA Faces Rulemaking Petitions and Litigation As Greenhouse Gas Endangerment Decision Nears." Marten Law, February 27. http://www.marten-law.com/newsletter/20080227-ghg-endangerment.

Tocqueville, Alexis de. (1848) 1990. *Democracy in America*. Vol. 1. New York: Vintage.

Treasury Department. 2008a. "TARP Capital Purchase Program: Senior Preferred Stock and Warrants." http://www.treasury.gov/press-center/press-releases/Documents/document5hp1207.pdf.

———. 2008b. "Treasury to Invest in AIG Restructuring Under the Emergency Economic Stabilization Act." Press Center, November 10. http://www.treasury.gov/press-center/press-releases/Pages/hp1261.aspx.

———. 2009. U.S. Treasury Department, Office of Financial Stability, Troubled Asset Relief Program, Transactions Report for Period Ending August 14, 2009. http://www.treasury.gov/initiatives/financial-stability/briefing-room/reports/tarp-transactions/DocumentsTARPTransactions/transactions-report_08182009.pdf.

Troyer, Ronald J., and Gerald E. Markle. 1983. *Cigarettes: The Battle over Smoking*. New Brunswick, NJ: Rutgers University Press.

Tullock, Gordon. 1967. The Welfare Costs of Tariffs, Monopoly, and Theft. *Western Economic Journal* 5(3): 224–32.

Tullock, Gordon. 1975. The Transitional Gains Trap. *Bell Journal of Economics* 6 (2): 671-78.

UN (United Nations). 1997. Kyoto Protocol to the United Nations Framework Convention on Climate Change. http://unfccc.int/resource/docs/convkp/kpeng.pdf.

UN Framework Convention on Climate Change. 2011. Status of Ratification of the Kyoto Protocol. http://unfccc.int/kyoto_protocol/status_of_ratification/items/2613.php.

Unfair Credit Card Fees.com. 2012. Merchants Payments Coalition. http://www.unfaircreditcardfees.com/.

Ungar, Rick. 2012. "Busted! Health Insurers Secretly Spent Huge to Defeat Health Care Reform While Pretending to Support Obamacare." *Forbes*, June 12. http://www.forbes.com/sites/rickungar/2012/06/25/busted-health-insurers-secretly-spent-huge-to-defeat-health-care-reform-while-pretending-to-support-obamacare/.

U.S. Census Bureau. 2013. Quarterly Summary of State and Local Tax Revenue. http://www.census.gov/govs/qtax/.

U.S. Department of Health, Education, and Welfare. 1964. *Smoking and Health: Report of the Advisory Committee to the Surgeon General of the Public Health Service.* Washington, D.C.: Government Printing Office.

USDA (U.S. Department of Agriculture). 1915. "Farmers' Bulletin," no. 663, June 5. Reproduced on Colorado Hemp Initiative Project, CO-HIP Library, as "1915 USDA Farmer's Bulletin: Cannabis Cultivation." http://www.levellers.org/cohip/library/usda.1915.html.

———. 2005. *Tobacco Yearbook 2005.* Electronic archive from the Economic Research Service. http://usda.mannlib.cornell.edu/MannUsda/viewStaticPage.do?url=http://usda01.library.cornell.edu/usda/ers/92015/2005/index.html.

Vaughn, Martin. 2010. "White House Recasts Bailout Funds Recovery." *Wall Street Journal*, May 5. http://online.wsj.com/article/SB10001424052748704866204575224830371640748.html?.

Verret, J. W. 2010. "The Bailout through a Public Choice Lens: Government-Controlled Corporations As a Mechanism for Rent Transfer." *Seton Hall Law Review* 40 (4): 1521–80.

Villegas, Andrew. 2010. "Conservative Target Rep. Betsy Markey on Health Law: 'I'm Proud to Have Voted for It.'" *Kaiser Health News*, April 16. http://www.kaiserhealthnews.org/Checking-In-With/betsy-markey-health-reform-vote.aspx.

Vlasic, Bill, and David Herszenhorn. 2008. "Detroit Chiefs Plead for Aid." *New York Times*, November 18, p. A1.

Volcovici, Valerie. 2012. "Court Ruling to Shift Greenhouse Gas Fight Back to Congress." Reuters, June 28. http://www.reuters.com/article/2012/06/28/us-emissions-court-idUSBRE85R0C120120628.

Wade, Nicholas. 2009. *The Faith Instinct: How Religion Evolved and Why It Endures*. New York: Penguin Books.

Wagner, Daniel. 2011. "Fannie Mae Seeks $8.5 Billion More in Federal Aid." *Newsday.com*, May 6. http://usatoday.com/money/economy.

Wagner, Richard. 2007. *Fiscal Sociology and the Theory of Public Finance: An Exploratory Essay*. New York: Edward Elgar.

Wallison, Peter J. 2008. "Cause and Effect: Government Policies and the Financial Crisis." American Enterprise Institute for Public Policy Research, Financial Services Outlook, November, Washington, D.C. AEI Online. http://www.aei.org/outlook/29015.

Walters, Joanna. 2011. "Occupy America: Protests against Wall Street and Inequality Hit 70 Cities." *The Guardian*, October 8. http://www.guardian.co.uk.world. 2011/oct/08/occupy-america-protests-financial-crisis.

Washington State Senate Committee Services. 2012. "Summary of Initiative 502 to the Legislature." http://www.leg.wa.gov/Senate/Committees/documents/Initiatives/2012/502Summary.pdf.

Wayne, Alex, and Drew Armstrong. 2011. "U.S. Won't Start Long-Term Care Insurance." *Bloomberg*, October 14. http://www.bloomberg.com/news/2011-10-14/u-s-won-t-start-class-long-term-care-insurance-sebelius-says.html.

Weisenthal, Joe. 2010. "Blanche Lincoln Made an Unpopular Vote on Healthcare, and Now She's Taking It Out on Wall Street in a Big Way." *Business Insider*, April 14. http://www.businessinsider.com/blance-lincoln-derivatives-ban-2010-4.

White, David. 2011. "Wholesaler Robbery in Liquor Sales." *New York Times*, April 4, p. A21.

White, Lawrence H. 2008. "How Did We Get into This Financial Mess?" Cato Institute Briefing Paper no. 110, November 18.

White House. 2011. "Executive Order 13563—Improving Regulation and Regulatory Review." White House, Office of the Press Secretary, Washington, D.C., January 18. http://www.whitehouse.gov/the-press-office/2011/01/18/improving-regulation-and-regulatory-review-executive-order.

———. 2012a. "Executive Order—Supporting Safe and Responsible Development of Unconventional Domestic Natural Gas Resources." White House, Office of the

Press Secretary, Washington, D.C., April 13. http://www.whitehouse.gov/the-press-office/2012/04/13/executive-order-supporting-safe-and-responsible-development-unconvention.

———. 2012b. "Statements on the President's Executive Order Supporting Safe and Responsible Development of Unconventional Domestic Natural Gas Resources." White House, Office of the Press Secretary, Washington, D.C., April 13. http://www.whitehouse.gov/the-press-office/2012/04/13/statements-president-s-executive-order-supporting-safe-and-responsible-d.

Will, George. 2009. "Bootleggers' Delights." *Newsweek/The Daily Beast*, February 13. http://www.thedailybeast.com/newsweek/2009/02/13/bootleggers-delights.html.

Wilson, Linus, and Yan Wendy Wu. 2011. "Escaping TARP." *Journal of Financial Stability* 8 (1): 32–42.

Wilted Greenery. 2011. *The Economist*. http://www.economist.com/node/21540996. Accessed September 8, 2013.

Wine Institute. 2012. State Shipping Laws for Wineries. http://wineinstitute.shipcompliant.com/Home.aspx?SaleTypeID=1.

Wiseman, Alan, and Jerry Ellig. 2007. "The Politics of Wine: Trade Barriers, Interest Groups, and the Commerce Clause." *Journal of Politics* 69 (3): 859–75.

Womach, Jasper. 2005. "Tobacco Quota Buyout." CRS Report for Congress RS22046, Congressional Research Service, Washington, D.C.

Wright, Robert. 1994. *The Moral Animal: Why We Are the Way We Are: The New Science of Evolutionary Psychology*. New York: Vintage Books.

Wutkowski, Karey, and Jonathan Stempel. 2009. "Goldman Sells Stock in 'Duty' to Repay TARP." Reuters, April 14. http://www.reuters.com/article/2009/04/14/us-goldmansachs-idUSTRE53D2Q120090414.

Yafa, Stephen. 2005. *Big Cotton*. New York: Viking Press.

Yandle, Bruce. 1983. "Bootleggers and Baptists: The Education of a Regulatory Economist." *Regulation* 7 (3): 12–16.

———. 1984. "Intertwined Interests, Rentseeking, and Regulation." *Social Science Quarterly* 65 (4): 1002–12.

———. 1999b. "Bootleggers and Baptists in Retrospect." *Regulation* 22 (3): 5–7.

———. 2009. "America's New Fuel Economy Cartel and Freedom to Choose." *Regulation* 3 (32): 6–9.

———. 2010a. "Lost Trust: The Real Reason of the Financial Meltdown." *The Independent Review* 14 (3): 341–61.

———. 2010b. "Much Ado about Pigou." *Regulation* 33 (1): 3–4.

———. 2013. "How Earth Day Triggered Environmental Rent Seeking." *The Independent Review* 1 (18): 35–47.

Yandle, Bruce, and Stuart Buck. 2002. "Bootleggers, Baptists, and the Global Warming Battle." *Harvard Environmental Law Review* 26 (1): 177–229.

Yandle, Bruce, Maya Vijayaraghavan, and Madhusudan Bhatarai. 2002. "The Environmental Kuznets Curve: A Primer." PERC Research Study RS02-1, Political Economic Research Center, Bozeman, MT.

Yost, Pete. 2012. "Court Leaves Ruling against Big Tobacco Intact." RN-T.com, *Rome News-Tribune*, July 27. http://romenews-tribune.com/view/full_story/1903104/article-Court-leaves-ruling-against-big-tobacco-story-intact?instance=home_news_lead-story.

Zacks Equity Research. 2012. "Auto Industry Outlook & Review-June 2012." Yahoo! Finance, June 26. http://finance.yahoo.com/news/auto-industry-outlook-review-june-182108430.html.

Zegart, Dan. 2000. *Civil Warriors: The Legal Siege on the Tobacco Industry.* New York: Delacorte Press.

Zywicki, Todd, Director, Office of Planning and Policy, Federal Trade Commission. 2003. Testimony before the Subcommittee on Commerce, Trade, and Consumer Protection of the House Committee on Energy and Commerce. *E-Commerce: The Case of Online Wine Sales and Direct Shipment.* 108th Congress, 1st session, October 30. http://www.gpo.gov/fdsys/pkg/CHRG-108hhrg90726/html/CHRG-108hhrg90726.htm.

Zywicki, Todd. 2008. "Bankruptcy Is the Perfect Remedy for Detroit." *Wall Street Journal*, December 16, p. A21.

———. 2010. "Will Congress Take Another Swipe at Credit Cards?" *Wall Street Journal*, January 5. http://online.wsj.com/article/SB10001424052748704905704574622722184163510.html.

———. 2011. "Dodd-Frank and the Return of the Loan Shark." *Wall Street Journal*, January 4. http://online.wsj.com/article/SB10001424052748704735304576058211789874804.html.

Index

Note to index: Following a page number, an *f* indicates a figure and an *n* indicates a note.

About the Authors

Adam C. Smith is an assistant professor of economics and director of the Center for Free Market Studies at Johnson and Wales. He has published articles in the *Journal of Economic Behavior and Organization*; the *European Journal of Political Economy, Social Choice and Welfare*; and *Public Choice*, as well as *Regulation* magazine. He is also a visiting scholar with the Regulatory Studies Center at George Washington University.

Bruce Yandle is dean emeritus of the College of Business and Behavioral Science and Alumni Distinguished Professor of Economics Emeritus at Clemson University and Distinguished Adjunct Professor of Economics, Mercatus Center at George Mason University. He is a member of the editorial board of the *European Journal of Law and Economics* and the academic advisory board of the *Independent Review*. Yandle is also the author of scores of journal articles and special reports, and has authored or edited 16 books.

Cato Institute

Founded in 1977, the Cato Institute is a public policy research foundation dedicated to broadening the parameters of policy debate to allow consideration of more options that are consistent with the traditional American principles of limited government, individual liberty, and peace. To that end, the Institute strives to achieve greater involvement of the intelligent, concerned lay public in questions of policy and the proper role of government.

The Institute is named for *Cato's Letters*, libertarian pamphlets that were widely read in the American Colonies in the early 18th century and played a major role in laying the philosophical foundation for the American Revolution.

Despite the achievement of the nation's Founders, today virtually no aspect of life is free from government encroachment. A pervasive intolerance for individual rights is shown by government's arbitrary intrusions into private economic transactions and its disregard for civil liberties.

To counter that trend, the Cato Institute undertakes an extensive publications program that addresses the complete spectrum of policy issues. Books, monographs, and shorter studies are commissioned to examine the federal budget, Social Security, regulation, military spending, international trade, and myriad other issues. Major policy conferences are held throughout the year, from which papers are published thrice yearly in the *Cato Journal*. The Institute also publishes the quarterly magazine *Regulation*.

In order to maintain its independence, the Cato Institute accepts no government funding. Contributions are received from foundations, corporations, and individuals, and other revenue is generated from the sale of publications. The Institute is a nonprofit, tax-exempt, educational foundation under Section 501(c)3 of the Internal Revenue Code.

CATO INSTITUTE
1000 Massachusetts Ave., N.W.
Washington, D.C. 20001
www.cato.org